A DAM COURTENAY is a Sydney-based writer and journalist who has had a long career in the UK and Australia, writing for papers such as the *Financial Times*, the *Sydney Morning Herald*, *The Age*, the *Australian Financial Review* and the UK *Sunday Times*. He is the son of Australia's best-loved storyteller Bryce Courtenay. He is the author of three previous books, *Blood Rubber*, *Amazon Men* and *The Ship That Never Was*.

THE
GHOST
& BOUNTY
THE
HUNTER

William Buckley, John Batman
and the theft of Kulin country

ADAM COURTENAY

ABC
BOOKS

Aboriginal and Torres Strait Islander readers are advised that this book contains images of people who have died.

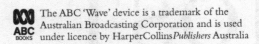 The ABC 'Wave' device is a trademark of the Australian Broadcasting Corporation and is used under licence by HarperCollins*Publishers* Australia

First published in Australia in 2020
by HarperCollins*Publishers* Australia Pty Limited
ABN 36 009 913 517
harpercollins.com.au

HarperCollins*Publishers*
Level 13, 201 Elizabeth Street, Sydney NSW 2000, Australia
Unit D1, 63 Apollo Drive, Rosedale, Auckland 0632, New Zealand
A 53, Sector 57, Noida, UP, India
1 London Bridge Street, London, SE1 9GF, United Kingdom
Bay Adelaide Centre, East Tower, 22 Adelaide Street West, 41st floor,
   Toronto, Ontario M5H 4E3, Canada
195 Broadway, New York NY 10007, USA

A catalogue record for this book is available from the National Library of Australia

ISBN 978 0 7333 4039 0 (paperback)
ISBN 978 1 4607 1172 9 (ebook)

Cover design by Peter Long
Cover images: (Foreground illustration) Sailor marooned on uninhabited island by Chris Hellier / Alamy Stock Photo; (Background illustration) Bonwick, James, 1817–1906. *The Wild White Man & the Blacks of Victoria*. 2d ed. Melbourne: Fergusson & Moore, 1863. Samuel Calvert 1828–1913, engraver.
Author photo by Christian Hagward
Map by Clare O'Flynn / Little Moon Studio
Typeset in Minion Pro Std by Kelli Lonergan
Printed and bound in Australia by McPherson's Printing Group
The papers used by HarperCollins in the manufacture of this book are a natural, recyclable product made from wood grown in sustainable plantation forests. The fibre source and manufacturing processes meet recognised international environmental standards, and carry certification.

To those who should be here: Nicholas Pfanner, Robert Foulcher, Christopher Aylward, Philip Parker, Romaine Youdale, Matthew Bracks, David Litherland, Harry McRitchie, Christopher Molnar, Sam de Brito, Sheila Browne, Kelly Stoker, Jaime Robertson. You are all greatly missed.

It's the first settlers do the brutal work. Them that come later, they get to sport about in polished boots and frockcoats, kidskin gloves ... revel in polite conversation, deplore the folly of ill-manners, forget the past, invent some bullshit fable. Same as what happened in America. You want to see men at their worst, you follow the frontier.

Thaddeus Cuff, quoted in *The Making of Martin Sparrow* by Peter Cochrane

You see Mr Hull, Bank of Victoria, all this mine, all along here Derrimut's once.

Evidence given by Derrimut to magistrate William Hull, 1858

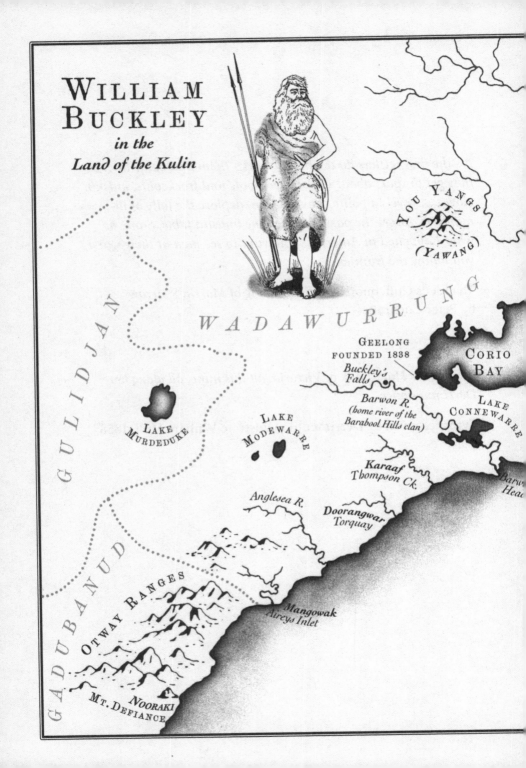

WILLIAM BUCKLEY

in the
Land of the Kulin

YOU YANGS
(YAWANG)

GULIDJAN

WADAWURRUNG

LAKE
MURDEDUKE

LAKE
MODEWARRE

GEELONG
FOUNDED 1838

Buckley's
Falls

CORIO
BAY

Barwon R.
(home river of the
Barabool Hills clan)

LAKE
CONNEWARRE

Karaaf
Thompson Ck.

Barw
Head

Anglesea R.

Doorangwar
Torquay

GADUBANUD

OTWAY RANGES

Mangowak
Aireys Inlet

NOORAKI
MT. DEFIANCE

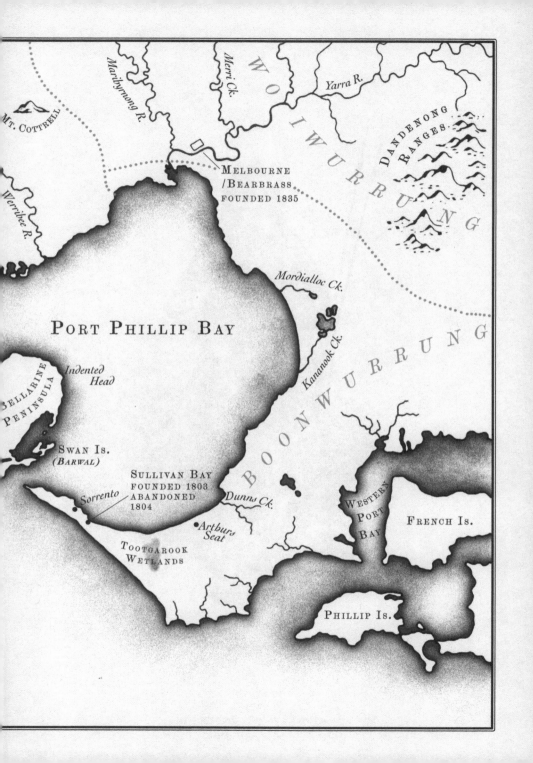

MT. COTTRELL

Maribyrnong R.

Merri Ck.

W O I W U R R U N G

Yarra R.

DANDENONG RANGES

Werribee R.

MELBOURNE
/BEARBRASS
FOUNDED 1835

Mordialloc Ck.

PORT PHILLIP BAY

Indented
Head

Kananook Ck.

BELLARINE PENINSULA

B O O N W U R R U N G

SWAN IS.
(BARWAL)

SULLIVAN BAY
FOUNDED 1803
ABANDONED
1804

Dunns Ck.

WESTERN
PORT
BAY

FRENCH IS.

Sorrento

Arthurs
Seat

TOOTGAROOK
WETLANDS

PHILLIP IS.

WILLIAM BUCKLEY.

Prologue

A T AROUND 2 p.m. on 6 July 1835, the ever-alert John Pigeon gasped and dropped his billy can. Pigeon was a well-travelled Aboriginal man from the southern coast of New South Wales. He had worked for the wealthy grazier John Batman in Van Diemen's Land for nearly a decade, travelled and walked with many tribes throughout the continent, and lived with the Palawa and European sealers on the coast. He had seen many things, but he had never seen this.

A giant appeared at the far end of the camp who was so clearly a white man and so clearly not. He was the tallest and most powerful human Pigeon had ever laid eyes on. He was middle-aged, his complexion ruddy and sunburnt, his grey beard falling below his chest. He held his gaze on the eight men in camp, with just the slightest hint of suspicion.

The man was shoeless and dressed in well-worn possum skins. In his left hand he carried a giant *mongeile*, a double-barbed spear ten feet in height, the most feared of all weapons. In his right a waddy or club, known as the *kudgeron*, designed to strike opponents on the head. At his feet, he had a number of boomerang-shaped *wonguim*, the first recourse in battle designed to break legs and inflict heavy wounds. He held these implements lightly and deftly, the way Pigeon's people did. His stance and bearing showed he knew how to use them, but his mien was unmistakably that of a white man. And yet only an Indigenous person could have come in so close to the camp without his noticing. White men knew nothing of stealth. Pigeon, one of Batman's most brilliant trackers, never missed a thing.

By Pigeon's estimation, this man had the bearing of a white *ngurungaeta*, an elder man of knowledge. There was no other name for what he now saw.

In a few moments, everybody in the camp had seen the man. There were a few gasps, then nobody spoke. The three white and five Aboriginal men sat transfixed, looking in wonder at each other then back at the apparition. There was no alarm. Nobody rushed to their guns. Nobody moved. It was as if a spirit had come to visit them, floating in from a place nobody could quite divine, hovering for reasons none could understand. An astonishing spirit, but not a harmful one.

The giant betrayed no emotion. Soon he sat at the edge of the camp, not far from where Pigeon and his men had set up their tents. He was impassive, almost motionless, looking askance at everyone. His war and hunting implements were now propped between his legs.

Eventually the stunned silence wore off, and the sprightly James Gumm, an ex-convict from Southampton, walked over to the man and started talking. He showed no signs of comprehension; it's probable he had some understanding of a working-class

Hampshire accent, but his tongue movements in relation to his upper palate had changed since he'd last spoken to a fellow white man. He couldn't remember – let alone form – the English words that had once come naturally. He also didn't want to say who he was – not just yet. He first wanted to figure out if these men were friendly. They cut up a piece of bread and handed it over.

Then he remembered. He later described it as a 'cloud passing over his brain'. 'Bread,' he said. It was the first English word he had uttered in thirty-two years.

The eight men started calling out words and phrases that they thought their visitor should know. They thrust objects in front of him, waiting for him to come up with the correct English terms.

Gumm asked the man if he could measure his height. In his bare feet, Gumm measured him at six foot five inches and seven eighths – not quite the height many have attributed to him at around six foot eight.

Gumm asked the question every man in camp must have had on his lips: 'Who are you?'

Still somewhat tongue-tied, the man pointed to the tattoos on his right forearm: the letters 'W.B.' alongside some basic renderings of the sun, the moon and something that looked like a mermaid with legs. 'William?' asked Gumm. The man nodded. Gumm persisted on the 'B' part of the puzzle but to no avail. 'Burgess?' The man did not respond. As an ex-convict, Gumm thought he knew a roughly drawn convict tattoo when he saw one, but these ones could have belonged to a mariner. Whoever the huge man was, it was clear he preferred to keep his identity a mystery.

He remained cautious but found them pleasant company, as they offered him food and gestures of assurance. Their chattering brought back old memories, as did the food. The fried tinned meat sat heavily in his stomach and must have reminded him of army and convict life, but the tea and fresh bread spoke of something else, a lost memory of home and hearth. The small things – bread, tea, salt and meat – were inflaming his senses, arousing old feelings. His old life, and the words that bound and formed it, were slowly returning, but he could express very little.

'Word by word I began to understand what they said, and soon understood – as if by instinct – that they had seen several of the native chiefs, with whom, as they said – they had exchanged all sorts of things for land,' he would later recount. That night, as his comprehension improved, he became increasingly alarmed at what he was hearing. These white people thought they had done a deal with the local Indigenous people, the Wadawurrung, and it related to a contract for landownership. 'I knew [this] could not have been … they [the Wadawurrung] have no chief claiming or possessing right over the soil: their's only being as the heads of families.'

He realised quickly enough that the whites – 'who knew nothing of the value of the country' – had duped the people he had lived with, who had nurtured him for decades. 'I therefore looked upon the land dealing spoken of as another hoax of the white man.' He had come here to warn the newcomers that they were in trouble, yet they had some strange notion that they had made a deal giving them protection.

The man knew nobody came onto Wadawurrung land without permission. This act required plenty of parley and plenty of gifts, and a readiness to have more to spare. He knew these transgressors had no idea that within a day or two, hundreds of Wadawurrung would be demanding huge compensation for their presence.

Only Pigeon understood. He was the big man's opposite: a black man who had lived with whites, who was now being asked by his white master to entreat with black people again. This had not been lost on Pigeon. Like himself, the mysterious man was a messenger, but Pigeon's job was to sow peace while the man brought tidings of war. Pigeon knew Batman had a very weak toehold on a strip of beach on the Bellarine Peninsula; he had not, in fact, signed a contract with the Wadawurrung people.

If Batman's eight men were to survive, they needed this giant man on their side.

Three nights after the man's arrival, Pigeon sensed the coming of many others. He smelled the smoke of their fires. They would be aggressive, and they would be demanding. Batman's little enclave was already surrounded.

Chapter 1

SOMETIME IN THE late 1790s, a young sealer was sitting on a rock shelf overlooking the southern coast of Victoria, smoking a pipe, his clothes spattered with blood and entrails. Around him were ten dead seal pups in various states of dismemberment. The rocks were splashed red, the colour trickling into nearby pools of water. The sealer had a look of contentment.

He did not know it, but he was being watched by Indigenous people. What did they think of this strange pale person? The man could pour forth smoke from his mouth. The men and women who populated this part of Bass Strait had never seen a man made out of fire.

Not long afterwards, they saw another white man. He wasn't able to walk in a straight line, and he shouted at the sun while drinking from a thin, bright bucket. He vomited all over himself, then peeled his outer layer off and washed it in the sea. This pallid person was definitely a man. Again, the locals kept their distance.

Rumours of the white men's arrival had come from the north and now moved south from tribe to tribe, speeding along the bush telegraph via the messenger men, the *waygeries*, who told of the bizarre feats and strange ways of these newcomers. Information was also transmitted via smoke signals and message sticks. It wouldn't have taken long for news of the white men's doings in Port Jackson to filter down to the south-easternmost corner of the continent.

Soon, the interlopers were arriving there in greater numbers. Sealers and offshore whalers were beginning to populate the coastal fringes of Bass Strait around Portland Bay, Cape Woolamai and Wilsons Promontory.

Who were these men? Debates were held among the coastal Boonwurrung people, who populated parts of Port Phillip and Western Port. Many believed they were spirits of their own kin returning to country with special powers. The Boonwurrung people of Mornington had heard that the white men could kill someone with thunder from their eyes; they sent invisible spears across great spaces that tore holes in a body.

It was a Gunditjmara tribesman from the Warrnambool area who reported the great white birds swimming on the ocean. Not long afterwards, in 1797, the Krauatungalung people of East Gippsland made the initial contact when they helped a group of shipwrecked sailors cast ashore near what would one day be Lakes Entrance.

As the century turned, European ships began haunting the southern coasts in greater numbers. The Indigenous people still thought they might be huge birds or trees of the sea, with branches that moved and swelled with the wind.

*

THE FIRST EUROPEAN ship to formally sight and bring back news of Victoria's west coast is thought to have been HMS *Lady Nelson*, a brig under the command of James Grant, who sailed past in December 1800. The ship later returned under John Murray, who traversed Bass Strait and 'found' Port Phillip, which the Boonwurrung called Narm-narm, in March 1802. It was not an auspicious occasion. Murray's men believed they were being ambushed, and a broadside was shot from the deck of their ship into a group of fleeing Boonwurrung. Two local men were wounded – and possibly killed. It was the first recorded incidence of violence on that coast. For the Boonwurrung, it was likely the first time they had seen firesticks shot in anger.

The French arrived a month later and received a far friendlier response. The *Naturaliste*, one of two vessels in the Baudin expedition surveying Australia's coastline, had stopped at Western Port. There the Boonwurrung couldn't contain their curiosity about the pale men, and Captain Pierre Bernard Milius obliged, removing his clothes to show his manhood. They then inspected his entire body, clothes and teeth. Milius sang and danced for them. It was an early show of French-style détente.

Ten weeks later Matthew Flinders, the man who would circumnavigate New Holland and identify it as a continent, arrived aboard the *Investigator*. He rowed to Mornington Peninsula and climbed up the great granite giant now known as Arthurs Seat (Momo), named by Murray after a set of hills just outside Edinburgh. From here Flinders could see not just the vast spread of Mornington's coastline, but also the unbroken green meadows of the Bellarine Peninsula across the bay. On the opposite shore he climbed the hills now known as the You Yangs, which look over the place the local Wadawurrung called Djilong – now known as Corio Bay. Here, at the peak he bestowed with his surname, he could see the shape of the harbour ahead of him, and behind him the hinterland stretching for fifty miles to the north-west, as far as Mount Macedon.

Flinders was mesmerised. He had seen more of the continent than most but never land of this type. The English, of course, counted their own island as pristine, and anything that resembled it was considered to be of similar high calibre. This landscape was closer in appearance to an English park than the tangle of wattle and eucalyptus Flinders had seen elsewhere, and he reported his findings to London with great enthusiasm. He knew he was looking at perfect grazing land.

Flinders met with the Yawangi, a clan of the Wadawurrung – who greeted him cheerfully. He noted that one had a piece of metal in a bag. These people, he thought, had probably traded with white men before.

In late 1802, HMS *Cumberland* arrived, bringing NSW Surveyor-General Charles Grimes. He was unimpressed by Port Phillip until he rowed up a great river in the north, which would one day be known as the Yarra. In his opinion the northern end of the bay – more populated, more fertile and with abundant fresh water – was the obvious choice for a colony.

By the time the old merchantman *Ocean* arrived on 7 October 1803, the many-winged birds, with their crews of ghosts, were well known to the coastal people. Two days later, in came HMS *Calcutta*, a 1100-ton monster more than twice the size of the *Ocean* and the largest ship ever to have sailed to New Holland. She was a former East Indiaman, built of teak, which had been converted into a convict transport. She was carrying over 400 people, including 299 male convicts, 30 wives and children of convicts as well as a large contingent of marines, crew and civil staff.

While the locals may have been awed by her size, the Europeans on board were equally in awe of the landscape. They had come from Portsmouth via Tenerife, Rio de Janeiro and the Cape of Good Hope. Nine convicts had lost their lives on the six-month journey, but in the early days of convict transportation this was considered reasonable 'attrition'.

Now gazing out at their new world, passengers rich and poor, free and unfree, convict and settler alike were of one opinion: this was El Dorado in the South Seas. 'Upon entering this spacious harbour, nothing could be more pleasing to the eye than the beautiful green plains with lofty trees which surrounded us,' wrote Third Lieutenant Nicholas Pateshall. 'In short, the country appeared more like pleasure grounds than a wild savage continent.' First Lieutenant James Tuckey also waxed lyrical, describing the scenery as 'nature in the world's first spring'. 'The face of the country ... is beautifully picturesque, swelling into gentle elevations of the brightest verdure and dotted by trees as if planted by the hand of taste ...'

Among the convicts was William Buckley, who also marvelled at the landscape. To its port, the *Calcutta* had passed Point Lonsdale (Gowaya) and to its starboard, Port Nepean (Boona Djabag), then cruising past the Bellarine Peninsula, Buckley must have felt he had crossed the Earth and found himself in an alternate England, a version cleaned of its vice and corruption, stripped of its industrial decay.

Buckley hadn't been mistreated on the voyage, even if his transportation for handling stolen Irish cloth (an offence considered punishable by death) was – in his opinion – grossly unfair. En route he had been invited on deck to work with the sailors and officers, who weren't overly harsh towards their convict charges. 'It was as far from suffering as could be expected,' Buckley would later write in his memoirs. 'At a time when prison discipline was generally carried out by coercion, and the lash and the rope were, in too many instances, considered too good for all who had been convicted.'

In those days, a man of around five feet seven inches was considered tall, so Buckley was gargantuan, standing just shy of six feet six inches. He had a head of bushy black hair and a low forehead with eyebrows overhanging his disproportionately small eyes. He had a short snub nose and a face scarred by smallpox, typical of his generation. His stature was of 'erect military gait'; he was strong, powerful and highly athletic.

In every other way, he was the archetypical convict: a former tradesman from Cheshire with no literacy skills, and with an almost unquenchable desire to escape. He was a true 'liberty or death man', the convict's credo that many uttered and others had scratched on their bodies – but relatively few acted on. We know something of his feelings because he committed them to print many years later with the help of a newspaper editor, John Morgan, who added much of his own voice to these memoirs and many of his own predilections to those of Buckley. But Buckley's character shines through. Like every other convict he had no qualifications for escape. The quiet giant was fresh off the boat with no backwoods experience. He was, by trade, a bricklayer and former soldier who had seen action against the French in Holland. Growing up on a farm in England hadn't bestowed bushcraft.

*

THE TWO GREAT WHITE BIRDS, moving north, turned towards the southern end of the bay and came to a halt about eight miles from the heads. For several days, they sat motionless on the water, side by side, moored a fair way offshore, on the lower south-east hook of Port Phillip – present-day Sorrento – which the Boonwurrung called Bullanatoolong. It was the home of the Burinyung-Ballak clan who called the strip of land from Port Nepean to Boneo, Tootgarook. They were now about to look right down the length of Mornington Peninsula, which the people here called Wamoon. From the ships there were a few comings and goings to shore. Then, all of a sudden, they began disgorging huge numbers of people and materiel.

The *Calcutta* was terrifying in herself, but she brought something the locals had never seen before: the ghost women. This could only mean one thing. Unlike their predecessors, these intruders were not planning to leave.

The tallest and strongest man in the colony had been chosen specifically for tasks like this. Colonisation was backbreaking work, and men like William Buckley were needed to bring in the hundreds of cases of stores, which had to be hauled at low tide. It was difficult and dirty work – men were often shoulder deep in water, carrying large boxes above their heads to a distant shore. Buckley was used to a life of drudgery and must have known it would be like this. Whenever the hardest physical tasks were assigned, he was the first man chosen.

What the Boonwurrung were witnessing was the second-largest land invasion of New Holland ever attempted by the British, led by an experienced officer and administrator with first-hand experience in colonisation. The new colony was to be run by the former Judge Advocate of New South Wales, David Collins, a colonel in the Royal Marines who had been on Captain Arthur Phillip's first voyage when it arrived in Port Jackson fifteen years earlier. It was Collins who had decided the infant colony should be placed at the south-eastern side of the bay. He named it Sullivan Bay.

A missionary, John Bulmer, later heard a song directly from the Boonwurrung that recorded the tribespeople meeting white settlers or seeing them approach: *'Mundhanna loornda kathia prappau. Muraskin mundhanna yea a main.'* ('There are white men long way off with great noise. Guns there sailing about.')

Within only a few weeks, the settlement took shape. It ran along the beach for about four hundred yards, naturally capped at each end with yellow and white sandstone bluffs. The western side of the settlement was designated convict and soldier territory, where many calico tents had been placed just above the shoreline with sentinels in positions surrounding the convicts. Here also lay the storage tents and a half-built munitions battery. At the eastern side of the beach lay the pens for pigs and other livestock. The officers' and settlers' tents were all clustered there, and at the top of the eastern cliff stood Collins's headquarters: less a tent, more a marquee. Two cannons were looking out to sea, and between them was a large, constantly flapping Union Jack.

Once the stores had been brought to dry land, Buckley's assigned job was much more to his liking. As a bricklayer, he would mostly be involved in working on the construction of a magazine and a storehouse. He was considered something of a 'mechanic' (anyone with hands-on building skills was considered such), and this was where his prowess worked for him; he was classed among the skilled lime-burners, builders and carpenters, and given some freedom of movement as the job required work beyond the main boundaries of the settlement. He could build his own hut and live outside the immediate range of the sentinels – by contrast, the labouring convicts were placed under more focused supervision.

Before too long, settlers were ransacking bird nests, as well as fishing extensively for crayfish; some were even pilfering artefacts from nearby camps. We know that Collins, who had encountered the Eora people in Sydney, was extremely wary of the new colony overindulging in the local people's resources. He issued what some have described as Australia's first environmental protection order, along with rules relating to local women. He reminded the colonists that taking 'spears, fishing spears, gum, or any other articles from the natives, or out of their huts, or from the beach where it is their custom to leave these articles' was robbery and would be punished as such. He also tackled what might have been the chief cause of frontier conflict throughout the British colonies – any violence towards a local woman was punishable by death: 'If any of the natives are wantonly or inconsiderably killed or wounded or if any violence is offered to a woman, the offender will be tried for his life.'

*

ESCAPE FOR A British convict in the early nineteenth century wasn't just about surviving in the wilderness. It was also about overcoming a certain deep-seated, entrenched fear. Out there, the convicts were told, you'd be taking your chances with man-eaters. It was one of the best pieces of propaganda the British – and, indeed, most Europeans – had ever invented, a fear so indelibly stamped into the convict psyche that it was rarely questioned.

A certain word first entered the English language in the mid-sixteenth century by means of Spanish explorers. Christopher Columbus used the word *canibales* to describe indigenous people of the Caribbean Islands who were rumoured to be eaters of human flesh. The name stuck: 'cannibal' became a popular term in Britain to describe any colonised people, whether they were of the British Empire or from the New World.

But in this new southern colony, most of the meetings between the British and locals were peaceable. In only one instance was there any difficulty. A group of Boonwurrung attempted to steal from a boat – however, no violence ensued. From this incident the colony's churchman, the Reverend Robert Knopwood, divined what everyone thought was obvious: 'We have great reason to believe they are cannibals,' he would write later.

This understanding of indigenous peoples would last into the Victorian era, when Morgan was ghostwriting Buckley's story in the late 1840s. It was this well-promulgated fear that 'stayed' so many itchy convict feet. But there were some, like Buckley, who were desirous enough of their liberty to ignore the propaganda. A bolt for Sydney, around six hundred miles distant, was what the convicts called 'China travelling': fleeing north without a map. China, it was widely thought, was attached to the top of Australia. Buckley wasn't quite so naive to believe that China was in marching distance, but he reckoned he had as good a chance as any of making it to Sydney. Where else was possible? In 1803, with the country beyond Sydney barely settled, a ship from Port Jackson was the only way out of New Holland.

The colonists didn't realise that the local people, who lived in one of the most bounteous parts of the continent, did not need to be cannibals: the land provided them with everything. The Boonwurrung were part of a greater 'confederation' of culturally similar Aboriginal tribes south of the River Murray who populated the area around and inland from Port Phillip Bay. Known collectively as the Kulin people (Kulin means 'man'), they represented forty language groups and clans who had been occupying the region for many tens of thousands of years. The Wadawurrung inhabited the west of the bay, around the Bellarine Peninsula through to the Otway Ranges in the south-west and as far north-west as Ballarat. The Boonwurrung were custodians of the slice of Port Phillip Bay east of the Werribee River, the Mornington Peninsula, around Western Port and as far east as Wilsons Promontory. North-east of the Boonwurrung were the Woiwurrung (many still adopt an alternative name – the Wurundjeri), who populated the area around the Yarra River and its tributaries; together with the Boonwurrung, they were part-custodians of the land that would one day be called Melbourne. There were also the Taungurong to the north of the Woiwurrung, and the Djargurd Wurrung who held sway over land north of the Wadawurrung.

The clans intermarried, fought with each other and did tribal business. One moment there was peace, another there was trouble, but through it all the bush telegraph never faltered. The messenger men, the *waygeries*, were always given safe passage by all Kulin tribes in all areas, so they could tell their vital news and stories. The coast was always being watched, and smoke signals foretold the arrival of white men to people further inland, many of whom wouldn't see the invaders for years.

The three tribes around and inland of Port Phillip would first bear the brunt of white incursions: the Wadawurrung, the Boonwurrung and the Woiwurrung. They held sway over significant slices of the bay and many miles into the interior. The boundaries moved and shifted a little over time, but the borders, marked by the Indigenous understanding of their respective country, had been respected for many thousands of years. However, white people ignored territorial protocol, moving without regard for each tribe's boundaries. There had been the odd skirmish but no one had seriously challenged these ghost-like people – and, until now, the ghosts had never seriously challenged them. But with the arrival of the *Calcutta*, they may have well believed they were witnessing the coming of a catastrophe.

Chapter 2

WHEN THE CALCUTTA's First Lieutenant James Tuckey was asked by his commander to survey the northern extremities of Port Phillip, he may have been wondering why. It was November, only a month after their arrival, and yet Tuckey already knew that whatever he found would never be good enough. Collins, for reasons of his own, had made it clear only a few weeks after arriving in the bay that he had his heart set on settling elsewhere. Here at Port Phillip, they were only play-acting.

History doesn't give any specific reason for Collins's early rejection of Port Phillip, but it may have been that his instructions from Governor Philip Gidley King in New South Wales had been far too demanding. The British wanted multiple functions from this second colony. The initial instruction was to form a settlement to serve as a depot for a growing seal-skin industry in Bass Strait, but that was just a small part of the remit. The authorities wanted it to be a military base as well. The French had long been surveying this part of the coast, and everyone knew that war with Napoleon could reignite at any moment. Indeed, officials in New South Wales had yet to be informed that the Treaty of Amiens, which had sustained a fragile peace between Britain and France, had already been broken in May that year. Britain was again at war with France. This second colony wasn't only required to be militarily advantageous, but had to yield good timber to build more warships for His Majesty's Navy.

The needs for this port didn't stop there. King was worried about food supplies and increasing convict numbers being pushed out from Britain and Ireland. Port Phillip was believed to have a better climate than Sydney for raising wheat and, if this second colony was successful, it would allow King to divide the very large numbers of convicts now streaming into Sydney.

Collins was being asked to do the virtually impossible: to discover and found a self-sustaining penal colony, all the while creating a seal-fur trading entrepot and a timber yard for the navy. The land had to be bounteous with clearly navigable sea lanes as well as being well-sited strategically for commercial and military purposes. Part of Collins's job was civil, part of it commercial and part of it military. At least he had been given a choice: if Port Phillip didn't meet these requirements, he had been given carte blanche to go elsewhere.

The newly named Sullivan Bay in the south was a perfectly delightful spot visually, but hardly the best place for a settlement. It was among the least habitable parts of Port Phillip for European purposes, despite the fact that the area was an important source of shellfish for the Boonwurrung. The shallow water gave the local people easy access to a wide rock shelf, and today there are still middens containing cast-off blue mussels and top shells. But in a region rich with good soil and freshwater sources, Collins had opted for one of its least fertile parts – a barren and sandy beach where they obtained briny water by sinking barrels into the sand that filtered out the salt.

Here was the rub: Collins, ultimately a military man, saw the immediate strategic advantages of this position only eight miles from the port's entrance. If he had chosen the more fertile northern and western sides of the bay – areas which had previously been recommended by Grimes and Flinders respectively – his ships would have needed to deal with problematic currents. It was said that Collins never knew of Grimes's report, which showed the advantages of the Yarra; that may be true, but Collins never explored the bay to any great extent. He had opted for first-rate shipping lanes that would produce only a second-rate colony. The threat of war against France, trumped everything. The Treaty of Amiens, signed in March 1802, was little more than a chance for both sides to re-arm for further warfare. War with France came first. The physical and material needs of his four hundred settlers were of secondary importance.

Although considered relatively lenient by the standards of the day, Collins was an officer in both name and nature, and he intended the British class system to operate as effectively here as in any part of the Empire. The old world and its affectations were alive and well in the new one, and deference and due regard for people's stations in life were magnified in this small, semi-constructed enclave at Sullivan Bay. To those in the higher echelons of the settlement, it mattered little where they resided as long as their lifestyles were unaffected. A classic example of this state of affairs was Collins's directive on washing duty, apparently only fit for the wives of the lowest class of soldiers: 'The commanding officer directs and appoints the following women to be employed in the following manner: The wife of Private William Bean to wash for fifteen persons, the wife of Private George Curley to wash for fifteen persons and the wife of Private James Spooner to wash for fourteen persons.' While the soldiers' wives washed for the gentry (and presumably the ladies), the latter did plenty of what was then described as 'cavorting'. The captain of the *Calcutta*, Daniel Woodriff, often entertained, and 'all the officers on board', according to Third Lieutenant Pateshall, 'were very merry'. All the most important men had a cook, and the very best produce landed on their dinner tables.

In character, the Reverend Robert Knopwood typified the predilections of the upper class. He was a Cambridge man and a part of the Prince Regent's racy set, and his diary suggests that his main fixation at the bay was nursing his constant hangovers. For a man of God, he had some very earthly and irreverent tastes, including fishing, hunting and womanising. He was said to have a mistress among the women 'on call' and was unofficially in charge of the entertainment for the higher born gentry and ladies, a role he took on with relish.

Collins, too, had his peccadilloes. He was considered liberal by nineteenth-century standards, and it was strongly rumoured that he had done a deal with one of the convict's wives – possibly he offered favours and a reduced sentence for her husband, in exchange for her sexual services. In his diaries, Knopwood recounts several occasions when Collins dined alone with a 'Mrs P'. She was Hannah Power, the wife of an Irish forger, Matthew Power, who had brought a printing press to the colony.

*

FIRST LIEUTENANT JAMES TUCKEY approached the western shore of Corio Bay with two boats, grounding the first on the beach and making sure that the second remained just offshore. As he and his men began setting up camp, three Wadawurrung men approached unarmed and in apparent good humour. Tuckey and his men had taken care to hide their firearms, leaving them on the boat that remained just offshore. The two parties were thus unarmed.

At first it seemed like the perfect welcoming. Tuckey's men offered fish, bread and blankets to their three visitors, who soon departed. One boat left to carry on the survey, while Tuckey and his men finished setting up camp for the night.

Within an hour around forty more men appeared. They were from the western shores of the bay – present-day Geelong – headed by a great chief; he was, in Tuckey's words, both 'masculine' and 'well proportioned', his air 'bold and commanding'. The chief was what the local people termed a *ngurungaeta*, an elder of high position. He was hoisted over the shoulders of two of his men, and around him others were clapping and shouting. He wore a necklace of reeds and several clumps of human hair strung across his chest, and his head was adorned with a beautifully arranged crown of swan feathers. The rest of the men were covered in war paint, its distinctive red, white and yellow clays streaked across their bodies and faces. Many of the chief's men had a bone cut through the septums of their noses, but he had by far the longest, around two feet in length. Each carried a spear pointed with a sharp bone, and in the other hand perfectly carved oval-shaped wooden shields.

In his diary Tuckey wrote that the atmosphere grew increasingly hostile, and he sensed an ambush. Some of the Wadawurrung surrounded the tent while others congregated beside the beached boat, milling around the oars, masts and sails. 'Their intention to plunder was immediately visible and all the exertions of the boat's crew were insufficient to prevent their possessing themselves of

THE GHOST AND THE BOUNTY HUNTER

tomahawks, axes and saws,' Tuckey wrote. He said his men attempted to intercede by sharing out food and blankets, but this had little effect as more arrived on the scene. At one point a ship's mate was manhandled by one of the warriors, who held him fast in his arms. The other boat, which had seen trouble brewing from afar, was now moving towards the shore at speed. 'For God's sake, fire!' someone called from the shore, and the approaching men shot over the heads of the locals.

The advancing Wadawurrung seemed to pause, some fleeing behind trees and others back up the beach. But the vast majority regrouped and returned to the scene, holding their ground. From there the scene deteriorated into what would become a typical confrontation between the two races on the new continent. The men on the boat shot directly into the crowd, and by Tuckey's reckoning four were wounded. The Wadawurrung men ran in every direction.

The melee was now turning into a battle, as another large group of men, who had hidden behind the hill above the shore, began converging on the scene. About a hundred men were now marching down the hill at a steady pace, screaming and gesticulating. Each warrior was armed with at least one spear, and some even carried bundles of spears. At about a hundred yards from Tuckey and his men, they halted.

Tuckey saw an opportunity. Moving briskly he offered several cloaks and necklaces as well as some of the spears which had been left behind, to the man who appeared at the head of the column. It was a useless gesture. Emboldened, perhaps by the apparent unwillingness of Tuckey's party to fight, this man, possibly another chief, ordered his men to move forward. Tuckey and his men cocked their rifles for the coming assault but the Wadawurrung chief, just like the first, showed no fear: 'His countenance and gestures all this time betrayed more of anger than fear and his spear was at every moment upon the point of quitting his hand,' Tuckey wrote.

The white men continued to make efforts to explain that if his men came any closer, they would be fired upon. But it was to no avail, as the warriors first moved forward and then tried to outflank the invaders.

It was a well-known practice for British soldiers fighting with indigenous peoples to aim for a senior warrior as a means of weakening collective morale. Three muskets were thus trained on one of the most outwardly aggressive of the warriors, from about fifty yards. The man was killed instantly by two shots, and the Wadawurrung immediately dispersed, leaving their dead comrade behind.

It will never be known whether the Wadawurrung men had deliberately confronted Tuckey and his party in great numbers in an attempt to drive the invaders away. If this was so, it had the desired effect.

Chapter 3

WHEN TUCKEY'S REPORT came back to Collins, he became convinced that the inhabitants of the entire region were incurably hostile, rendering Port Phillip essentially uninhabitable. It was the kind of confirmation Collins wanted. He duly relayed his findings to King in New South Wales: 'Were I to settle in the upper part of the harbour which is full of natives, I should require four times the force I have now to guard not only the convicts, but perhaps myself from their attacks.' To wit, Port Phillip Bay, which had some of the most fertile land ever seen on the new continent, was entirely unsuitable for the Empire's purposes.

When Collins's about turn became officially known two months after first settlement, convicts and colonists alike despaired. He had selected the least prosperous part of the bay and now, based on a single skirmish, he was abandoning the bay altogether – and yet this landscape screamed bounty. This was a perfect recipe for discontent among the colonists. What had it all been for? The tallest man in the colony now realised some kind of escape had to be planned and executed very soon, or it would become impossible. The seeds of a plan were beginning to sprout.

As Christmas 1803 approached, the colony was in emotional turmoil. Ever since the commandant had declared they would be leaving Port Phillip, rumours had spread of a major breakout of convicts – possibly even a mutiny. While stoked more by fear than reality, there was truth in this gossip. The half-built colony was in the process of unbuilding itself, and in the confusion tensions were heightened.

December brought searing heat. There were flies by the thousands by day and mosquitoes biting at night. Members of all social classes succumbed to sickness, but this had little effect on Collins's determined quest to abandon the area. He ordered there be no rest days, which meant the convicts were in gangs working from sunrise to sunset. 'Carry on' was the message delivered from above. The women were still undertaking domestic work, creating vegetable gardens with the help of their children, but there was a sense of unease.

Like many others, William Buckley watched in dismay as the colony he had helped to build unravelled. By early December he was part of a team ordered to build a 380-foot jetty for the next operation – reloading onto the ships all the stores they had recently unloaded.

To everyone except Collins, this all seemed like an anticlimax. They had been prepared to make this country work. As the wife of one officer, Mrs Hartley, remarked in a letter to her sister, 'My pen is not able to describe the beauties of this delightful spot.' The colony, she muttered, was being abandoned 'at the whim of the governor'. She ended the letter: 'I parted from it with more regret than I did from my native land.'

With fewer able-bodied men on watch, Collins couldn't maintain the usual standards of security. Buckley, chafing for freedom, knew he needed to act soon. He decided to bolt for Sydney that month.

What did he have going for him? Added to his immense strength were qualities of self-reliance and resilience. When he had fought in the army his height had guaranteed him a position as a 'pivot man'; in the heat of battle soldiers needed someone to rally around, and Buckley had been that man. He was calm under pressure and battle hardened. While determined in character he was also gentle in nature, emotional and sometimes given to self-doubt. He wasn't one who found self-expression easy, but underneath it all there was grit, resourcefulness and determination. Buckley was the archetypal gentle giant. He believed – perhaps naively – that whatever this new continent threw at him, he could handle.

All the 'cavorting' among the colony's wealthiest denizens wouldn't have gone unnoticed by Buckley and his fellow convicts, nor the fact that the officers and their men were frequently drunk. In fact, to improve morale Collins had offered them double rations of grog. The hardworking convicts, of course, received nothing. Across the board, a climate of sickness, despondency and ennui prevailed.

Among the inmates' ranks were a number of radicals who held their greatest rancour for members of the upper crust. There was one George Lee, mentioned by Tuckey and Collins as a man of 'considerable education and abilities', who was granted special dispensation for being something of a gentleman. He was given a hut and light duties, but Lee abused his role, as Collins put it, by 'misapplying the leisure' that he had been given and 'endeavouring to create dissatisfaction among the prisoners'. Lee had apparently written some scurrilous verse about the officers. 'I would rather take to the bush and perish sooner than submit to the torture to please the tyrants, the ignorant brutes placed over me as slave drivers,' he reportedly said when asked for his views on colonial life. When

Collins asked Knopwood to inquire more deeply into the man's background and current activities, it became obvious that Lee was a firebrand, influential and dangerous. Immediately he was put in a gang for hard labour. But he was influential, and his punishment did not deter the convicts. It hardened their resolve to flee.

In the end, though, it was just Lee and his mate David Gibson who bolted. Lee stole a gun and made a desperate run for it. He was never heard of again, believed to have (as Collins would describe in his periodic reports to King) 'perished in the woods'. When Gibson returned a few weeks later, he was unrecognisable. He stumbled into the camp, raised his hands and practically walked into the leg irons awaiting him. The flogging he received was a blessing compared to the rigours of the bush.

Despite their failure, Lee and Gibson had succeeded in igniting the first wave of desertions. Gibson's wretchedness, after his bush ordeal, did not discourage them. They all knew that if they were transported south to Van Diemen's Land, escape would be next to impossible. By December, as Buckley and a group of friends were contemplating their breakout, fourteen people had already fled. Anyone who relished liberty, anyone who truly believed the 'liberty or death' credo, would make a run for it. 'I determined on braving everything,' Buckley wrote. This, he said, was due to his 'unsettled nature' and his 'impatience of every kind of restraint'.

And so it was that William Buckley, Dan McAllenan, George Pye, Jack Page, William Marmon and Charlie Shore plotted their escape, hoping that just after Christmas, with the rum ration doubled, most of the sentinels would be off their guard, if not drunk.

Buckley and his troop didn't look to abscond across the hinterland. That way, they thought, lurked countless savages. The band of convicts would begin their escape in the backwoods behind the beach and then double back to the coastline. They would then head north for about fifty miles to the top of the bay, and from there they would cut across country and head direct to Sydney. Their greatest hope for survival was a fowling piece – a rather ramshackle gun that McAllenan had secreted – to shoot possums and kangaroos.

Christmas passed, and all was quiet in Sullivan Bay. At nine o'clock at night on 27 December, six men went on the run with a few tin pots, an iron kettle and a second-rate gun. They had just a few days' rations between them. A green, beautiful but ultimately alien wilderness awaited them.

Chapter 4

BUCKLEY AND HIS CREW had only just crept their way into the woods behind the encampment when they heard shouts from the sentinels followed by the sharp crack of a rifle. Their hopes of putting distance between themselves and their pursuers were foiled, but they carried on. The six men ran into the woods as fast as their legs could take them. A posse of soldiers was coming. In the race for freedom, it was every man for himself.

Buckley increased his pace, and Pye, Marmon and McAllenan responded. They'd barely covered a few hundred yards when the air resounded with thunder followed by flashes of lightning. Within seconds, there was heavy rain.

When Buckley heard the report of a rifle, he looked back to see Shore writhing on the ground, badly wounded. Page had stayed with him, deciding not to risk the run. It was now just Buckley, McAllenan, Marmon and Pye.

They pressed on, heading back onto the coastline and running north along the sand in the darkness, skirting dunes at speed, every now and then crossing minor streams that emptied onto the beaches.

Occasionally a bolt of lightning illuminated the territory ahead but mostly all they could see was sea, sand, trees and rocks amid a haze of rain and sweat. The creeks slowed them as did the rocks around the headlands, and there were marshlands to negotiate as well.

Just before present-day Rosebud, they found themselves trudging across the onomatopoeic sounding Tootgarook Swamp (Boonwurrung: croaking frogs), which reached to the sea and extended several miles inland. The atmosphere cleared, the humidity dropped and, after four hours on the run, the men paused to gather their wits. They had shaken off their pursuers. Their clothes were dripping from rain and exertion, and it was only now they realised four had become three – Marmon had been unable to keep up and had turned back for the settlement.

'We now pushed on again until we came to a river, and near the bay; this stream the natives call the Darkee Barwin,' noted Buckley. This has been identified as present-day Kananook Creek, but that would mean they had run more than twenty-five miles, the equivalent of a marathon, in around six hours: not impossible but very difficult over wet sand, swollen creeks and wetlands. It's most likely that they stopped at either Dunns Creek, a few miles to the north of Arthurs Seat, or Sheoak Creek, which drains from Mount Martha.

When daylight came, Buckley realised he had become the natural pivot man for his troop. It was now just he, McAllenan the Irish horse thief, and Pye – a convict who had been convicted for stealing sheep in Nottingham. Neither Pye nor McAllenan had military experience. Both were still exhausted, their bodies stiff, but they fell in line with Buckley, who was determined to move relentlessly northwards. They knew their provisions would barely last more than a few days, so they had to conserve their strength. But the weather grew steadily hotter, and their pace began to slacken. At some point, they threw away the kettle.

Buckley was leading the men into places few white men had seen or experienced. En route they passed the clifftop scrubs of Mount Martha, Mornington and Mount Eliza (Berring-wallin). Hugging the beaches were the banksia woodlands, and in other areas ancient stands of moonah trees twisted into bizarre tendrils by the heavy coastal winds. The three men were passing through Boonwurrung lands and had yet to meet any of the locals, whom they feared greatly.

By the third day they were negotiating an array of swollen creeks that drained through ferny areas, shaded forest and, in some cases, heathland that was dense with shrubs. According to the Morgan–Buckley account, at present-day Mordialloc they came to either a deep river or a swollen creek that could not easily be forded. Buckley's immense size and strength came into play. Part-swimming, part-walking, he took all their provisions and clothes across, then returned to piggyback Pye and McAllenan. They were now about fifteen miles from present-day Melbourne.

The going was getting easier as they headed north, the heathland and scrub diminishing and the topography ahead changing to more open pastures of kangaroo grass studded with the dandelion-like murnong (a food source also known as the yam daisy), with only a scattering of trees. But as they approached the Yarra River, the ground grew wetter and boggier, dotted with lagoons and the occasional swampy impasse. They were now in the lands of the Woiwurrung. It looked like a vast green estate owned by the landed gentry, which Buckley had seen in England, only this one was studded with natural lakes, marshlands and billabongs.

Here Buckley seems to have lost his sense of time. In the memoir he reached the south bank of the Yarra on the second day, but it's likely he and the others had been travelling for four days. The only place to cross the river was at the falls, a precarious line of rocks that could be braved at low tide. This was by far the widest river they had crossed. As they reached the other side they could see gently undulating hills. Behind these hills they would find extensive green plains running to the west and south-west, with only one prominent feature. These were the dark hills known as the You Yangs, which seemed to arise from nowhere, crowning the surrounding basalt plains. Reaching them would be about a day's walk from the top half of the bay.

Buckley's plan was to see the lie of the land from the top of these hills, the You Yangs that had so enchanted Flinders. But to get there, the men had to negotiate the mudflats and boggy fens around the top of the bay. While they trudged along, they came upon an intensely blue natural lagoon, only a foot or so deep, filled with clear salt water. It was here that Port Phillip Bay had found one of its last refuges, at this point giving way to the fresh water of the Yarra and its surrounds.

As the men approached the hills to the west, the ground hardened and the sparsely wooded grasslands took over. They passed the present site of Werribee township. They had walked from early that day to reach Flinders Peak by early evening, and morale was slipping. That night they finished all their provisions. 'We had not divided our rations properly,' Buckley stated. 'We had not taken the precautions necessary to avoid starvation.'

On that bleak night on top of the You Yangs, the men had to make a decision. Going north to Sydney, the original plan, now seemed senseless. The only obvious choice when daybreak came was directly ahead of them: they would make for Corio Bay – the site of present-day Geelong – a neat little sandy beach that could be plainly seen from the You Yangs. They hoped to sustain themselves on shellfish. Buckley wrote, 'I told my companions that we must make for the beach to look for food, for death was certain.' His decision was prompted by sheer hunger. Even if he had known the direction of Sydney, all he could see were plains and bushland, and he may have known there were sealers and whalers along the Bass Strait coast who might accommodate escaped convicts.

The men didn't know it, but they had already crossed all the clan territories that bordered Port Phillip. As they approached Corio Bay, they noted the same evenness of the green plains that appeared to be cleanly cut. Unbeknown to them, the landscape had been nurtured, shaped and farmed by the firestick. Not only did the use of fire promote regrowth, but it also stimulated the tuberous edible plants such as the murnong. This plant was a prime staple of the locals, as was the ubiquitous kangaroo grass that could be made into a kind of flour. A later settler, Edward Curr, would remark in the 1840s how the local people set fire to grass and trees as the seasons demanded. '[The Indigenous people] were tilling the land and cultivating pastures with fire.' The local people understand how fire was not necessarily a killer but a giver of life. Animals such as the kangaroo, emu, wallabies and wombats were aided by the autumn burnings before the winter rains, so that new mothers would have fresh grass in the spring with which to nourish their young. This was farming of a type that Buckley, born in rural Cheshire, could not have comprehended at first. There was no need for provision, no call for winter storage or for a plough to rupture the soil, and the land never needed to lie fallow. The Wadawurrung knew exactly what their lands would yield.

We don't know if the three escapees were spotted by locals around this time, but it is more than likely. These people would perhaps have been as upset at the intrusion as any European farmer who sees a stranger trespassing on his land. Access to country had to be negotiated. Normally they would punish transgressors, but many Wadawurrung were still greatly reticent to approach white men. The invaders were still generally believed to be supernatural, the ghosts of possibly hostile ancestors. The three men may have been avoided, but they were probably tracked and closely watched.

After another day's walk, the escapees arrived at Corio Bay extremely hungry, but Buckley's decision proved sound. They followed the coast as it headed south and then wrapped around to the east. While they walked they collected mussels and oysters, and discovered a well of fresh water; they made an unsatisfyingly small meal of the shellfish, but they had no skins with which to retain the water. They drank as much as they could and moved on. At one stage they noticed a little village of sturdy huts, but this only filled them with apprehension. They were constantly afraid that they would encounter local people. They pressed on both wearily and warily.

The next day they skirted the Bellarine Peninsula as it thrust east and then curved south towards Indented Head (Bengala) and St Leonards (Nearnenulloc). They kept to the beaches, passing the area now known as Portarlington while combing the sand for anything edible. At night they forded Swan Bay at low tide, wading across to Swan Island (Barwal). They had almost come full circle, the first white men to have walked the circumference of Port Phillip Bay from the south-east to the south-west.

At Swan Island, Buckley said they found an edible gum – it may have been that naturally rendered by the acacia tree – which they placed over the fire until it was soft and palatable. When morning came, they could survey much of the terrain they had crossed on the other side of the bay, but there was something else. Almost due south, they could clearly see the *Ocean* sitting calmly just off Sullivan Bay. It was now a few days into the new year. The ship was only about ten miles along their line of sight. This was all too much for McAllenan and Pye – that way lay food, shelter and survival.

All three men tried to attract attention by starting fires and hanging their shirts from trees. It seemed to work: a boat left the opposite shore and was moving in their direction. Halfway across the bay, the boat stopped dead, tacked to starboard and headed back to shore. The currents may have been too strong. McAllenan and Pye started screaming at the boat while it kept pulling away. 'The dread of punishment was naturally great,' Buckley recorded, 'yet the fear of starvation exceeded it.' It was later reported that the fires had been seen at Sullivan Bay, but as the soldiers in the boat had approached they'd changed their minds, believing it to be started by the locals. The escapees' fires were henceforth ignored.

Buckley wrote they lasted another six days living on whatever they could scavenge from the coastline, before McAllenan and Pye resolved to return by foot. They had continued signalling to the camp across the bay but to no avail. 'They lamented bitterly,' Buckley wrote. The two men strongly entreated him to return with them, but the big man remained steadfast. He believed that with a bit of luck and perseverance, he could make his way through this country. It was a case of them needing him far more than he needed them. 'To all their advice and entreaties to accompany them, I turned a deaf ear, being determined to endure every kind of suffering rather than again surrendering my liberty.'

Buckley's companions left with some bitterness but no acrimony. He had made his decision. He was now alone, it seemed, in this strange but beautiful landscape, the untarnished England of his imagination.

McAllenan made it back to Sullivan Bay. He surrendered on 13 January, reportedly suffering from severe scurvy. As Collins noted: 'Upon the 13th January, one of the wretches surrendered himself at the camp, having accompanied the others, according to his calculations, upwards of a hundred miles round the extensive harbour of Port Phillip.' McAllenan brought back the Commissary's fowling piece and stated that he had subsisted chiefly upon gum and shellfish. Pye was never seen by white people again.

It didn't take Buckley too long to recognise his extreme vulnerability. He fell into a severe melancholy. Any idea of making it alive to Sydney had been sheer folly, and even if he had succeeded he would probably have been incarcerated.

The liberty Buckley had so hankered for had now become the source of his pain. He was, he wrote, experiencing 'the most severe mental suffering for several hours'. Freedom, as he put it, 'now made the heart sick at its enjoyment'. It carried heavy penalties. He would continue his 'solitary journey', he wrote. He would not speak to another white man for the next thirty-two years.

Chapter 5

WILLIAM BUCKLEY WAS just twenty-three years of age, an Englishman in a landscape he found beautiful but forbidding. He was overcome with a sense of bitter nostalgia, not quite comprehending how it had all come to this: 'I thought of the friends of my youth, the scenes of my boyhood, and early manhood, of the slavery I had suffered and the liberty I had panted for …'

He was no doubt thinking of his idyllic, if relatively impoverished, childhood in rural Cheshire. He was born in 1780 in the tiny town of Marton, where a handful of families owned a few small plots of land. The Buckley family was run by his mother, Eliza. Nothing is known of his father, but his mother re-wed and, in time, Buckley had a brother and two sisters. The family enjoyed a modicum of freedom and security. But twin factors were having a deleterious effect on the English countryside: a rapidly encroaching industrial revolution and the war against revolutionary France.

For the previous fifty years rural England had been transformed by the parliamentary acts of enclosure, which allowed the local gentry to agglomerate the common land. Enclosure was England's version of the American events captured by John Steinbeck in his novel *The Grapes of Wrath*; families who had once owned their means of production were forcibly evicted. By some quirk of fate or oversight, Marton had been spared – for a time.

The Buckley family did what British rural people had always done: they grew oats, corn and potatoes, and milked cows. But by the late 1780s their bucolic fairytale, poor and simple as it was, was becoming an anachronism. All the land in and around Marton was demarcated, forcing the tiny community to disperse. The village, famous for its giant oak, would survive. But much of the lands around it would be sold cheaply to the largest local landholders and used to feed a growing army. It was state theft by any other name, and the powers that be felt it was justified as the war with France intensified.

Those who had been labourers with land became labourers (or beggars) without it, seeking onerous and badly paid work wherever it could be found. Enclosure destroyed the rural working class and would sow the seeds of discontent for the class wars of the next century. In late eighteenth-century England it was widely said that you were either a grandee or a slave. There was nothing in between.

In the late 1780s a very young William Buckley was sent away to Macclesfield, a town five miles north of Marton, to be brought up by his mother's grandparents. Macclesfield was witnessing first-hand the rapidly growing gap between rich and poor. It was an interesting town – one account, in *The History of Macclesfield*, says there was 'a furore of party spirit' around this time. A growing tradesmen class showed some sympathy with the left-wing revolutionary tactics of the French Jacobites, a movement that threatened Britain's ancient class order, and one that was strongly condemned by local churchmen and politicians. It's difficult to know whether this affected young William, but he may have carried some memory of social resistance that inspired him to demonstrate it later in life.

We also don't know if he and his siblings were kept together, but it is believed that the very tall William was well treated by those around him and enjoyed growing up in a bustling market town, close to a thickly wooded forest and a countryside of open plains that stretched all the way to the moors of the Peak District.

Buckley never mentioned any schooling, a luxury mostly denied to the rural poor. At fifteen he was illiterate and was apprenticed to a local bricklayer, Robert Wyatt. Here, he later said, his woes began. His dislike for the job was palpable but given his strength and height – by then well over six feet – it appears he was highly suited to the work. For young William, however, it was awful servitude: there were 'hardships and punishments, unnecessarily and improperly inflicted'.

*

AFTER FOUR YEARS WITH WYATT, William Buckley enlisted in the militia. Britain had been at war with France for five years and this would continue – with one small hiatus – for another seventeen. Threats of an invasion of southern Britain sparked fears that 'Boney' might come at any moment, and the government, aided by the press, stoked the fears of all. Young men like Buckley, powerless to shape their own futures, felt duty bound to sign up. He had to choose between the drudgery of bricklaying or the glory of king and country.

In villages and towns across the nation, thousands of men were called to arms and dozens of amateur volunteer forces were formed. By the end of the century nearly 400,000 men were in readiness for an imminent French invasion – more than twice the size of the then standing army. This line of national defence would remain in place until Napoleon's defeat at the Battle of Waterloo in 1815.

As a nineteen year old, Buckley may have had grand notions of being heroic on the battlefield and becoming either a corporal or a colonel – though he later admitted to not knowing the difference. Also in his reflections, he mentioned he had no inkling of the dangers, trials and suffering he was about to endure in the army. Soldiering, he would discover, wasn't all that different from the life of a bricklayer. But this form of drudgery was far more dangerous.

In July 1799, the government legislated to reduce numbers in the militia to make men available for the expeditionary army, and they were given a £10 bonus to join. The British were planning an August attack against the French in Holland to help support a Dutch counter-revolution to restore the ousted William V – an uprising that never fully eventuated. Buckley had already received a bounty of ten guineas with the militia and now took the £10 bounty, volunteering in the Fourth (or King's Own) Regiment of Foot at Horsham Barracks, about forty miles south of London.

The regiment was commanded by a lieutenant-general, the Earl of Chatham, who was considered lazy and feckless. But he was Prime Minister William Pitt's brother, which merited deference. He was often described as 'the Late Lord Chatham' because he would lie in bed till late in the day, keeping his men waiting.

The Morgan–Buckley account doesn't dwell on his military service, but we know he was involved in the second wave of landings in northern Holland, arriving on the Dutch coast in late September. On 2 October, he played his part in an attack on the town of Bergen, which was successful. Four days later, Chatham ordered another attack towards the village of Egmond aan Zee. Chatham had no prior knowledge of the countryside nor the strength of the enemy, and threw his men into the sector with limited military intelligence. This was catastrophic for Buckley's regiment, which was asked to take rough swathes of land in extremely difficult conditions against nimble and experienced French infantrymen who were well 'dug in'. To make matters worse, the rain bucketed down and mingled with fog throughout the copse-woods and villages, making it impossible for the soldiers to distinguish anything clearly.

Buckley and his men fought over high, broad sandy dunes, which felt like a maze of never-ending, crumbling hills, and through it all the men were scattered and picked off like flies. The highly adaptable French infantry, far more experienced than Chatham's militia-filled brigade, took pot shots at will, retreating swiftly into the mist as the hapless British attempted to advance.

Buckley's regiment didn't receive reinforcements, because nobody knew that Chatham's men were already fighting. When a soldier from another regiment was sent up a nearby church tower with a telescope to investigate what was happening in Buckley's sector, he recorded no activity other than mist and haze.

Even with a limited line of vision and on slippery, sandy turf, Buckley was deemed an asset. He could always be seen, so the men naturally rallied towards him. His formal role was as a pivot placed on the outer flanks of a moving line. When commanded, he was the first to wheel the line into a new position without halting – but in sand dunes half obscured by mist, it's hard to know how the British line held any identifiable formation.

Buckley's regiment suffered many casualties that day: 496 killed, wounded and captured, including three lieutenant-colonels.

Chatham's entire division lost about 630 men at a conservative estimate, nearly half the 1400 British casualties, and a fifth of the 3200 total casualties. In the melee, Buckley received a musket shot to his right hand. Chatham wasn't spared, receiving a spent musket ball to the shoulder.

Eventually the expeditionary army was evacuated, under an agreement with the French to withdraw peacefully. The Dutch campaign was considered a wasteful effort, and the Dutch showed no inclination to side with the British. The wounded Buckley, incapable of fighting, was relieved to be going home.

*

As the century turned, Buckley lived at Fort Amherst barracks in Chatham near the Kent coastline. He was now without any real purpose.

Radicals and firebrands stalked the British political landscape. Napoleon was in the ascendant. There were food riots throughout 1801 and 1802, and the government under William Pitt was increasingly paranoid. After the Irish Rebellion of 1798, the government had decided to suspend the legal right of habeas corpus – anybody could now be held prisoner without proof of wrongdoing. This was a period when a man appearing to be radical or seditious could be gaoled without charge. There were spies and informers everywhere. The great romantic poet and artist William Blake was famously tried and acquitted of sedition in 1803 for telling a soldier who had invaded his garden, 'Damn the King, and damn all his soldiers, they are all his slaves!'

The army, too, wasn't impervious to radical voices. One of the most influential was Colonel Edward Despard, an Anglo-Irish officer suspected by the government of just about everything, from having a connection with Irish rebel militias to being in league with the French. Despard was well known to mix happily with all ranks, among whom was almost certainly a young William Buckley.

In Despard's former role as superintendent of the Bay of Honduras, he had distributed lots of land equally to people of all races. If this wasn't galling enough to the authorities, he had the temerity to marry a woman of colour and bring her to England at a time when slavery was still British policy.

Despard's small acts of empathy and natural charisma made him a hero for some and a suspect to others. He had all the swashbuckling traits of a seasoned British soldier, backed by a distinguished military career in the American War of Independence. He counted Lord Horatio Nelson, commander of the British Navy in the Mediterranean, as a close friend. In truth he was less a radical, more a political evangelist. Disaffected young soldiers rallied around his notions of freedom.

Like many of this time, Despard had read Thomas Paine's banned 1791 political tract *Rights of Man*, which the British government considered to be a treasonous publication. In it Despard recognised his own conviction that popular electoral mandates should be the basis of government. He had committed himself to a peaceful campaign for political reform, but his enemies were sure – or at least claimed to be sure – that it was far more insidious. He was arrested without any real proof and held for three years without charge. When habeas corpus was revived, he was released, and by then he had become the great liberal cause célèbre of his time. He would eventually be executed for high treason in 1803, despite the courtroom appearance on his behalf of Admiral Horatio Nelson.

William Buckley was no revolutionary but, in this climate of suspicion, mere sympathy with the wrong types was seen as treasonous. In other ways, his career had been on track: he'd received an extra bounty based on his extended service and 'the good opinion' of his officers. But the extra money may have caused him to be more careless, and he fell in with the wrong crowd. As he later put it, he was associating with 'several men of bad character in the regiment' owing to his 'improper education'. These men 'gradually acquired an influence' over his conduct, and there were scenes of 'irregularity and riotous dissipation'. Whether this was a reference to carousing or politics, he didn't mention, but no doubt he was spending time with those who attracted official attention.

When, in early 1802, an unknown woman purportedly approached him inside the barracks and asked him to carry a bolt of cloth to another woman working inside the garrison, he thought nothing of it. Within a few moments, he was arrested. 'I do not know, to this hour, the precise character, or extent of my sentence,' he wrote in his memoirs. Was he a political prisoner or a common thief? There's another story in which he was indeed culpable – in that version, Buckley, alongside a certain William Marmon (the very man he escaped Sullivan Bay with, who had been a fellow soldier in his regiment) had broken into the shop of a Mr Cave in Wareham and stolen two pieces of Irish cloth.

Buckley claimed to his death that he was innocent, and that he didn't commit the burglary but it's possible he may have been asked to fence the cloth. Other possible scenarios come to mind – that he had been suspected of some kind of political conspiracy and this woman may have been used as a lure to incriminate him. The powers that be may have felt the need to have the big man – whose sheer size made him appear dangerous – under lock and key.

On 2 August 1802 at the Sussex Assizes, Buckley received a death sentence that was commuted to gaol for life. A few days earlier he had been a free man, and now he was back in a more onerous version of his old bricklaying job. He was carting and laying bricks, but this time as part of a prison gang working on riverside fortifications at Woolwich in East London. His physical strength and building ability were assets to the project, and his supervisors noticed this. His recollections of this time are tinged with sadness – his liberty had been snatched away and his status as a criminal had ended all contact with his family. He would never see any of his relations again.

He was a mechanic with skills and strength, the type badly needed for the new colony. When selected for transportation, he saw this as an opportunity not just to restore his character but to find his freedom as well. On 28 April 1803, the *Calcutta* departed from Portsmouth under the command of Captain Daniel Woodriff, accompanied by the *Ocean*. Buckley, like most of his fellow transportees, had virtually no clue where he was going or what he was in for. He just knew it had to be better than this.

Chapter 6

I N LATE JANUARY 1804 the *Ocean* left the half-made settlement at
Sullivan Bay minus all those convicts that Collins believed had
'perished in the woods'.

David Collins had been given a free hand to go where he wanted,
but he would think carefully before commiting to any location. He
would have remembered his early tenure at Sydney Cove sixteen
years earlier, and the desperate circumstances that had prevailed
in that infant colony. In his *An Account of the English Colony in
New South Wales* he wrote of the 'great despair' of Sydney that had
reached well into the 1790s. In July 1790 there were 488 on the sick
list and 143 deaths. The next year another 160 people died, and
in 1792 when the salted meat supplies ran out, 450 people died
of disease and malnutrition. The increasingly crowded settlement
at Port Jackson had to evacuate hundreds of convicts to Norfolk
Island. Even by 1795, the colony was barely self-sustaining: they
couldn't harvest enough fish, and by July that year had run out of
all salted and fresh meat. Sydney was on starvation rations for its
first few years.

Collins must have known that starvation wasn't just possible in any colony that he was to form but that it was highly probable. With his Sydney memories still fresh, he was being extremely cautious. He had been told a suitable settlement might be possible on the Tamar River at Port Dalrymple, near present-day Launceston, but he sent out an emissary who returned deeming it unsuitable. Apparently the local people were hostile, and the Tamar held little prospects for a colony. In this Collins would be wrong – again. That very year, 1804, Lieutenant-Colonel William Paterson would set up camp nearby, creating one of Van Diemen's Land's most prosperous settlements. But Collins sailed on to the Derwent where he joined Lieutenant John Bowen at the embryonic Risdon Cove settlement, established the previous September.

When he arrived on 15 February, Collins looked on aghast. Lieutenant Bowen's chosen site was not to Collins's standards, as the fifty or so settlers hadn't made enough progress, and as Collins soon learnt, there had been a terrible fight with the local people in which an unknown number of Indigenous people, the Palawa, were said to have been killed. Immediately taking charge of the situation, Collins moved all the settlers to a more suitable site on the western shore of the Derwent, downriver. This time he got it right. The cove was an excellent site, with a good port, running fresh water nearby, and the shelter of what would later be known as Mount Wellington. He named the new settlement in honour of the then Secretary of State for War and the Colonies, Lord Hobart.

But the first few years in the settlement then known as Hobart Town were difficult. Collins was given little official support, as the British government was still preoccupied with Napoleon. Collins sent twenty-three despatches to England, which were ignored. Then the colony's management became more difficult overnight when the British government ordered him to receive four hundred settlers from Norfolk Island. In one fell swoop, the population of Hobart Town doubled. Collins was told to provide them with houses, farms and convict labourers, and then, as an aside, was given a serious rap over the knuckles for spending too much public money. He was forced to obtain food from the government stores at Sydney and to purchase supplies from visiting traders. Supply ships rarely came, and a lack of food and equipment dogged Hobart Town's early years just as they had Sydney's, but Hobart Town developed at a much faster pace than that northern colony.

This had less to do with Collins's administration than with the abundant resources available. Here, unlike in Sydney, the most dogged and resourceful could provide for themselves. Convict hunters were living year round in the bush, capturing food aplenty and regularly bringing in surplus for the colony.

The Hobart coat of arms shows both a forest kangaroo and an animal that no longer exists: the Tasmanian emu. When it comes to extinctions on the island, most speak of the thylacine, commonly known as the Tasmanian tiger, but there were others. The Tasmanian emu was smaller than its mainland cousin, and once European dogs arrived on this dingo-free landscape, the emus' days were numbered. The city's coat of arms reads: *Sic fortis Hobartia crevit* – 'By this means did Hobart prosper'. Without these two hapless creatures, the colony may not have survived.

In the early 1800s Hobart Town was also becoming the natural home port for hundreds of sealers and whalers, who were already spreading out to all areas of the island and across the Bass Strait to the southern shores of the mainland. But something else kept the colonisers' interest. Some parts of the island had been crafted by the Palawa, for at least thirty thousand years, as they had applied their own brilliant form of fire management to create some of the best pasture lands in the world. These great grasslands, known then as 'grassy woodlands' by the British, were also readily accessible, and close to ports and estuaries; to the invaders, they seemed perfect for sheep and cattle. The landscape was similar in aspect to that of Port Phillip, though with far greater amounts of virgin forest. Here again, the colonists felt they had been granted an Antipodean version of mother England.

The convict hunters in Van Diemen's Land spread throughout the midlands region, which stretched between the northern and southern settlements in Launceston and Hobart Town. They soon evolved into pastoralists. On their perfectly manicured pasturelands, sheep and cattle multiplied, and within ten years of Collins's arrival there was a distinct – if slightly disorganised – grazing industry, almost exclusively run and managed by convict settlers. These weren't elite landowners and squatters, but rough men who let their livestock graze wherever they wished. Within a few short years, traditional British beef and mutton was back on the local menu, supplementing the kangaroo and other native foods. Within fifteen years of the founding of the colony, there would be around 170,000 grazing animals – twice that of New South Wales.

It may be hard to believe now, but until 1820 in Van Diemen's Land, the semi-nomadic, convict hunter-pastoralists shared the land with the traditional owners. The two peoples negotiated food and resources, and while there were frequent imbroglios and misunderstandings, the newcomers and the Indigenous people generally found ways to coexist. The Palawa loved the settlers' tea, flour and sugar, and bartered for their dogs, which they adapted to their own needs almost overnight. At a time when most guns were inaccurate at more than fifty yards, dogs became the most valuable hunting tools in Van Diemen's Land.

In this distinctly penal colony, free settlers hadn't been actively encouraged, but that was about to change. After 1815 and the defeat of Napoleon, the British needed to find pursuits for all those officers and gentlemen now being discharged from the army. Knowledge of the island's bounty spread back to Britain, and in 1820 a commission of inquiry chaired by John Thomas Bigge, a judge and royal commissioner, agreed that land grants in the colonies should be given according to a settler's starting capital.

Only when the government started handing out parcels of land with 'exclusive ownership' attached did the largely pragmatic and often uneasy coexistence between convict graziers and the Palawa start to fall apart. Suddenly the concept of private property, which the convicts had rarely had for themselves even when freed, was transplanted to Van Diemen's Land. A new breed of aggressive pastoralists, who brooked no trespassing, arrived with the intent of replicating the socioeconomic order of rural England – the order that had displaced William Buckley and his family from Marton. The local Indigenous people, as ever in Australian history, would soon be fenced off from the lands that had been their birthright for untold thousands of years.

Not all arrivals with dreams of verdant land were British born. Among those enticed by the prospect of acreage was a man from Parramatta who was vastly superior in bush knowledge to any of his grazing peers. His name was John Batman.

*

JOHN BATMAN'S START in life was inauspicious. He was Australian, born in Rosehill, Parramatta, to William and Mary Batman on 21 January 1801. His father was a Yorkshire cutler and grinder who had been transported in 1797 for receiving stolen saltpetre, used in the manufacture of gunpowder. Mary paid her fare to Australia and brought their two children, Maria and Robert. When William obtained his ticket of leave, he went on to establish a timber yard at Parramatta. He and his wife, devout Methodists, would go on to have another four children, all of whom were baptised at St John's church in Parramatta in 1810, the year that William's sentence expired.

Young John, who attended John Tull's elementary school, was described as 'sufficiently literate for any practical purpose' as well as being highly sociable and 'of fine physique'. One contemporary description of him as a youth was that he had considerable intelligence and vigour 'with a merry eye, a handsome face, and a flattering tongue to please the other sex'. Rather than avoid the local Aboriginal children, John showed no discrimination – they were his pals and playmates. It was part of his Methodist upbringing to mingle with all peoples, and he grew up conversant with their cultural idiosyncrasies and their knowledge of the land.

At fifteen, John and his younger brother Henry were apprenticed to James Flavell, a blacksmith and wheelwright, in Sydney. Both young men enjoyed the rough and tumble of Sydney. John was a chancer who tried his luck at everything – and, if it suited him, showed no loyalty. Within a few months Flavell and his associate William Tripp were sentenced to hang for stealing clothing from a neighbour's house. John had few qualms about bringing evidence against Flavell that led directly to his death.

John Batman.
from an old print in the possession
of his grandson, Mr A. B. Weire.

Portrait of John Batman by Charles Nuttall (c.1912). No authentic contemporary portrait of Batman is known today. This portrait was drawn 'from a likeness supplied by his grandson'. (National Library of Australia)

In his late teens he had become a 'jack-of-all-trades' farmer. The brothers could have returned home to Parramatta, as their father was prospering there, but they wanted to stay in the heart of the colony, where all the action was. Rumours spread that John had taken up with a number of girlfriends as well as married women.

Little is known about John's last few years on the mainland, although it is believed he left New South Wales because he had an affair with a young orphan named Elizabeth Richardson. In 1821 she became pregnant and named John, then just twenty, as the father. In early May 1821, the Orphan Institution Committee (which was responsible for Elizabeth) suggested John marry her, but he refused. When he was asked to pay £50 for the orphanage's expenses, his father stepped in and the amount was reduced to £25. Whether or not John was the father, his involvement with Elizabeth would have been deeply embarrassing for his father, a devout Christian, who may have asked his son to leave Parramatta so that the family could save face in the community. Three days after the committee made its final decision, John and Henry left New South Wales for Van Diemen's Land. It was 29 November 1821.

Almost certainly with the financial backing of their father, John and Henry bought property at Kingston in the north-east part of the island, near Ben Lomond. This mountain is dominated by an alpine plateau around five thousand feet high and surrounded by precipitous escarpments. Henry became a wheelwright near Launceston, while John took up as a grazier on a farm said to be large in acreage but agriculturally poor. In 1823 the government contracted him to supply meat, and through hard graft he was able, the next year, to graduate from a leasehold to a grant of six hundred acres in the area.

*

FOR BATMAN AND other new so-called gentlemen settlers of the island, there was, in 1824, one persistent problem: a growing infestation of bushrangers. Some had escaped from Hobart Town; others had escaped penury from Macquarie Harbour, an inlet on the west coast where the most recalcitrant and escape-prone prisoners were detained in horrific conditions.

Among the two most feared were Thomas (also known as Mark) Jeffries and Matthew Brady, the latter often termed the 'gentleman bushranger'. They both knew how to work the bush, but otherwise they couldn't have been more different.

Brady had famously escaped by stealing a whaleboat and, with the help of a sailor-convict, out-sailed the Macquarie Harbour pilot who set out in pursuit. He and his fellow escapees alighted several days later just south of Hobart Town, beginning a life of ransacking the wealthy settlers who were now colonising the countryside. Brady's signature style was to rob the rich as heavily as possible (especially those who mistreated their convicts), taking their food, horses and munitions. By contrast, he kept the poor afloat, robbing them lightly and often with great care – and with impeccable manners. He was handsome and beloved by women, as close as Australia ever had to the dashing Dick Turpin style of highwayman who had roamed the English countryside a century before.

Jeffries was an entirely different matter. He was sent down from Scotland and started life in the colony as an executioner and a flogger of fellow convicts. With this curriculum vitae, he took bushranging to new heights of depravity. Like Brady he was one of the very few to escape Macquarie Harbour. During his overland bolt from the west coast, it was said that he either ate or murdered four of his accomplices. As a bushranger, he murdered a man then kidnapped his widow and their baby, dashing the infant's head against a tree and violating the woman. For a short period he was part of Brady's gang. While Brady had a number of desperados with him, he couldn't abide Jeffries's constant abuse of women and ejected him from his crew, calling him a 'dehumanised monster'.

The style and verve of a bushranger didn't matter to the humourless Lieutenant-Governor George Arthur, who looked on with loathing at the growing menace of escaped convicts. To the commercially minded Arthur, they were bad for business and a nuisance of the highest order. Arthur, a distinguished soldier in Britain's battles against Napoleon in Spain, was a former lieutenant-governor of British Honduras, who had come to the new colony to bring God, order, punishment – and profit.

Soon after his arrival in May 1824, Arthur was running the penal colony with great exactitude and extreme rigour, but he wasn't just a capable administrator. He looked upon the island's rich pastures and arable land as a source of wealth not only for himself, but for the great and growing Empire he diligently served. Over the next decade he would become the biggest (and most silent) landowner on the island and its richest man. In public he played the part of a dispassionate and formidable regulator, but privately he was lending money to wealthy but clueless new settlers at extortionate rates of interest. To Arthur there was no ruling the land without returns accruing from it, and he would tolerate neither bushrangers nor the Palawa standing in the way of 'progress' and economic growth.

As has often been quoted, when Arthur offered the reward of twenty-five guineas for Brady's capture, Brady – who knew exactly what kind of man Arthur was – sent out his own missive. Brady's rejoinder was crafted in Arthur's own bureaucratic style: 'It has caused Matthew Brady much concern that such a person known as George Arthur is at large. Twenty gallons of rum will be given to any person who will deliver this person to me.'

Brady's enormous charm and charisma endeared him to the mostly convict population, but not to the settlers whom he was robbing with virtual impunity. He was a brilliant and crafty bushranger who could strike and disappear into the back country in moments. But John Batman, ambitious and with a strong desire to become a player on the island, believed that he exceeded Brady (indeed any bushranger) in bushcraft. The young man from Parramatta could see clearly where his next move must be.

Chapter 7

I T WAS IN the early days of 1804 that William Buckley had made
the momentous decision to remain free, but his escape wasn't just
about freedom – he yearned for a life that he controlled, a destiny
he could shape and influence. As he'd grown into adulthood, he
had never been able to get away from the unrelenting onslaught of
economic imperatives, the forces of war and the paranoid politics of
his age. His life had been made up of rapid changes of circumstances,
where the smallest indiscretions had the widest ramifications. One
moment he was a highly regarded and rewarded soldier, the next
he was carting bricks in disgrace. Before he knew it, he was on his
way to an unknown and strange land, and now he was deeply in its
embrace, with few resources and no destination. Here nobody could
tell him what to do. He couldn't be influenced or prejudiced. In the
most bizarre way, he had been granted his wish.

He took a course west along the coast of Bass Strait, with only one
purpose – to survive, and in this he would be remarkably lucky. The
southern coasts of Victoria were among the most naturally blessed
regions on the continent. He would have plenty of shellfish, lobsters

and berries if he was resourceful enough to find them. On the downside, his clothes and shoes were fraying, and he needed some form of shelter and a supply of fresh water. He had a firestick, which allowed for warmth and cooked food, but McAllenan had taken the gun, so Buckley couldn't shoot for game despite the incredible array of birdlife around him.

The land, formerly the arena for his escape, had taken on a new significance: it had to be the source of his sustenance. As he left Swan Island, he crossed flat marshland and was soon confronted by a howling southern wind that came off the ocean and the never-ending crash of surf. The sun was still very warm, and the sand was hot. After a few hours of trudging across the marshland, he heard human voices, not close but not too far away either.

By his estimate there were about a hundred Wadawurrung based in a camp by the Barwon River, and some were moving in his direction. Buckley ducked for cover and made for another part of the river away from the beach, where he felt he could observe and not be observed. But while crossing a creek he accidentally extinguished his firestick. The nights were mostly warm, but a fire was always a welcome friend in the wilderness – now even that had been snuffed out. Fire made what he had foraged 'palatable', he said, but it was also a means of 'preserving his health under the great privations to which I was subjected'.

Buckley managed not to attract attention and kept moving. He was tired and hungry, and his skin was heavily burnt. Still fearing he might be spotted, he wrapped himself in leaves and branches but that night slept badly. 'It was a miserable night, my clothes being wet, and the weather cold, it being the early part of the spring that year,' he noted. Actually it was still summer – he probably had no idea of the seasons in the southern hemisphere, or that the weather patterns, influenced by the Antarctic, were volatile. Temperatures could shift at any moment.

Buckley said he came across a considerable supply of abalone, which the Wadawurrung called *kooderoo*. It proliferated on the rocks of the southern coasts of Australia and was an important subsistence food for the locals. The inside of the shell is shiny, from silvery white to green-red mother of pearl, and it would prove to be among Buckley's most valuable food sources.

Without fire he had been forced to eat the abalone raw, a decent meal for the first time in days but one that caused a tremendous thirst. He piled abalone in his pocket and crossed over Thompsons Creek, which the locals called Karaaf. He needed fresh water, but so far he had remained close to the coast and all the creeks were salty. He must have realised that inland was a better place to find drinking water, but he felt safer on the beaches – inland were forests and scrubs and, of course, the camps of Indigenous people. The beach allowed him space to see and time to react. Fear of the unknown was keeping him coast-bound.

He tried licking dewdrops from branches, but the few he extracted only seemed to make his thirst all the more pressing. He trudged on the next day and night, finding shelter in the long grasses or by covering himself with reeds and rushes. The abalone were scarcer, and he was getting progressively weaker. To make matters worse, his walk for survival was loaded with fear – he believed he'd seen dogs following him. He flinched at noises and saw shadows at night. He was terrified of an ambush.

Perhaps a week after leaving his comrades, Buckley was debilitated and depressed. He could find nothing to eat and there was no sign of fresh water flowing into any of the beaches. He also felt he had moved into a hotter climate zone, but it's likely his body was now less able to deal with the pressing heat of January. 'I laid myself down at night in a state of total exhaustion,' he recounted.

The next day he pressed on, summoning reserves of strength he didn't know he had. Late that day, he fell asleep in a space between two large rocks. The tide came in so quickly, or so he thought, that he was woken by a wave washing over him. He rushed to the back of the cliff and stayed there, exposed all night, shivering while he waited for the tide to recede. He had begun to rant at non-existent people, railing at his own misfortune. He wandered all the way down to the Anglesea River, by which time he hadn't drunk water or eaten in three days.

His luck turned at the most crucial time. He was shuffling listlessly down the coast when he came upon a recently abandoned camp and, by chance, a smouldering piece of wood. He now had a firestick that he held on to for dear life, although he had nothing to cook.

He had now reached the Otway Ranges, a wet, lush and bounteous region, covered in cool rainforest, that offered abundant bush food. Here he finally decided to head slightly inland, and within a few hours he had discovered a wild raspberry that grew in profusion, hanging from high bushes. Soon he came across a well that held clean, fresh water; he had never drunk so heartily of anything in his life. 'The Almighty indeed, appeared that day to favour me,' he wrote. 'Especially, I thought, in pity to my sufferings. For I also found a great supply of shellfish so that I had found food, fire and water.' Buckley considered it a sign and a deliverance – he finally had the trinity of essentials to keep him alive.

He was now at Aireys Inlet, known to the local Wadawurrung people as Mangowak. Each night he was able to start a fire and cook various shellfish. He came across hollowed-out trees and found areas that had been deliberately burnt – these and the water well were clear evidence, if any was needed, that locals were close at hand.

Buckley stayed about a week in the area, sheltering in a small cave. It may have been about two or three weeks since his companions had left him, and he had covered about sixty miles down the coast. He decided to move on, a decision that he never explained; he may have felt that he was too close to the locals, and that further south there may be fewer people and even better resources.

Buckley carried on for another two days and was eventually rewarded for his efforts. He came across Nooraki (Mount Defiance) where he felt he could make a home. Here was a rocky hill about a mile in length with a very long overhang. It wasn't exposed to the sun, and the tide neither waxed nor waned just below it. Fresh water was streaming down its face, and its formations afforded some shelter from the elements as well as cover from potential enemies. Nooraki was also a welcome rest stop, as his body was covered in bruises and sores.

The area appeared to have everything he needed for subsistence. There were a variety of shellfish on the coast and a proliferation of a purple-flowered succulent now known as pigface. There were two sources of fruit – a black and a white berry – but the pigface, creeping everywhere, was the real godsend. Not only is the entire plant edible both cooked and raw, but it also has medicinal qualities: its thick leaves can be used like aloe vera to lessen stings. This food source nurtured Buckley back to relative good health, while to him it tasted just like watermelon.

He was now able to build a hut of sorts from sticks, branches and leaves, and within a few weeks he was as robust as he had ever been. 'I remember a fancy coming over me, that I could have remained at that spot all the rest of my life, but this solitary desire was but temporary,' he explained. 'For it was never intended that man should live alone, so implanted in his nature are social feelings.' These sentiments were a sign that Buckley had reached beyond mere survival; that his most basic needs were being satisfied. He was now in need of company.

*

WE DON'T KNOW exactly how long it took for Buckley to make his first contact with the Wadawurrung, but it was likely a few months into his sojourn.

'I was gazing round from my Robinson Crusoe hut upon the surface of the waters,' he wrote, 'when I thought I heard the sound of human voices and on looking up was somewhat startled at seeing three natives standing on the high land immediately above me.' The three men, clad in possum skins, were all armed. Buckley made for a rock crevice, but his language in the memoir gives the impression that he instinctively knew these people held no threat. They had noticed his tracks to and from the beach and seen his simple habitation: 'They were soon on my track, and shouting what I considered to be a call for me to come out. I resolved to do so.'

For a split second Buckley felt he was done for, but the looks on their faces revealed otherwise. According to him, their expressions were those of clear wonder and respect. The three men moved hesitantly towards him, obviously a little afraid but seemingly overwhelmed by curiosity. They reached out to touch his hands and then, satisfied that he was warm and alive, began to strike their chests and cry.

Buckley had no idea what was going through their minds – they were all in uproar, screaming and wailing, each man touching him all over as if to prove he was real. Buckley initially thought this was a precursor to some kind of mischief – in fact, these men appeared to be rejoicing. Buckley was struck dumb. It was as if he was a long-lost friend suddenly returned to them. He couldn't have known it at the time, but he had been recognised, or so the men believed.

They examined his hut and made themselves at home, one man building a large fire while another threw off his possum rug, dived into the sea and returned with an enormous crayfish that he threw on the flames. Buckley had no idea why he was given the best portions of crayfish meat.

With the meal finished, the men wanted him to follow them out of his camp. Buckley said he was nervous, but decided to consent. Two men went ahead of him and one followed. For several hours they walked inland, and Buckley lost his bearings. Eventually they came to a pair of lonely huts – 'two small turf cabins' as Buckley described them – each just wide enough to allow two men to sleep. Buckley felt trapped, as if he'd been gulled by the men, even though there was no cause for alarm. He thought it might be possible for him to leave in the depths of night, but his 'guard' – really just his bunkmate – didn't sleep and was constantly mumbling.

Buckley remained sceptical of them, with no desire to do their bidding. He had no experience of the Indigenous people, and was still of the English cast of mind that they were by nature treacherous. He was wondering if this was all a ploy designed to have him taken somewhere, and he was right – for all the wrong reasons.

The next day the men asked him to follow them; they wanted to celebrate the arrival of this man with their tribe. Buckley, who had no idea what was intended, resisted strongly. 'Mustering all my resolution, I intimated a refusal that I would not do so. After a warm discussion by signs, and to both parties, by sufficient sounds, they apparently consented that I should remain.' But Buckley wouldn't get away so easily: the Wadawurrung men wanted his worn-out stockings as an 'assurance offer'. Buckley still resisted. The men pushed him harder, striking their chests and stamping, while he held out.

One of the men left and returned with a basket of reeds, in which he had placed a number of berries. He was offering to barter them for the stockings, but still Buckley refused. This was a pivotal point for him, his form of hard negotiation, as he felt he had to remain strong and give them nothing. He was resolved to demonstrate to these people the kind of tough man they were dealing with, a show of strength in case more crucial confrontations ever arose. In both Indigenous and white society, his size and strength remained his strongest bargaining chips.

Exasperated by the white giant who refused to compromise, the three men walked off into the bush as night fell. Buckley had made his point, but he had unknowingly declined what he had been seeking: society and sustenance.

*

BUCKLEY'S WANDERING CONTINUED, probably for several months. He was extremely lonely, at one point returning to where he had left the Wadawurrung men who had shown him nothing but kindness and interest, but he could find no signs of human activity. As he wandered aimlessly, time and space no longer seemed to matter.

At night he endured eerie nocturnal screams that forbade sleep. As he put it, his mind was suffering 'for want of relaxation'. The minds of the strongest men, he wrote 'would fail in such circumstances'. But he didn't completely lose his wits, and he kept feeding on berries and succulent shrubs, finding water as it pooled in small holes in the ground.

He had no way of knowing that the *Calcutta* and the *Ocean* had left Sullivan Bay less than a month after his escape. He decided to return there, but he was asking the impossible of himself. The coastline was by this time numbingly cold, while the ocean, as he described it, was in such a white and unbridled fury that he could no longer scavenge the rocks. Whenever he found accessible shellfish they were never in such profusion as he remembered them. These few raw shellfish were his 'wretched meal', as he described it. He was back in familiar territory, his health steadily declining for lack of a sustainable diet. He could barely move at night and could only endure short distances by day.

Then Buckley made a discovery that would change his life forever. He came to Spring Creek (in present-day Torquay) which the local people called Doorangwar. Just beyond it he saw a great mound of earth – clearly the grave of an important person. He had no desire to disturb it, but then he noticed that a very long, thin and well-formed wooden rod had been inserted into its peak. This implement could be life saving: it was possibly a walking stick, but it could be used to spear fish or hunt. He knew he was desecrating a grave but felt he had no choice when he extracted it. Was it a desecration in Aboriginal eyes? Almost certainly yes. In any other situation, it would have been considered an insult to the deceased – but this was no ordinary situation as Buckley would soon find out.

The Bellarine Peninsula, which he had last seen six months earlier, was now returning into view, and he felt glad to be back in reasonably familiar surroundings. He found himself at Karaaf, the first big stream he had forded after leaving McAllenan and Pye on Swan Island. This time, however, it was flowing far more swiftly, and the effort of swimming across nearly overcame him. He crawled into the bush where he lay down exhausted, fearing he would 'not see the light of another morning'. This was only a slight exaggeration – his strength was leaving him. He 'prayed long and earnestly to God for his merciful assistance and protection'. The signs were pointing to his imminent death: 'All night the wild dogs howled horribly as if expressing their impatience for my remains,' he wrote. 'Even before death, I fancied they would attack me.'

A day later, at the edge of a lagoon amid the flutter and cluck of swans and ducks, Buckley suddenly went limp. He stumbled, fell sideways to the ground and lost consciousness.

Chapter 8

I N APRIL 1824, John Helder Wedge was one of the new settlers to Van Diemen's Land's northern region, taking up fifteen hundred acres on the Lakes District. He was only twenty-seven when he arrived fresh from England to work for Arthur's regime, marking out and surveying all the land that had been granted to settlers. Within a year of arrival, he had been robbed at gunpoint by the gang led by Matthew Brady.

To pursue the bushrangers, Wedge secured the services of two convicts who worked as trackers. However, it was soon clear to him that this was pointless: Brady was too fast and too crafty for them. Convicts may have been tough and able to live off the land, but they lacked any real tracking ability. In despair, Wedge approached John Batman.

Wedge was in luck: Batman was also angry about the growing bushranger menace. At that meeting, both men decided they would form vigilante groups under the auspices of the administration, which would provide them with guns and horses. This was no small risk – if a bushranger knew that someone was working with the police, they could face severe reprisals. Brady and Jeffries were well enough connected with the convict population to work out who was helping the authorities.

One night in January 1826, Wedge's nephew John Darke was staying in a settler's hut on the River Nile, a tributary of the South Esk River, when Jeffries appeared about a hundred yards away. He walked slowly towards the hut, his two latest captives walking just ahead of him, bound by the wrists, stumbling as he prodded them forward.

Darke didn't wait. As soon as Jeffries came into range, he began discharging his musket. The men exchanged a volley of shots, and Darke managed to graze Jeffries's throat with a bullet. When Jeffries retreated, Darke sprang after him. He searched all night along riverbanks for any sign of the bushranger. Worn out by morning, he approached a hut where he hoped to rest. Breakfasting there were a group of men who welcomed him in – but just as Darke was drifting off to sleep, a young Indigenous man who worked for the settler James Cox came running in with news. Jeffries was approaching again. 'Having been up the three nights before and walking the bush and without sleeping, I rolled myself in a blanket and had been asleep about ten minutes,' Darke later related in a letter to his uncle John Wedge.

A number of the men concealed themselves until the bushranger came into range, which was when Darke allegedly leapt from his bed naked and ran into the fray. 'Parsons was up to him first and presented his gun. Jeffries begged for mercy, and I, coming up, prevented the men from hurting him [Jeffries] – he was well armed but did not fire.'

Darke claimed in his writings that after capture, Jeffries was contrite and within a few minutes started relating some of his more recent crimes. 'He had killed Russell and lived eight days on his flesh, and had five pounds of it left when he robbed Miller's hut,' Darke wrote. Jeffries was supposed to have fried the man's flesh together with some mutton. 'He told me of the seven murders and how he meant to have committed many others.'

Jeffries was later taken to Batman's property, where he was plied with further questions. Apparently the bushranger was equally contrite in Batman's presence, confessing to all his crimes down to the last detail. He was then taken to Launceston Gaol.

By February 1826, Brady had returned to the north where he commenced raiding near Launceston, and Governor Arthur offered rewards to anyone who could capture him. For a settler, the reward for bringing Brady back dead or alive would be either one hundred guineas or three hundred acres of land; for a convict, there was the lure of a full pardon and passage to England. This was a temptation few convicts could ignore, even those who sympathised with Brady's Robin Hood style of plunder.

Brady had been causing enormous trouble in the district. First he and his gang had attacked the house of wealthy settler Richard Dry, seizing his white carriage horses among many other things. Then Brady had headed south for the Tamar River, burning en route the wheat and stockyards of Thomas Kenton. Wedge's posse, on the alert, were now heading that way.

When three men betrayed Brady to the authorities, the gang was ambushed around Patersons Plains. Brady was shot in the leg, the bullet entering his calf and passing upwards to his lower thigh – but with the help of his gang, he still managed to escape.

The news quickly spread through the region that a wounded Brady was at large. The local white settlers formed small detachments to range across country. One party passed directly over Brady and his men, who were concealed in a deep ravine. Brady then doubled back, moving towards the pursuers but slightly around them. He didn't know that in doing so, he was heading directly towards John Batman and his men.

Brady, severely incapacitated, had a makeshift pole to help him walk, and his difficult movements may have warned animals. Not so far off, near the North Esk River, Batman watched a herd of cattle rush down a nearby hill, disturbed by something higher up. He reconnoitred at higher ground but found nothing. The next dawn he returned and witnessed cattle again stampeding down the hill. As he gained the height, he saw at some distance a man clearly limping, in pain. Batman cooeed for his men. Brady knew what this meant – he was about to be pincered.

As Batman approached with his gun raised, Brady dropped his own to the ground. 'I would not normally surrender to soldiers but you are a brave man and I submit to you,' he allegedly said to Batman. Legend has it that Batman was wearing a top hat and frockcoat when he caught Brady, the latter supposedly relieved at being trapped by a true gentleman. But given Brady's natural antipathy towards the monied class, it's more likely that he saw in Batman a serious rival, not to be trifled with.

For Batman, this was the turning point in his career: he was about to become the colony's most celebrated bounty hunter. However, this didn't turn out to be quite the triumph he had hoped. The capture and arrest of Brady and his men were celebrated in the press, and Batman was rewarded with a parcel of land and an appointment as special constable and pound keeper, the latter role affording him the right to impound cattle that had wandered onto private or government land.

But what Batman really wanted was land – a great deal more than what he received after capturing Brady. Land was the currency of respectability, and Batman yearned for respect. He applied for a large grant based on the work he'd done at his property in Kingston – and his new-found status. Yet his prowess wasn't enough for Arthur. The governor held out.

Batman's lack of respectability was working against him. He wasn't a gentleman, and in Arthur's mind he hadn't been behaving as one. In fact, he had been living in sin with an uncompromising Irish convict, Eliza Callaghan (also known as Eliza Thompson). Originally sentenced to fourteen years' transportation for passing a counterfeit banknote in London, she had run away from the police superintendent in Launceston and taken up with Batman. Arthur's rigid moral tone pervaded the colony, and as long as Batman was cohabiting with an escapee, he wouldn't be granted any further land expansion for his sheep and cattle. Eliza had also given Batman two illegitimate children, which did nothing to further his cause.

'Pending the survey of the Island His Excellency has not the power to comply with your request,' was Arthur's contrite reply to Batman's petition. It was a rejection Batman would never forget.

*

BATMAN HAD LONG had dreams of being a large landowner. A year before his capture of Brady an article in the *Hobart Town Gazette* in February 1825 had set his heart alight. It told of great pastures on the mainland. For months afterwards, the landowning gentry of Hobart Town and Launceston discussed what they had read. The article reported the exploits of Captain William Hovell and Hamilton Hume, who had travelled from Sydney to Western Port in October the previous year. Hume was an old schoolfriend of Batman's from Parramatta. He and Hovell claimed to have discovered the best pastures ever seen in New Holland: abundant grazing land for untold miles, along with copious fresh water.

But the two men were describing an area on the western side of Port Phillip Bay, not Western Port. Hovell's longitude measurements had been wrong – he was a degree out. The two men would later fall out over this, as Hume insisted the grasslands were in Port Phillip, but Hovell would not concede. This disagreement was of no interest to Batman, however – to him, the article had kindled a dream. Hume's own account, which Batman later read avidly, would profoundly change his ambitions. As the nineteenth-century Anglo-Australian historian George William Rusden wrote: 'The overland journey had stirred him [Batman]. Bushman as he was, he knew that Hume was right about Port Phillip Bay.' Hume had done his homework before leaving – he knew that Western Port Harbour had two islands, while Port Phillip's harbour had none.

A year on from the article and Batman was now a local hero in and around Launceston, and he was gathering a coterie of like-minded people whom he believed might be of service to his ambitions to expand. These included Joseph Tice Gellibrand, the island's former attorney-general who had fallen out of favour with the governor and was now a wealthy lawyer; William Gardner Sams, the Sheriff of Launceston; and Henry Arthur, the governor's nephew, who would later be appointed collector of customs in Launceston. There was also the constable Anthony Cottrell and the merchant Joseph Solomon.

The untamed potential of Hume and Hovell's 'Western Port' had been imprinted on colonial minds. Batman and Gellibrand would often talk over the possibilities of acquiring mainland pastures. The ever-garrulous Batman, adventurer and raconteur, seemed to believe it was his destiny to take this land. He would hold court at the Cornwall in Launceston, a pub owned by John Pascoe Fawkner. There he spoke with his growing coterie about the verdant possibilities less than a few days' sailing across the Bass Strait.

The quiet landlord who eavesdropped intently on their banter knew more than any of them about the lands they were discussing. Fawkner had been at Port Phillip Bay as a ten year old with his convict father on the *Calcutta*. Even as a young boy he had found it painful to leave that land – and he had always harboured a desire to return. 'It was primal,' Fawkner later wrote of Port Phillip. 'Like before the beginning of time'.

But Fawkner never partook in the pub discussion. He wasn't interested in joining Batman's entourage, so he kept his dreams of mainland emigration to himself. He'd always been an outsider, a self-made man who had set up a number of businesses with dogged determination, seeking no outside help. He trusted nobody and had a natural scepticism of the power base Batman was so obviously cultivating.

As it happened, the NSW government sent out a small army contingent to Western Port in 1826, spurred on by fear. The French had been sighted in the area, and the British responded by sending out a small detachment. The settlement, around today's Corinella, was a failure, and was abandoned thirteen months later. Hovell, who had been asked to lead the venture, now conceded to Hume that he had been wrong all along: the Arcadian landscape they had visited in 1824 wasn't Western Port at all. The problem was that without a map reference, neither man could determine the location of these now legendary Elysian Fields that had so inspired Batman and others. It was an uncertainty that wouldn't be resolved for another eight years.

Hume and Hovell had in fact passed through present-day Geelong. The fields that so inspired Batman were the lands of the Wadawurrung.

Chapter 9

I T WAS SOMEWHERE in these very lands that, a couple of decades earlier, William Buckley was lying close to death. The Morgan–Buckley account says he was half-dazed and unable to move, only just able to perceive that two local women had cautiously approached him. 'These women went in search of their husbands, with the intelligence that they had seen a very tall white man,' he wrote. 'Presently they all came upon me unawares, and seizing me by the arms and hands, began beating their breasts and mine, in the manner the others had done.'

Pastoralist James Dawson, an amateur ethnologist who spoke the Djargurd Wurrung language, wrote an alternative, far less dramatic version of Buckley's first meeting with the Wadawurrung, Many years later – in the 1860s – an Indigenous woman at Framlingham Aboriginal Station claimed to be Buckley's wife and described how a giant had been stalked by one of her tribe. The woman, known as Purranmurnin Tallarwurnin, related how easy their tracker had found this task. The white man had left huge tracks in his wake.

The tracker believed Buckley was a transgressor and an enemy but kept his distance for a while, perhaps owing to Buckley's size.

Eventually the tracker approached Buckley with caution. The giant was apparently in rude good health, sunning himself on top of a small hillock after a swim in the nearby ocean. The tracker soon gathered others from his tribe who looked on, puzzled by the white man's insouciance. Buckley showed no apparent interest in them, not even glancing in their direction; he didn't even bother to move. According to Tallarwurnin's account, 'They were very much alarmed. At length one of the party, finding courage, addressed him as *Muurnung gurk* (a man who had died and now returned to his kin). The man asked his name: "Are you Kondaak Baarwon?" Buckley replied by a prolonged grunt and an inclination of the head, which those assembled around him took to mean yes. They made a *wuurn* (small hut) of leafy branches for him, and lit a fire in front of it, around which they all assembled. He was then recognised as one of the tribe.'

Buckley had been rescued by the Wadawurrung Balug clan of the Barrabool Hills, one of twenty-five clans that formed the Wadawurrung people. The Morgan–Buckley account says that Buckley was immediately seen as a *ngamadjidj*: a word understood by all the people of Western Victoria to mean a ghost of one of their dead kin who had returned. The first group of men he had met months before had almost certainly seen him this way, and it is this perception that was almost certainly the key to his survival. In many of the tribes of southern Australia, the elder men used to say that the forms or spirits of the dead went westwards, towards the setting sun. When the tribes saw white men arriving by sea from that direction, they surmised they were dead relatives, reincarnated, coming home.

Others were more precise about the movements of the reincarnated. Katherine Kirkland, who lived at 'Trawalla' station in Wadawurrung country with her family from 1839 to 1841, recalled that the 'natives have some strange ideas of death: they think, when they die, they go to Van Diemen's Land, and come back white fellows'. Near Melbourne, William Thomas observed that at the death of Rubertmuning on 25 April 1840, his kinfolk came to his deathbed and comforted him, saying 'he would soon be at Van Diemen's Land and come back again'.

To the Wadawurrung, it seemed Buckley was one of their own, returned to them from the south.

According to this interpretation of events, without knowing it Buckley had plucked the spear from the grave of a great warrior, who had been killed along with his daughters by a rival group. The presence of the spear was proof enough to the tribe that their man had come back from across the seas to revisit them. This may have been normally considered a desecration of a grave, but Buckley was one of their own returned to them, and this was not an issue. He was, after all, desecrating his own grave. This heralded a great rejoicing – it was one of the strangest moments of Buckley's life.

In the Morgan-Buckley account, he was so physically weak that men had to carry him to a spot where they could adequately treat him. The men in particular were touching and grasping him, sometimes beating his chest and sometimes beating their own; all the while, they were emitting what Buckley described as a 'hideous whine'. The women cried and wailed, tearing at their faces and pulling out tufts of their hair.

Buckley was soon offered a concoction of acacia gum and water, fed to him out of a bowl fashioned from bark. The men gestured to him not to move as they left him alone for a moment; when several of them returned, he was treated to some large, fat grubs (*verring*), harvested from the roots and dead parts of trees. These, he noted, were delicious.

Buckley had not quite realised it yet but he was now practically family – or at least made to feel this way. He was experiencing a kind of reverse wake. In the history books he is the first man to have been seen this way, but it wasn't unknown during the early years of settlement for other Europeans to experience the *ngamadjidj* phenomenon, as it was backed by some widely held and important beliefs throughout many parts of Indigenous Australia. According to these beliefs, the cosmos was finite and the Kulin could not conceive of other countries, or states. You were either kin or you were not. If not, then you were on what is often described as 'a cosmological periphery'. This is where the unknown resided.

The people who lived in and around Port Phillip had different words to describe people on this cosmological edge: *mainmait*, *warragull*, *myali* and *gulum gulum*. These meant 'wild blackfellows', people who were foreign, spoke a language they did not understand and with whom there was no intermarriage. Everyone felt a natural antipathy towards all distant tribes.

For Europeans to be here, they must have had some link to or had known of the land in a previous life, because it was impossible for anyone to come to a country they did not know because everyone had strong spiritual bonds to the land. There was no conception that anyone could leave their homeland. So Buckley, recognised as kin, must have resided there or known of it at some point.

Pale skin was also closely aligned with Kulin experiences of death. Bodies were often laid to rest on platforms in trees, where they were gently embalmed with smoke; these cadavers turned pale and, in time, would become chalk-white. Not only did some local Indigenous people believe that white people were resurrected former kin, but also that they themselves might become white people after death. There is a famous story, told by the magistrate William Hull, of a local Indigenous man condemned to death in 1842. Hull told how just before the man was executed, he consoled himself with the expectation that he would come back white. 'Very good. Me jump up whitefellow: plenty sixpence,' he was alleged to have said.

It seems that for many Indigenous people to see a white person as kin and not a dangerous stranger, it would only take a small mannerism – a body tic, a certain stance or even just a smile – to inspire recognition. Buckley had the dead man's spear, so, in the eyes of the Barrabool Hills clan, the Cheshire bricklayer was a deceased clan member returning to country. There would be many other examples of this phenomenon in years to come. One squatter in the 1840s, Charles Gray, was identified as the husband of an Indigenous woman and the father of her three children; he was then called Tirrootmerrie. Another squatter, Colin Campbell, was identified as a man who had fallen from a tree forty years earlier; he became Kerappunnen.

Buckley, mistaken for the man with the spear, was named Murrangurk, and that was how he would always be seen. He recounted that as night fell the wailing and crying abated slightly but never really ceased, and he felt his old fears of savages. He was so deeply out of his depth he wanted to escape, but with so many people fussing around him, this was impossible. There were six men and two women, in all, who continued their jubilation for much of the next day. Still fearful, and dumbfounded by the reaction to his presence, Buckley found it impossible to sleep.

He was left even more aghast by what he saw the next morning, according to the Morgan–Buckley account: 'The women were all the time making such frightful lamentations and wailings – lacerating their faces in a dreadful manner. [The women] were covered in blood from the wounds they had inflicted, having cut their faces and legs into ridges and burnt the edges with fire sticks.' This custom, if accurately described, appears reminiscent of the self-flagellation and mortification of the flesh historically practised by some Christian sects; in fact, self-harm has been practised in a variety of contexts by many religious and spiritual groups worldwide. It seems clear that Murrangurk's perceived return was a deeply spiritual experience for the people around him.

For years afterwards, Buckley would regale his adopted clan with stories about England, trying to explain that he wasn't a returned tribesman but rather transported from afar to this new land for life. But his explanations never seemed to matter to the Wadawurrung. His British past was what had happened while he was a dead man; now he was Murrangurk, the man who had flown over the southern seas, experienced many things, and rejoined them.

Whichever way you look at it, Buckley had been returned to the land of the living.

Chapter 10

WILLIAM BUCKLEY WAS now in the care of the Barrabool Hills clan, who were based around the lower western bank of the Barwon River. Among other Kulin people, the Wadawurrung are known as 'the People of the Water', although many of them inhabited areas quite far inland.

Buckley soon found there was nothing his new-found clan wouldn't do for him. The way he described it, they seemed to anticipate almost all his needs. They knew he was thirsty and handed water to him; when they could see he might be hungry, those delicious grubs or acacia gum would appear. 'I was, to them, an object of the utmost care and solicitude,' he remarked. 'They never allowed me to walk any distance unattended – and if I happened to leave them for a little, Blacks were immediately sent in search for me – when tears were often shed on my reappearance.'

Buckley thought the best approach was simply to cooperate as best as he could, making sure he never gave offence, and 'yield to them at all times'. He had just experienced a major reversal in fortune: after having to scavenge what he could, he was now heartily catered for. His survival was a top priority of his clan – it was as if they had found a long-lost friend. He couldn't be put in danger, was never asked to fight, and was absolved from all disputes. He would be wrapped in the very best possum rugs.

This was all very convenient for Buckley, but he admitted to having some initial trouble accepting his situation. Many of the clan, he said, 'would be good-looking, did they not make such horrid frights of themselves'. Initially he was disconcerted by the way the Wadawurrung plastered their hair and daubed their faces and bodies with pipe-clay and ochre. Most would anoint their bodies and hair with animal fat, then toast themselves in front of a fire allowing the oil to absorb into their skins. To protect themselves from the cold they might mix red clay with the oily fat of emus or water fowls, possums, or that derived from eel skins or grubs, and smear themselves all over with the mixture, an alternative to clothing.

Buckley soon learnt that in summer the men wore very little other than a garment resembling a short apron, formed of furred possum skin strips that hung from a skin belt in two bunches, one in front and the other behind. In winter the men would add a large kangaroo skin, fur side inwards, hanging over the shoulders and down the back like a cloak; it was fastened around their necks by the animal's hind legs and fixed with a kangaroo's hind leg bone. In contrast, at all times of year the women covered their backs and shoulders with a possum rug that reverted to a blanket at night. Around their waists was a garment resembling a short kilt, made up of the neck feathers of an emu tied in little bunches to a skin cord and then fastened. In wet weather they would change into kangaroo skins. Women also knitted headbands and coloured them with ochre. Necklaces were strung with shells and kangaroo teeth, swan and emu feathers. They often wore rings suspended in their nostrils, made out of the bones of birds. Men had straight, knobby bones through their nostrils. Buckley came to understand that among the Wadawurrung, the wearing of ornaments made a person more fashionable and attractive.

Buckley was also confronted by cultural differences to do with hair. When a man's beard was almost full grown, he would either singe it with a firestick or pluck it off with a mussel shell. And everyone in the clan had a strong aversion to grey hair, plucking out each strand as soon as it emerged. 'Every hair of the head appears to be deranged, or out of temper with its owner,' Buckley wrote. 'And well it may be, for it gets frightfully cut and hacked about, sometimes by shells, and flints, and such like ...' He couldn't get used to the idea that within unkempt body hair were 'living tormentors' – but he never explained what these were, and fleas and lice only arrived in Australia after the invasion of white men.

If his new friends weren't quite yet to his taste, the same can't be said for his new environment, which when he arrived was turning on its spring bounty. It was ruggedly beautiful yet perfectly and purposely nurtured, a landscape graced by countless generations who had moulded and cultured it into a home. All around Buckley were myriad acacias and eucalypts, and waterbirds such as the magpie goose and the brolga that dived into the streams and rattled the trees. The great red rivergums and swamp gums shared space with the blackwood and drooping she-oaks (*ngarri*). As the river snaked its way to the coast, the trees gave way to a proliferation of cherry ballart, its squat green leaves dotted with edible red berries, and the coastal banksia with its orange floral cones. Never far away was the kangaroo apple (*koon-yang*), which sprouts a profusion of vivid purple blossoms through the spring and summer.

It was a place Buckley would always love and cherish. He would always be welcome here.

*

BY HIS SECOND NIGHT with the Wadawurrung, Buckley must have believed he was in wonderland when he was treated to the first of many corroborees. It appears this one was devoted to him. He didn't know that, of course, and later he provided the observation – perhaps ghostwritten by Morgan – that as soon as a fire was lit he assumed he was about to be eaten.

As the sun weakened, two men walked the guest of honour to a prime position overlooking proceedings, and asked him to rest and watch. Then, much to his surprise and arousal, he saw that the women had shed their garments and assembled naked in front of him. A few kangaroo teeth were fastened to their hair and above each ear, and projecting beyond each of their foreheads was a thin piece of wood with coloured feathers tied to its end. On some women, perhaps the more senior, a band of white cockatoo feathers was fastened there as well.

The men now joined the group, all painted in white pipe clay sourced near the Barwon River, armed with clubs more than two feet long. Buckley wrote, 'They had run streaks of white clay around their eyes, one down each check, others along the forehead down to the tip of the nose, other streaks meeting at the chin, others down the middle of the body down each leg.' Buckley was terrified – in the half-light the men looked like skeletons prancing around the blazing fire. The incisor teeth of a large kangaroo were fastened into some of the men's hair, while others – perhaps the most important among them – had their heads circled by fur bandanas with the dark quill of a swan tucked in over the right temple. Still other men had the tail of a wild dog woven into their hair, the tail falling down their backs. Their necks were circled with kangaroo teeth.

The women started proceedings by beating their hands slowly on possum rugs stretched tight between their knees. Some of the rugs contained shells that jingled to the beat. Its speed and intensity increased gradually, then a man seated in front of them began chanting a plaintive lament to the same time signature. Corroborees were often staged to mark special events. He may have been singing of the return of Murrangurk. Meanwhile the other men had assembled into a tight column, and within a few minutes it was their turn. They beat hardwood sticks together, each of which was about nine inches long and an inch or so in diameter, rounded and tapering at each end to a point.

As the minutes became hours, the intensity of singer, stick-beaters and drummers didn't falter. The men kept their feet wide apart and their knees slightly bent, and their hands were never lowered, always at the same height as the shoulders. The men's thighs had a quivering motion Buckley had never seen before. While to him these people were making a 'frightful noise', he was nonetheless impressed by the perfectly choreographed sound and dance.

There was, Buckley said, a 'leader of the orchestra, a master of the band' who kept the rhythms tight and the movements synchronised. It's likely that he was a chief song maker, an elder known for his prowess in this area. Song makers were in charge of communicating with and transmitting ideas from the ancestral world, as the song lyrics were the words of the spirits of dead relatives. The elder man, Buckley wrote, 'marched the whole mob, men and women, boys and girls, backwards and forwards at his pleasure, directing the singing and dancing, with the greatest decision and air of authority. This scene must have lasted at least three hours, when as a wind-up, they gave three tremendous shouts, at the same time pointing to the sky with their sticks, they shook me heartily by the hand, again beating their breasts as a token of friendship.'

*

AFTER THE CORROBOREE Buckley slept soundly, no longer afraid of his companions. The next day he went to bathe in the Barwon some distance from the camp, causing concern when the clan couldn't find him for a few minutes.

He returned to much consternation – he hadn't understood that this was the day when he would meet Murrangurk's family, who lived a few miles distant in another camp. After he was ushered over to them, he witnessed more of what to him seemed like histrionics, but he found quickly that he had gained a family willing to give him safety and total devotion. He was now considered to have a sister, a brother-in-law, two nephews and a niece; in his accounts, he never provided their names or descriptions. For a meal they gave him the best tubers that could be found in the region, as well as the acacia gum and his first taste of possum. It was also his first piece of meat since Pye and McAllenan had left around a year earlier, and it sent him into raptures.

Buckley was now clothed as a Wadawurrung man, his filthy, torn jacket exchanged for a possum pelt. His sister took the jacket, which he said made her look quite fetching. This exchange of gifts, he said, cemented real kinship. 'These interchanges of attractive civility

88

had great effect in cementing our family acquaintance,' is how he described it. Reciprocity is one of the cornerstones of Wadawurrung culture – and indeed all Indigenous cultures across Australia – and when someone enters into kinship status, an entirely new set of rules comes into play. Buckley would have to learn these rules; for example, when an animal was eaten, specific portions were allotted to specific family members. This was a turning point in his life, and he knew instinctively that it was his duty to understand the laws of reciprocation to which he was now beholden. Breaking those laws, some experts claim, would be almost akin to a Westerner breaking commercial law. Kinship was etched deeply into Kulin governance.

What Buckley never quite got used to was the love given freely and constantly by his new family. Until now no one had ever embraced him so warmly or showed emotion so openly, not even his family in Cheshire.

*

THE MOST COMPLETE account we have of William Buckley's life with the Wadawurrung comes from the 1852 autobiography, *The Life and Adventures of William Buckley*, ghostwritten by newspaper editor John Morgan and published about forty-seven years after the events described above. A briefer version of Buckley's life story was ghostwritten much earlier, in 1837, by the Reverend George Langhorne, a missionary in Melbourne whom Buckley was assisting as a translator. At that time he spoke only halting English, which helps explain the brevity of Langhorne's account. However, the voice in *Reminiscences of James [sic] Buckley* is widely considered closer to Buckley's than that in the Morgan memoir. *Reminiscences* didn't see the light of day until 1911 – not surprisingly, as it reads like a patchwork of memories.

Morgan's book, by contrast, is a Robinson Crusoe tale in the Antipodes and clearly positioned as such. Langhorne had been writing when relations were still reasonably strong between the races in a colony just beginning to get on its feet; Morgan was writing at a time when the city of Melbourne was well established, the state of Victoria had just come into being, and much of the damage to Kulin culture in the Port Phillip area and beyond had been wrought. Morgan wanted a bestseller, and in much of his account he had no compunctions portraying the Wadawurrung and other local people Buckley encountered as lower forms of humanity.

While neither Darwin's term 'natural selection' nor Herbert Spencer's phrase 'survival of the fittest' existed back in 1852, many so-called 'doomed race' theories about 'stronger' races replacing 'weaker' ones abounded in Europe. The white people who went along with this can't be excused by the fact that they lived in different times. After all, some nineteenth-century Europeans saw through the racist theories – those like James Dawson, an amateur anthropologist appointed as a local guardian of the Indigenous people in the Camperdown area west of Melbourne, who spoke the language of the Djargurd Wurrung (a Kulin clan of the north-west), and his daughter Isabella Park Taylor. Both had an abiding respect for the Kulin, and in 1881 Dawson published a work entitled *Australian Aborigines: the languages and customs of several tribes of aborigines in the western district of Victoria, Australia.*

There were other sources even closer to the Wadawurrung. William Thomas was the Assistant Protector of Aborigines in the Melbourne/ Westernport/Mornington Peninsula area (Boonwurrung country) from 1839 to 1850 and lived in their camps – and was later appointed Guardian of all Aboriginal people in Victoria, a position he held from 1850 to 1867. He spoke Wadawurrung, regularly dealt with them, wrote about their ceremonies and translated in the courts for them. There were also men like George Augustus Robinson, who became Chief Protector of Aborigines in the Port Phillip area in March 1839, who scrupulously chronicled his travels and impressions in the region. Robinson, Thomas and Dawson were white men who were immersed for decades with Aboriginal people. These were men who daily conversed, frequently travelled and awoke on country with the Kulin – not long after Buckley had done the same.

The Morgan–Buckley account is often sensationalist and to modern readers' eyes, disrespectful in its depiction of Indigenous culture. On the question of its value as a primary source, scholars have made varied responses. Many believe that its literary embellishments render it utterly unreliable. There is no archaeological evidence to support its story, and over the years some researchers may have rejected its veracity on this basis alone. But in the 1880s, the historian Edward Curr said that 'Morgan's *Life and Adventures of William Buckley* gives a truer account of Aboriginal life than any work I have read.' Marjorie Tipping, who wrote the Buckley instalment in the *Australian Dictionary of Biography*, stated that in her view this account was 'close to fact'. One of Australia's most renowned anthropologists, Lester Hiatt, was quoted as saying that the account presents 'a much higher degree of consistency with modern understandings of Aboriginal social life ... than inconsistency'. And in 2002, the eminent writer and environmentalist Tim Flannery wrote in an introduction to the account that 'It has been ignored or mentioned only in passing by historians because it is so at odds with contemporary preconceptions.'

My view is that the Morgan–Buckley account includes insight into the everyday lives of Indigenous people in the region but the depiction of internecine violence (some of which I relate in the following pages) demands serious scepticism. Much of that has been deliberately exaggerated by Morgan. The weight of evidence clearly suggests that all of the Kulin tribes put a strong emphasis on interdependence. Melinda Kennedy, a Wadawurrung woman, told me in an interview that in addition to holding tribal meetings, neighbouring and allied tribes would usually gather to discuss important issues on an annual basis at a place with mythological or cultural importance. The incessant warfare described by the Morgan–Buckley account, she says, is false. Bruce Pascoe, an acclaimed writer and broadcaster of Indigenous descent, agrees: 'The violence is overplayed and much of it occurred after contact simply as a result of the invasion's disruption,' he said to me.

Why did Morgan overplay these aspects of Buckley's experience? Sales were one reason, but there were political motivations as well. In the 1850s, many British people wanted to justify what their Empire had recently done to the Aboriginal population in less than two decades. If these people could be cast as savage, then they could also be deemed in need of Christianising. This was a perverse attempt to relieve collective guilt.

While the following sections trace Morgan's account, I have tried to draw from as much anthropological and/or Indigenous evidence as possible. There is, however, no way around the fact that most of this evidence is derived from white men who observed Indigenous people in Victoria during the half century after European settlement in 1835. We have very little oral, written or archaeological evidence of events before that period. The writings of Thomas, Dawson and

Robinson shine above and beyond other scholars, many of whom relied on questionnaires (as they did not speak the languages) or on second-hand reports from settlers. When in doubt, I defer to them.

*

THE MORNING AFTER Buckley met his new family, he was woken by raucous shouting. The camp at the Barwon was astir, with women and children running in all directions. At the centre, a large group of men appeared to be throwing insults at each other. There was much finger-pointing and fisticuffs, and soon some long wooden spears were produced and brandished.

At this point Buckley's family ushered him from the camp into woods about a hundred yards away. From there he watched the men position themselves in a single file, each one targeting an opponent symmetrically opposite. Some men had hunting spears about twice their height; others had implements around five to six feet in length. Buckley wrote, 'The spear which they use is from ten to fifteen feet long, and is made of a solid piece of wood, very sharp at the point with rows of teeth; these jagged spears known by the tribe as *karnwell*, could not be easily extracted from either man or beast.' The smaller *daar* spears were flung with throwing sticks to increase their speed. They were made of two pieces of wood fastened together with the sinews of a kangaroo, and sharp points of white flint were glued on each side with gum. The throwing sticks had a handle at one end to thrust the spear, and a hook at the other in which the tail of the spear was inserted. Boomerangs, known as *wangaam*, were also part of the weaponry, and for his defence each man was equipped with a large oval-shaped shield of wood from the inner parts of a gum tree; these shields were planted squarely opposite an opponent, covering a good deal of the bearer's side and flank.

There was no commander on either side, nor were any orders issued. Without warning or signal, both sides let loose, the spears flashing through the air at astonishing speeds. Buckley now saw something he had never seen before – straight, light, almost noiseless missiles passing in continuous opposite and horizontal streams. How could so few people keep so many spears in flight for so long? As the missiles crossed, men were dancing and weaving around them with almost impossible dexterity.

Buckley was a veteran of the war with the French but he had never seen such an intense, set-piece engagement at such speed and at such close quarters. Spears were flung with pinpoint accuracy, the combatants stepping nimbly around them. One man raised his foot casually as a spear impaled the very spot his foot had filled a split second earlier. No man faltered nor showed the slightest sign of fear.

Then a cry went up, and both sides stopped immediately. One of the women – and Buckley never explained how any of them were caught in the melee – had been fatally speared just under her right arm, while a man had been wounded by a spear in the thigh. After only a few minutes, the fight was over. The women came out to tend to the wounded man, and the camp returned to apparent normality. Buckley sensed that the fight had been more a show of strength than a real battle, and he couldn't shake the idea that men had been practising a craft not resolving a feud. It seemed too perfect, too choreographed – and yet someone had been killed.

The family of the dead woman threw her body on a large fire, then heaped on more wood so that the corpse was burnt to ash. 'This done,' wrote Buckley, 'they raked the embers of the fire together and struck the stick she used to dig roots with upright at the head.'

This fight was the first of many Buckley claimed to have seen throughout his years with the Wadawurrung. He wrote that at first he couldn't understand why a show of togetherness at the corroboree was often followed by a show of aggression. Deaths caused by these skirmishes were accompanied by great lamentations, but from Buckley's perspective the people affected then moved on very quickly. He came to believe that in nearly all cases the feuds were either about women among closely aligned tribes and clans or about more serious matters with foreign tribes with which his clan had little or no association. In the latter instance, this would amount to more intense warfare, which could be related to 'payback': a belief that a foreign tribe had deliberately created mischief and sorcery to compromise the tribe. According to Buckley, the fights caused by women seemed to occur most frequently, as whatever indiscretions had occurred during a corroboree had to be settled promptly the next day. 'They [the fights] were occasioned by the women having been taken away from one tribe by another which was of frequent occurrence,' Buckley explained, 'at other times they were caused by women willingly leaving their husbands, and joining other men, which the natives considered very bad.'

In one intertribal fight, Buckley wrote, his tribe won the day but lost two young boys. The vanquished tribe seemed to retreat, then returned that night for a surprise attack, removing the legs of the boys' corpses. Buckley was disgusted, even more so when he came to believe that the enemy tribe had eaten the legs. According to Buckley, someone killed in their prime of life was of spiritual value to the aggressor, and when eaten, their limbs were thought to offer strength and power.

This isn't the only tale of apparent cannibalism in the Morgan–Buckley account. But many believe Buckley's allusions to the practice were part of his ghostwriter's attempt to sensationalise his experiences. Buckley may have witnessed the sacrament of people rubbing a slain person's body fat or kidney fat onto their skin, and Morgan then converted this into a highly exaggerated tale of cannibalism. According to Marguerita Stephens, a well-regarded writer on Australian colonial history, there is practically no evidence of either cannibalism or infanticide among Indigenous people, both of which were accusations often levelled against them: 'As with cannibalism, discourses on infanticide most often inhabit the terrain of the unseen.' Stephens wrote that the 'witness' might see only a fragment of the event 'and then imagines the rest in the act of appropriation. Like the cannibal of the (missed) colonial encounter, infanticides remain uncaptured.'

Chapter 11

S LOWLY BUT SURELY, William Buckley was transforming from an English bricklayer and soldier into someone conversant with Wadawurrung culture. A year on and he was picking up scraps of language. His family spent hours helping him to pronounce words and phrases, but it would be some time before he could speak clearly.

The more he absorbed the language, the better he could play his role in the tribe. It appears he cherished this highly: he was a kind of go-between who settled disputes and sought peace when other men confronted each other. As he was never treated as a combatant, this role was accepted by his fellow clansmen.

Buckley was learning the clan's paths, their habits and their caring-for-country practices. He gradually became adept with a spear as a half-capable hunter. The country waxed in some parts and waned in others, and he grew accustomed to its cycle of renewal and return. It had always been this way.

But the language couldn't have come easily to him. Experts say there's no proof he ever became fully conversant in it, although anecdotal evidence suggests that his speech was eventually comprehended by all the Kulin tribes. Wadawurrung language expert Stephanie Skinner says that Buckley wouldn't have had the same facility with the language as a child would have: 'Adults tend to use declarative memory and similar memory pathways and storages for bilingual learning.' Children can more easily overlap the Wernicke's and Broca's sections of the brain, which are dedicated to language learning, speech and comprehension. Buckley may also have struggled with the fact that the Wadawurrung language has a different sentence structure from English: the verb comes first, then the subject and the object. As Skinner explains, 'Instead of saying in English "Lisa has a kangaroo", it would be "Has Lisa a kangaroo".'

The name 'Wadawurrung' literally translates as 'no lip language' – *wada* meaning 'no' and *wurru* meaning 'lip/language' – so Buckley would have found it difficult to pronounce. The language frequently involves a 'velar' approach: using the soft palate to pronounce sounds such as 'k' 'n' and 'ng'. English has this too, but it is far more prominent in Wadawurrung and used in different ways. When the settler John Helder Wedge came to Port Phillip in the 1830s, his field book included a list of vocabulary from the region, which contained the following entry: 'white man – amajaic'. This is the earliest recorded variant spelling of *ngamadjidj*. Many nineteenth-century European recorders of Kulin languages were unable to hear the 'ng' sound at the beginning of words; sometimes they substituted an 'n', but usually omitted it. According to Skinner, 'Saying that Buckley would have found it difficult to speak Wadawurrung in a way that was understood does not mean that he didn't learn it quickly – but it would have been a considerable time before he would be fully understood by Wadawurrung people.'

*

THE BARRABOOL HILLS CLAN had the Barwon as their home river, and this wasn't unusual for their people. All Kulin tribes based themselves along the river systems of Victoria. The River Murray from present-day Albury to the River Lindsay in the west was heavily populated; the Goulburn, Loddon, Avoca, Richardson, Glenelg and Wimmera rivers also gave refuge to many tribes. As the seasons changed and important food sources came into being, they all moved accordingly. Buckley described their semi-nomadic lifestyle; they made temporary shelters as they moved using 'mere branches of trees thrown across each other with slips of tea-tree and with pieces of bark placed over as an additional shelter'. In half an hour a fully functioning campsite could be established.

Buckley gave the impression his clan was highly nomadic, but this wasn't true of all clans. In some cases several clans lived in one area and may have moved only sporadically, as everything they needed was in one place. They often built solidly constructed villages that may have contained around twenty to thirty huts, each of which could hold ten to twelve people. On these sites, there were often extremely sophisticated dams, the net-fishing was prolific and the game plentiful.

In contrast, Buckley said his clan would wander far afield for whatever its people needed. They would hunt and gather as individual families in small numbers, giving them greater mobility and flexibility. Highly important was the local descent group, a kind of extended family that had its own stretches of territory, and curated local ceremonial and sacred sites. These groups were patrilineal – traced through the father's line – which meant that married women went to live with their husbands' families. When the clan was hunting for food, it wasn't uncommon for a number of descent groups to band together as they ranged the country.

And so it was that Buckley's band, which probably held between twenty to sixty people, would move across a well-defined territory, combining a nomadic existence with longer stays at more established camps. Buckley said he would journey with them to Lake Corangamite, the largest lake in the western district, where on Vaughan Island in spring they could reap a harvest of swans' eggs. As Buckley described it, on those occasions his belly was so full he was practically on the verge of vomiting. They also journeyed to Lake Modewarre about fourteen miles from present-day Geelong. At other times they were in the Otway Ranges, where they swapped food with other tribes. But there was always a return to the Barwon and the environs of Geelong.

Buckley came to know the rocks, landmarks and vegetation as the clan knew them – stalwart friends that were always available and always had been. There was practically no creature that didn't make a meal, and his people knew when and where to find them. Brushtail (*walert*) and ringtail (*barnong*) possums, koalas (*ngaanbulmum*), emus (*kawir*), kangaroos (*goim*), wallabies (*goy-in*), wombats (*ngurr-ngurr*) and grubs (*verring*) as well as fish and eels (*buniya*) were on the menu, as were large ants living in trees (Buckley called them *kalkeeth*) that were eaten with relish. He watched people beat the trees with tomahawks to determine the ants' location based on hollowness. Once they were located, someone would cut a deep notch in the bark while another person reached into the tree to pull them out. They placed the insects in bark panniers and roasted them. They were seasonal as well – arrive too late to the feast, and these ants would have metamorphosed and flown away.

Buckley reported that his clan sent small boys and girls feet first down wombat holes. The wombat would naturally escape to the back of its burrow, which the child would locate by feeling its fur with his or her feet. 'Having discovered the lair,' Buckley explained, 'they called out as loud as they can, beating the ground overhead, whilst those above are carefully listening, their ears being pressed close to the earth.' When they had learnt the wombat's location, the men above ground sliced the part of the earth that marked the extremity of the burrow, then dug back from the spot with sharp sticks until the hapless creature was found stuck between the child's feet and the back of its home. 'The poor things are easily killed, for they make no resistance to these intrusions on their haunts,' Buckley wrote. 'There is, however, a good deal of difficulty in making these holes, and in getting down so deep to them – so that it is a sort of hunting for food of which the natives are not very fond.'

There is a story told by a white settler to the region in the 1840s of how a Wadawurrung guide was able to find native honey, '...the native sticks a piece of feather or white down to it [a bee] with gum, and then letting it go, sets off after it as fast as he can: keeping his eye steadily fixed upon the insect, he rushes along like a mad-man, tumbling over trees and bushes that lie in his way, but rarely losing sight of his object, until conducted to its well-filled store, he is amply paid for all his trouble.'

The settler watched his Wadawurrung guide find the tree, but it had been marked: the tree had been claimed by another member of the clan. The guide told the white man he couldn't extract the honey from this tree; he had not been given the right permissions.

The Kulin knew what would come with the seasons. At the end of November, came the *karl-karl*, locusts which would gather around the local box trees. The Wadawurrung clans called them *yerring-*

yerring and would gather up the locust dung from the base of a tree and eat it with relish as a form of honey. William Thomas said he was able to gather a 'quart' of this substance from below one tree. It was said to be delicious.

As for hunting kangaroos, there was, Buckley said, 'considerable dexterity used'. Sometimes fire would be used to 'smoke' them and smaller mammals out, or the hunters would place themselves at particular spots while herding the kangaroos into corners where they could be speared without difficulty. But finding them wasn't always easy: *goim* were intelligent and sensitive, able to hear and smell the hunters coming from miles away. Their ears were attuned to danger, and they often crossed streams to avoid detection.

Stories were told to the early settlers of 'grand battues' ('great beatings' in French) which involved beating woods and bushes to flush out game. Large numbers of men from different tribes agreed at a certain time to form a giant ring, sometimes fifteen to twenty miles in diameter. They would then slowly march in on a central spot, beating the countryside and thereby enclosing kangaroos and emus in their giant human noose. One of the appointed places was said to be Mustons Creek, a few miles east from its junction with the River Hopkins. All the women, children and old people would be encamped there waiting for the human noose to close in on the hapless animals. Once surrounded, they could be easily slaughtered. A great corroboree and feast would ensue, with any remaining flesh equally apportioned among all the tribes involved.

The kangaroos and emus were the prize catches, but Buckley's band also ate wild dog (*warragul*). When offered the leg of a dog, he turned up his nose and instead took the leg of a kangaroo – he couldn't bring himself to eat a canine. His band seemed to find this extremely amusing: 'No doubt they thought my having died and been made white had strangely altered my taste in such matters,' he wrote. The Kulin were known to love their trained dogs, which were valued for their ability to sense outside danger, but dingoes in the wild were considered no different from other game.

Buckley would learn to skin animals with mussel shells, and to stretch and dry their hides in the sun. 'I would prepare the sinews for sewing together for rugs and to trim them with pieces of flint,' he wrote.

Buckley also took to possum hunting, working with his brother-in-law to fetch them from trees. To determine if a possum was up there, they would breathe hard on the bark to see if any hairs were still attached; if they were detected, it meant a possum was in residence. Buckley's brother-in-law would cut a notch as a foothold and begin climbing, notching repeatedly as he ascended. The animal was dragged out of its hollow and thrown to the ground to be killed by Buckley waiting below. Buckley was no climber but became quite adept in his role as possum executor.

There was plenty of fishing as well, which Buckley explained would often be conducted at night. People would mesmerise the bream or salmon with a flaming torch that lured them to the surface where they were speared with ease. Eel fishing took place in the lakes west of the Barwon and at the place that would one day be named Buckley Falls, also on the Barwon just west of present-day Geelong. Here, according to Buckley, the eels were big, fat and succulent. As the water flowed through the many rocks and cracks in the slow-running falls, people eased the eels into conical nets. If this method didn't yield enough, people would simply dip worms on a string to lure them in or pluck those wriggling beneath their feet.

The Wadawurrung were expert at constructing fish and eel traps. When more white men arrived decades later, they noted that on just about every stream there was some form of strong woven fish- or eel-catching net. Lake Bolac, south of the Grampians, was one of the most celebrated places for eels. The locals would wait for the autumn rains that forced the fish to travel down creeks and streams towards the sea. The various clans would each be allotted a portion of a stream on which to catch the eels, and in pivotal places they had constructed elaborate stone weirs that diverted the eels into waiting baskets. Other methods diverted smaller eels into spawning ponds, from which they were harvested when fully grown. The eels would be smoked, otherwise their natural oils quickly degenerated their flesh, and were one of the most important trading materials for the Wadawurrung.

In winter, Buckley's clan would move away from the coast to take shelter from the winds that blew off the southern waters. Most of these winter camps were on higher ground, flood-free land that was sheltered from the weather. The clan constructed durable huts known as *wuurn*, and such camps could be occupied for months. Dome-like houses on solid wood frames were noted in the 1830s by white explorers. In the 1860s, a white squatter and experienced bushman G.S. Lang admired the proficiency of local hut-building after witnessing Wadawurrung men construct them with ease: 'One of our overseers, a very ingenious man, singularly skilful in overcoming mechanical difficulties, I saw over and over again attempt the construction of a hut, native fashion, under the direction of the blacks, and with a blackfellow beside him building up another, as an example. But he never got his edifice to stand the weight of the turf, and it generally fell before he had the framework completed, of course to the intense amusement of the natives.'

Women gathering edible roots using digging sticks. Sketch by John Wedge, 1835. (Federation University Australia Historical Collection)

Near these dwellings were elaborate fisheries. John Batman, when he first came to this country in the mid-1830s, was amazed by the extensive use of weirs and fish traps, and noted the housing around them; these were, he understood, permanent villages with local food sources. There were also places, such as the McLeods Waterholes west of the town of Drysdale, that offered alternatives: lakeside plants and freshwater mussels.

But while animals were an important source of sustenance, the most vital staple for the Wadawurrung was the flora collected by the women. They gathered roots, plants, fruit and berries, along with a variety of tubers. The murnong, with their radish-shaped roots, were the most important of these; they're seasonal – bitter in the winter, sweet in the summer – and can be eaten raw or baked in an earth oven. Another commonly eaten tuber was the finger-shaped water ribbon (*palango warngare*), which is very sweet when cooked. The small-leafed clematis – also known as the peppery yam or *tarook* – was used as a poultice to treat aching bones, and it was also administered for headaches by inhaling the vapour from its crushed leaves. The pink bindweed is another edible taproot that the Wadawurrung ate during the colder months, when the murnong was still too young and bitter to taste.

There were many more edible plants, including orchids, daisies, warrigal cabbage, native geranium, bulrush shoots and kangaroo apples. The latter could be used as a woman's medicinal plant, perhaps to ease menstruation. There were native-named plants such as *bol-kom-bop-ba*, a small green plant with a leaf like a turnip, which when eaten, is said to act as an emetic. There was fruit from pigface and the native raspberry, and seasonal nuts and seeds. Acacia gum from the black wattle (*warour re rup*) was a common food that Buckley relished and was said to aid digestion, while the gum of the yellow wattle was used to cure stomach complaints and salve burns. Gum that came to be known as 'blackfellas chewing gum' was derived from a small to medium sized Eucalypt and either eaten or made into a flavoured drink.

The Kulin used everything they could. The acacia that produced gum was also the source of many wooden implements. The dried cones of the silver banksia (*wurrak*) were used as drinking-water strainers and also stuffed with coals for use as spot burners for firesticks, while the flowers were made into a cordial. The blackwood (*burn-naa-look*) was an essential tool tree: fashioned from its wood were boomerangs, clubs, spear-throwers and parrying shields. Its medicinal outer bark was used for joint pain, while its inner-bark fibres were made into fishing-net strings. She-oak wood was also used to make boomerangs, clubs and digging sticks, while the stringybark had its bark removed to create canoes or shelter, and its medicinal sap was used for burns. The yellow gum (*bi-et-mai*) was another tough timber used for digging sticks and parrying shields, and it was said to have magical properties. There was also the manna gum (*larrap*) with timber used for clubs and shields, and leaves made into a poultice to alleviate backache.

Animals, too, sometimes had two or three uses. The *goim* and wallaby were for eating, but their sinew and teeth were used for adornments, their rib-cage bones could be used as tools, and their smaller leg bones as sewing needles. Both kangaroo and possum pelts were made into ceremonial cloaks – a single cloak was composed of about sixty pelts – while possum fur was made into a type of football and its pelts also woven together into rugs. It's no surprise that the echidna (*mon ngarrk*) was eaten as well, and its sharp quills became necklace adornments. The quills also had a role as natural lancets, when trying to remove infections from wounds. The Kulin would debride the wound with a quill, which would then be closed and covered with a layer of gum from a eucalyptus or acacia tree and placed over the sore as a salve. The elder man Barak of the Woiwurrung, who knew Buckley, was once unhappy with the treatment he received from a burn and requested what he called 'the blood of the tree'. Burns were also treated with melted fat, after which a fine dust made of possum fur and red ochre known as *wheerup* was sprinkled over it.

Buckley too received medical attention. The Wadawurrung had no bandages, but after receiving a laceration to his head, the women bound the wound in possum skin tied with possum sinews. There was, indeed, a use for everything.

*

SOME WHITE COMMENTATORS have said that Buckley regressed, that he fell from the advanced state of the agricultural and industrial revolutions into a more primitive hunting-and-gathering existence. But Buckley never mentioned this as being part of his cultural shock. The former farm boy from Cheshire was thriving as both a forager and a farmer in Wadawurrung country.

The Kulin nation had discovered myriad farming technologies that proved highly efficient. The local people had little need to store food, knowing the land would replenish itself. The European method of planting just a few types of seeds, plucking out weeds and watering the crops – as well as nurturing a few animals – was pointless to Indigenous people. In Wadawurrung country, a crop never failed: if one food source was lacking or scarce, the band of people would just move to another. And there was no need for livestock. The dingo was the only native mammal that could be domesticated, and it was highly valued as a hunter and a sentinel that could warn of the approach of evil spirits.

Buckley had entered a society that anthropologists now largely agree was among the most egalitarian the world has ever known. In Indigenous life pre-colonisation, there was no such thing as succession. Most serious disputes weren't about ownership but encroachment. They hinged on the fair and equitable sharing of resources. Outsiders could not 'invade' other people's lands – the idea of dispossessing a tribe of its land made no sense at all. Likewise the rights and obligations over a particular resource were always known – they had been fixed over time and delineated by a deep sense of spatial awareness.

The agricultural revolution in the northern hemisphere had given rise to the idea of private ownership, while in Indigenous culture ancient sharing laws forbade private property except for weapons and tools. A man had his spear, a women her cooking utensils and digging stick, and everyone had their own clothes.

When a band needed a specific food, they always understood which tribe controlled the land it came from. Taking an eel without permission was a transgression but not an usurpation. Buckley recounted an expedition made by members of his tribe deep in the north of the Otway Ranges, travelling hundreds of miles to exchange their eels for the other people's roots. 'We carried our fish in kangaroo skins, and reaching the place of rendezvous, we found about eighty men, women and children gathered together,' he noted. The transaction was done with great formality and care, as two men crossed simultaneously from each tribe to the other carrying bark panniers filled with food. The negotiations were concluded only after the equivalent number of panniers had been exchanged. It was fair trade, Kulin style.

Perhaps the best example of exchanges was for axes – by far the most important working tool for Indigenous men. At the Mount William stone quarry, strangers were not allowed to enter and could not take stone until the fair exchange had been made. Those without rights to Mount William would have to negotiate a price for their needs with those who had the rights. Reed spears from the Goulburn

River reed beds and possum rugs were recorded exchanges for Mount William's much coveted green stone. The exchange rate was recorded by a settler as one possum rug for three pieces of stone.

This society wasn't about taking, but giving – he who gave the most, was the most revered. There were no IOUs, no tit-for-tats, no special favours, only reciprocal obligations handed down by time, which everybody understood. If a person had a patrilineal right to access a particular resource, they could access it. If they did not, then access wasn't possible or had to be bestowed by someone who did. People would go through protocols and procedures to access, for example, stonework for axes or a pond bursting with eels. You might be refused or allowed, but if you simply went and took it, that would be the crime. Under Judeo-Christian law, if a person is convicted of a crime they literally do the time, but among the Kulin a perpetrator's uncle could be more severely punished than the perpetrator, who should have been taught the rules of reciprocity. In these societies, including the one in which Buckley was ensconced, the people of a particular line were meant to keep their people in check.

The Kulin were taught from childhood the immediate punishments both moral and physical that would result from a wrong action. Tribal law was in effect internalised as part of each child's education, and the sanctions meted out meant there was no need for an elaborate set of laws or a judicial system. If matters became complicated, the male elders of each band (known as *arweets* among the Boonwurung or *ngurungaeta* among the Wadawurrung) would weigh in, and at larger tribal meetings these men – who could be religious leaders, song men or even great hunters – would judge crimes as well as make determinations. As many scholars have said,

Indigenous governance was far more about education and learning than it was about empowering a government.

The Kulin had no need for maps, as they knew their country through songs and stories passed down for countless generations. They had names for every river, mountain and waterhole over thousands of square kilometres, and they believed many of their ancestors were alive in rock formations, billabongs, ghost gums and stars. In country, there was no such thing as wilderness. A person could never be alone or lost either literally or metaphysically, as their country was always with them.

However, if something was unknown or from outside the known limits of country – including anyone whom the locals described as being on the periphery – it was deemed by definition to be harmful and unwelcome, perhaps the product of sorcery. Foreign tribespeople were ascribed with morally reprehensible characteristics and behaviours, including cannibalism. The widespread use of words like *mainmait* (wild blackfellows) was acknowledged by white nineteenth-century observers, including squatters and protectorate officials. Deaths within a tribe, even natural ones, were often attributed to the influence of an exterior person or hostile being. The Kulin were always wary of payback or revenge. Distant tribes, those with whom there was no linguistic or spatial attachment, were considered the source of all evil. Someone had to be responsible, and retribution needed to be taken; Buckley recounted that this could take the form of revenge expeditions.

Joseph Parker, whose father was Assistant Protector responsible for the Loddon district of the Aboriginal Protectorate from 1839 until 1851, recalled that the Djadjawurrung believed in two forms of death: one natural and one superstitious: 'They did not believe in death from natural causes, except in the two extremes of life – old age and infancy,' he wrote. Any other form of death was always regarded as suspicious.

James Dawson was one of the first white observers to understand that deaths were often attributed to the malevolence of a distant tribe. Such foreign enemies were frequently blamed when a dying person believed they were the victim of an incantation. Dawson recounted one example: a corpse was suspended from a tree, and by watching the course of the first maggot that dropped on the ground from the body, the clan divined the source of the culprits. There was also a case in which a man was speared by another, and the dying man blamed a distant tribe of the north for directing the spear. The thrower of the spear was not deemed culpable.

Who would they blame? There were recorded cases when tribes decided to take a similar life to the one they had lost. So if a man died, the life of another man would be taken, and if that of a woman or child, a similar life would also be taken.

In the Morgan-Buckley account, intertribal warfare ranges in type and intensity. Some scholars think that the nature of the warfare depended on tribal propinquity. The Kulin people were an association of tribes, and this meant their customs, languages and personal relationships were often close. The bonds of kinship among neighbouring bands and clans meant such feuds rarely escalated into widespread warfare; the Kulin tribes tended to settle their differences with a fair fight between the disputing parties and little bloodshed. Neighbours may have been blamed for mishaps, but they were also often linked by blood and other types of respected traditional relationships. It is thought that in the remote past, the ancestors of the tribes now living in association were a single tribe, and that geography or separate interests may have contributed to their gradual division. Between Kulin tribes there were often what could be described as 'goodwill sabbaticals': a person from one tribe might live with another for a long time, learning their ways.

Buckley doesn't distinguish between associations and non-associations, although he mentions tribes further afield as the natural enemies of the Wadawurrung. Of course he was saved from being a stranger due to his identification as *ngamadjidj* or kin – without this, many scholars believe, he wouldn't have survived.

Buckley's clan gave him ample breathing space, as they believed he had simply forgotten the old ways due to his time away. He was an ingénue who would always be forgiven – and often laughed at – for not knowing social and cultural ambits. All the same, he had to grapple with a tribal- and family-based network of rules and regulations. Everyone was to some degree interconnected. He assumed the former rights and obligations of the man he'd replaced, and he would have to learn about this man's reciprocal relationships.

Buckley had been assigned the role of a lifetime – to take on the guise of someone he had never met, in a social network that differed vastly from anything he had ever known.

Chapter 12

LIKE MANY SETTLERS in Van Diemen's Land, John Batman was angered and frustrated by the power wielded by the island's despotic ruler and principal landlord, George Arthur. Batman realised the best way to advance was to cut the man out altogether. By January 1827 Batman had formed the Port Phillip Association and, with the help of Joseph Gellibrand, applied for a mainland grant around the Western Port area, where a small military outpost had been founded. It was an early tilt by Batman at gaining access to a slice of the mainland, and it had distinct advantages – this land was outside Arthur's remit. Batman and Gellibrand offered to pay the government the £5000 value of the livestock as a fee for taking sheep there. They wrote to the government in New South Wales:

> We propose to shift from this place 1500 to 2000 sheep, 30 head of superier cows, oxen, horses, &c. &c., to the value of £4000 to £5000; the whole to be under the personal direction of Mr. Batman (who is a native of New South Wales) who will constantly reside there for the protection of the establishment.

Under these circumstances, we are induced to hope
your Excellency will be pleased to grant us a tract of land
proportionate to the sum of money we propose to expend,
and also to afford us every encouragement in carrying out the
proposed object into effect.

The application was refused in March that year on the grounds that the land they sought wasn't part of the Nineteen Counties. Settlers were permitted to take up land only within these counties due to the dangers in the wilderness. Batman, who had single-handedly carved out his niche in the north-eastern backwoods, would have probably scoffed at this. The wilderness was his backyard.

Thwarted again, he kept buying up local land. He took on 1200 acres of land that had not been settled in his area and leased another 4200 acres of reserve land. He also decided to apply to marry Eliza, who had recently given birth to their third daughter. Batman knew he had to be obsequious when writing to the governor for permission to marry: 'Your memorialist therefore humbly prays your Excellency will be pleased to permit your memorialist to marry the said Eliza Thompson, there not being any lawful impediments thereto.' While Eliza's pardon wouldn't be gazetted until 1833, Arthur gave consent for their wedding. The lieutenant-governor would have known that Batman housed an escapee, but as with most matters in which Batman was concerned, his service to the state caused Arthur to look askance. He found a plausible reason to pardon the bride-to-be – the reason given was her last offence had been in early 1823, five years prior to their wedding.

Now Batman reapplied for the land he had petitioned the governor for. Arthur reversed his original decision (presumably based on Batman's nuptials), granting Batman a further thousand acres. It made him a significant landowner in the north-east of the island. He had been given 1600 acres by grant, had another three hundred acres under tillage, had a high number of workers, and owned some 250 cattle and nearly three thousand sheep. He even purchased another hundred acres from his brother Henry.

But for John Batman, it was never enough. He was never convinced of the land's worth. In his eyes the Van Diemonian hinterland was rough and imperfect – and he was well aware that just across the water lay a grazier's Eden, which the powers that be in New South Wales denied him.

*

As SETTLERS' PROPERTIES expanded in Van Diemen's Land, and greater swathes of Indigenous land were sequestered, the number of attacks on properties began to escalate. In 1826, Arthur declared all local people who resisted to be insurgents. Both the military and the police could now raid camps to arrest and detain any Palawa without reasonable cause. Many were shot on sight, including women and children, leading to escalations in retaliatory violence.

When in April 1828 a band of Palawa chased one of Batman's shepherds back to the homestead, he responded by taking eight men out to hunt them down. Journalists at the *Hobart Town Courier*, most likely using Batman as their source, described his discovery of smoke, whereupon he crept on his hands and feet to within twenty yards of the place before he was seen. He supposedly endeavoured to make them stop but to no purpose; one of them was in the act of throwing a spear at Batman, when he fired at them in his own defence. The man fell but got up again and ran off. Batman then pursued them and at last overtook a boy of about sixteen years of age, whom he took prisoner. The local people had fled and Batman recovered blankets, muskets, ammunition and knives. He learnt from the boy that a nearby shepherd had also been killed.

The boy eventually escaped, but the incident was one of many as warfare escalated throughout Van Diemen's Land. By late 1828 the fighting had become so vicious that Arthur declared martial law in the settled districts, labelling the Palawa as 'open enemies' of the state and giving them no protection under the law. The three previous governors had urged settlers not to harass the Indigenous people, but their best hunting grounds were in areas where Europeans wished to expand. Settlers and their servants would fire at the locals on sight. Bushrangers, too, were known to treat locals with atrocious savagery – one bushranger reportedly threw an old woman on a fire; another shot at a heavily pregnant woman. The locals were being brutalised, and they would respond in kind.

The Palawa were brilliant guerrilla fighters, and the island, part wooded, part grasslands, was perfect for this form of warfare. Their surprise attacks inspired fear. The more aggressive they became, the more they hindered occupation of their land. They would raid white people's homesteads in minutes and just as quickly melt back into the landscape. But it wasn't only their natural abilities and local knowledge that gave them an advantage – it was also their ability to adapt to white people's ways. Many had a rudimentary knowledge of English, enough to taunt settlers in language probably first heard from convict mouths.

And many Palawa had lived and worked on farms. They knew exactly where the firearms were kept and who was at home at any given time, as well as where the food was located. They had a good idea as to whether guns would be loaded. They would surveil a house, watching the comings and goings. In many parts of Van Diemen's Land, settlers' homes were positioned at the bottom of a valley overlooked by hills, perfect vantage points for Aboriginal sentinels. Their scouts would let off decoy fires in order to attract the attention of stockmen and shepherds; while these men went out to investigate, the Palawa would strip their homes bare. As one colonial writer remarked, 'These insidious depradators will watch a house for days and weeks that they have marked out for plunder, till they find the whole of the males absent, they then pounce upon the dwellings, and with a celerity incredible, plunder it of every article they consider valuable.'

There was a story told by George Augustus Robinson, one of a handful of white men with some command of the Palawa language. He noted how expertly the local people trained their dogs, which would bark or keep quiet immediately on command. Robinson was out in the bush one day when he and his Aboriginal troop found two feral pups. The pups were naturally cautious, barking and snarling at Robinson and his party, but the Indigenous men in his party managed to calm them. Within a few hours, they were fully tamed. The Palawa would use dogs to hunt down fleeing Europeans or just the opposite – to surround huts, ensuring the hapless occupants couldn't flee.

By the late 1820s, guns had literally lost their magic for the Palawa. They'd come to understand both the powers and limitations of the weapons, and they'd learnt how to use the powder and shot. Many became brilliant marksmen, while just as many were disappointed by the guns they procured – these firesticks, it turned out, were less accurate than a spear thrown at fifty yards. They could throw several spears while the white men reloaded. The Palawa also knew there was a second or so to wait before the flash of gunpowder and the eventual discharge of the shot, and they had just enough time to duck or find cover.

Fights between the settlers and the Palawa were often stand-offs that could last for hours. The Europeans knew that after their first shot at the locals, they would be extremely vulnerable to spears and waddies. And the Palawa goaded them. From the depths of the forests, the locals would call out in English, 'Shoot, you buggers, shoot.'

Chapter 13

B UCKLEY'S BAND WERE fishing along the coast when he noticed several tribal elders talking to two men he'd never seen before. They had marks painted on their arms, and a set of coloured feathers around their heads with longer emu feathers tied to their waists. These men were *waygeries*, messengers with virtual diplomatic immunity throughout Aboriginal lands.

These honoured ambassadors brought vital knowledge from great distances. Some wore red clay marks on their forearms to denote how many days they had walked to bring message sticks to their destinations. On these small sticks, notches showed which tribes were required for a meeting and how many men were needed from each tribe. A *waygerie* could be despatched or received by all tribes, and they were the only strangers from outside country who didn't need permission to pay a visit. Purranmurnin Tallarwurnin later told James Dawson that one *waygerie* she knew of was able to travel unmolested between the Grampian Ranges and the ocean, and between the Wannon River in the far west of present-day Victoria to the Leigh River just outside Geelong. His name was Weeratt Kuyuut, and he was reputed to be a great warrior as well as a renowned messenger and truthteller who was received everywhere with respect and hospitality.

In this case, the two men were painted in accordance with their message: their faces were red and white, the colours daubed across their cheeks and nose. This meant the Barrabool Hills clan were being summoned to a great meeting, a corroboree, a marriage or a fight; if they had been painted in white all over, the information would have related to an important death. Buckley was told that there was to be another honour fight over a woman, and the messenger was to be despatched to relay the news that the clan would accept the challenge. Four days later, the messenger returned to report that the place of confrontation had been determined.

Soon Buckley's band was again on the march, with all the men save himself coloured for war. As he walked with them to the appointed place, he noted that the men vastly changed their demeanour: they were no longer relaxed and fun-loving but had become tense and alert. He later realised that as they were travelling in strange country, they expected to be ambushed at any time. They would always sleep among the bushes and long grasses away from their main camp, often without any clothing and equipped with weapons; this was necessary to prevent surprise by enemies who would be attracted to the smoke of a campfire.

Whenever the clan made a camp, they would leave it spotless the next morning and incinerate all rubbish. Buckley learnt that if an enemy took possession of anything they had used – even the bones of animals they had eaten, broken weapons, feathers or pieces of skins – it could be used as a charm to produce an illness in the person who had handled it the most. Even someone's excreta could be used against them, and so it was concealed with the use of a *gunigalg* (an excrement stick).

It is believed that at a site near Mount Eccles in the south-west of Victoria, there were two very deep, well-like holes into which an enemy's excreta were dropped. A tiny speck of an enemy's faeces deposited in these holes would cause him to pine and die. For all these reasons, any clan on the move would never leave any trace of their comings and goings which might encourage sorcery.

Buckley discovered that his tribe looked out for the accoutrements of others, as these could be used as a form of insurance or to vent anger against an individual of another tribe.

In a few days, he and his clan came to a great open place where hundreds of people were assembled from five Kulin tribes. Each tribe lit fires and set up camp on the side of the meeting area that corresponded to their country. The men were all heavily painted in warlike hues when the fight commenced as planned. This time, several women were killed in the melee.

On its conclusion, a new matter needed to be discussed: Buckley himself. According to him, his presence – and obvious difference – had proved a major distraction. The Boonwurrung from the east of Port Phillip and the Woiwurrung from the north were there, people who had never seen the huge white *ngamadjidj*.

His clan escorted him into what had just been the battle zone, where a ring of warriors was formed around him of about a hundred and fifty yards in diameter. The different tribes were all seated in rows on the ground behind the circle. Then the elders of each tribe, the *ngurungaeta*, walked along and tapped everyone on the head with a piece of bark, asking them to identify themselves, their tribes and allegiances. Each elder advanced by turns into the ring, speaking loudly enough for all to hear.

Confused as ever, Buckley began to feel that he was somehow a part of a new quarrel. Was his presence unwelcome? Was he suspected of being an evil spirit or sorcerer used by the Wadawurrung for their own advantage? Perhaps the other tribes disputed his status as kin returned.

In the inner circle closest to him were a number of heavily armed men, coloured in war paint, who had recently killed and maimed people. It seemed they were the tribunal. Buckley thought he might be sacrificed, but after the elders spoke, the spectators remained silent, staring at the huge white man for what seemed like ages. He was apoplectic with fear, but he knew to stay defiant – to show them nothing.

The tension broke so quickly that Buckley didn't know whether to smile or faint. Perhaps it had been agreed that this giant white person was Murrangurk after all. Soon the warriors were laughing, shaking their spears about and jumping in all directions. The opposing tribes gave three cheers and dispersed.

But Buckley's nerves had been shattered. There had been nobody to explain or excuse him. Not even his own people had spoken – apparently they had been beholden to whatever law or protocol was being observed. Shaken, he realised that even a year in, he knew so very little about these people.

*

THE MORGAN—BUCKLEY ACCOUNT never speaks of the spirituality of the Kulin, which seems like a great oversight but is understandable given the general readership. Indeed, few Europeans showed any interest in the belief systems of Indigenous people until the rise of anthropology in the middle to latter part of the nineteenth century.

It's also possible that the Wadawurrung told Buckley not to talk of spiritual matters to outsiders, and that his doing so would have contravened their law. The late Wadawurrung elder David Tournier explained in the documentary film *The Extraordinary Tale of William Buckley* (2010) that Buckley wouldn't have been allowed to discuss sacred matters: 'He would have learnt to respect the law and the law was you didn't dare talk about certain songs, dances and stories. They would have been taboo.' Even if Buckley never adopted the Dreaming belief system, he would have been versed in how it related to the land. He simply would never have been accepted without this spiritual inclusion. The beliefs would have been everywhere, part of all personal and collective decisions and actions.

The Dreaming, sometimes called deep time, infused everything from the day an Indigenous person was born to their dying breath, and it continued when they moved into the spirit world. It was a period at the beginning of time, when beings – some of which were human, some animal and others supernatural – brought all species to life and from there ushered in all the things the people would know. These beings had fixed the world as it is; they were heroes of different shapes and forms who determined the spirit centres for everything human and animal. If a hero spirit was connected to the kangaroo, he may even have been able to take on its form. He would have performed ceremonies to foster the lives of kangaroos and maybe even left a stone to mark the site that would represent a great repository of kangaroo life or spirits. Other legends might explain how a hill got its particular shape, how a creek was formed, how the wattlebird found its wattle, or how a crow achieved its colour.

Among the Kulin people, the most prominent legend was about Bunjil, the eaglehawk. There are hundreds of stories related to his works and creations. One legend tells of how he cupped the sun and warmed the Earth. The Earth opened, and humans came out to dance. Other stories of Bunjil relate to his creation of everything in the Dreaming. He had fought and subdued the great snake Mindie, harbinger of chaos and disorder. But Mindie had never gone away: he lived in the north, and when disease or disaster came to the Kulin, it was always his doing. It was after Bunjil had overcome Mindie that he proceeded to make the land, animals, trees and grasses. He taught all of them what to do and how to behave. He gave men and women the law. He gave men weapons and showed them how to use them.

According to Wadawurrung beliefs, all animals and geographical features visible today resulted from the actions of ancestral beings. Physical features in the landscape such as Lal Lal Falls near Ballarat were created by Bunjil, who was said to have formed these places as physical reminders of his exploits and the laws that originated because of his actions.

Colonial observers of Indigenous culture such as Edward Stone Parker, the assistant protector in the Aboriginal Protectorate established in the Port Phillip District of New South Wales (now Victoria) between 1838 and 1849, wrote:

Bunjil is said to have been once a 'black fellow', and a remarkable locality is indicated as his residence when on earth. This is the deep and basaltic glen or hollow, forming the fall of 'Lal lal' on the Marrabool [Moorabool], near Mr Airey's Station. He is now represented as dwelling in the sky, and it is curious that they call the planet Jupiter 'Pundyil', and say it is the light of his fire. This

Pundyil is said to have found a single kangaroo, emu, and other animals on earth: that he caught them, cut them up, and by some mysterious power, made each piece into a new kangaroo, &c., and that hence the country was filled with these animals.

Bunjil was also the creator of moieties, a concept that doesn't translate into any Western religion. Moieties are divisions, and the word literally means 'halves': Bunjil was one part or half, while Waa (the crow) was another. Some clans were Bunjil, others were Waa. These divisions weren't designed to separate people but rather to unite them.

In 1909, Ellen Richards, who had a Djabwurrung mother, explained to the anthropologist R.H. Mathews that the land around Ballarat from Smythesdale to Geelong was Bunjil territory, and that the Waa people inhabited the area around Mount Emu and Skipton. Richards had several interviews with Mathews respecting the language and customs of her people. They knew exactly when, where and how to find food and water, the meaning and significance of different places, and which ceremonies needed to be performed where, when and by whom. They knew how to behave in certain areas, and where access was restricted or forbidden. Richards told Mathews about various ceremonies and the people involved in them, including those related to the initiation rites of a girl becoming a woman.

Other oral histories were shared with white colonists by Wadawurrung and neighbouring Kulin tribes about events between roughly one thousand and three thousand years ago, such as when Port Phillip was dry land. One colonist recorded the account given to him: 'Blacks say "their uncle" (unspecific for all progenitors) recalled when Hobson's Bay was a kangaroo ground. They say "plenty catch kangaroo and plenty catch possum there" and Murray [an Aboriginal man] assured me that the passage up the Bay, through which the ships come, is the River Yarra, and that the river once went out at the Heads, but that the sea broke in, and that Hobson's Bay, which was once a hunting ground, became what it is.'

Another account attests to how the Wadawurrung could, in one ancient period, 'cross, dry-foot', from one 'side of the bay [in the east] to Geelong [in the west]' until a time when 'the earth sank, and the sea rushed in through the heads, till the void places became broad and deep, as they are today'. This story about the inundation of Port Phillip Bay shows the depth and age of Dreaming stories.

Central to both spiritual and social life were the moieties. They were about bringing two halves together – for example, a Bunjil couldn't marry a Bunjil, they had to marry a Waa or another moiety. Other non-Kulin people had other moieties. The Gunditjmara people of south-west Victoria had Krokitch the white cockatoo or Kaputch the black cockatoo. Throughout the Kulin nation and beyond it was a way of ensuring a person married outside their kin, which doubled as a natural way to foster genetic diversity; a Bunjil woman would always go and live with her Waa husband's people. It also determined the roles played in ceremonies such as corroborees, and most importantly it created intricate kinships and relationships between sometimes fairly distant tribes.

The Dreaming stories linked people to each other but also tightly to their natural surroundings. They were guarantees of security and stability. If the people performed the appropriate ceremonies, observed the rules of kinship and marriage, and showed respect for sacred sites, then the seasons would continue, the food would be plentiful, animals would be abundant and the rains would always come.

Chapter 14

THERE WERE MANY others who had similar experiences to Buckley. Barbara Thompson was one such person. She was discovered in 1849 by HMS *Rattlesnake*, a surveying ship that has been in the vicinity of New Guinea. After the completion of their expedition they continued to Cape York, where, while collecting water, came upon a white woman among the native tribes. Once on board the ship she insisted on remaining and joined the journey back to Sydney. During the nine-week voyage her experiences were recorded by Oswald Brierly, the artist on board, who undertook long interviews with her to record her account. She had found herself on Muralug (Prince of Wales Island) and had been living with the Kaurareg Islanders and the Aboriginal people of far north Queensland. She had been instantly adopted into the family of a respected elder known as Pequi and recognised as his daughter, believed to have returned from the dead. Known as 'Gieowma' or the shortened version, 'Giom', she was integrated into the community and treated quite well.

Thompson's experience shares many parallels with that of Buckley. She too had been recognised as a deceased relative and welcomed into the tribe. Though she had only been with the Kaurareg people for four to five years she had almost forgotten her native English language and initially struggled to make herself understood to those who found her.

James Morrill (or Murrells) spent seventeen years with the Aboriginal people of Cape Cleveland, or what is now present-day Townsville. Though he never provided the name of the group he had spent time with, he only referred to them by the area of Mount Elliot. Later historians have identified them as the Bindal clan of the Birri Gubba (or Biri) people. In 1846, at the age of around twenty-two, Morrill was an experienced seaman having run away from his home in Essex, England, at a young age for a life at sea. He had joined the fourteen-man crew and seven passengers of the *Peruvian* in Sydney for the voyage to China. The ship encountered a storm a few days out from port, at the southern end of the Great Barrier Reef. They rode it out as best they could but at daybreak realised the full extent of the predicament they were in. They managed to construct a makeshift raft from the ship's masts after the loss of their lifeboats, their intention of remaining near the wreck was quashed when the raft was torn from its ties overnight leaving them adrift for forty days until they were blown ashore.

By this time only four remained and it was two weeks until they were discovered by the local Aboriginal people. The survivors were divided between the different groups of the area but were close enough to hear of each other regularly. Morrill outlived his fellow survivors and spent most of his time with the Bindal clan. In 1860 he made a failed attempt to attract the attention of a passing ship. Over the years interaction between Aboriginal people and white settlers became more common with regular bouts of violence, leading

Morrill to seek out white society as a means of survival. He made his way to the Burdekin (Mall Mall) River with his group though they discouraged his desire to seek out the white people. He approached a hut and was met with suspicion from two white people, who eventually took him in and questioned him. He remained for two weeks before returning to white society with his arrival in Bowen in February 1863.

Morrill negotiated land agreements between the Aboriginal people and the white settlers, though with some unease. He ended up in Brisbane with the aim of playing a role to protect the Aboriginal people and negotiate policy. A pamphlet written by Edmund Gregory, a local Brisbane printer, was published in 1863 describing Morrill's life with the Aboriginal people and his story appeared in many newspapers at the time. He did not reveal detailed information on Aboriginal customs and traditions though was well integrated into Aboriginal society. Morrill attempted to assist the Aboriginal people who had helped him but he was met with resistance from white settlers, and he, himself didn't fully settle back into white society.

Another to struggle to return to white society is the little-known account of Narcisse Pelletier, a French cabin boy who was marooned in 1858 on Cape York at the age of fourteen. The ship he had been on had run aground and he was left behind by the crew to fend for himself. He was discovered by local Aboriginal people, given food and water and was soon adopted as a son by one of the men, but he was not considered a relative returned from the dead. The name he was given was 'Amglo' or 'Anco' depending on historical interpretation. Pelletier spent seventeen years with his Aboriginal clan and was deeply embedded in the culture including receiving decorative cicatrices on his chest and arms, though he did not undertake any initiation ceremony during his time with them. In the account of his experience he referred to the people he lived with as 'Ohantaala' which is now recognised as the Wanthaala. His time with them came to a sudden end in 1875 when he was discovered by an English pearling lugger that was in the area for trade. Pelletier was invited aboard the ship and was encouraged to go by his Aboriginal father who had instructed him to collect the gifts being offered and make his escape.

Once onboard, he feared the guns the sailors held and thought he might be shot if he tried to leave. Unable to communicate with those onboard as he knew no English, he quickly relearned French and was able to speak with Lieutenant John Ottley, a French-speaking passenger on board.

He spent a month in Sydney as a curiosity before returning to France in August 1875. He was interviewed by Constant Merland who published his story which provided Pelletier with an income. An English translation appeared in 2009 from a reprint of the original publication. Pelletier struggled to re-adapt to life in France and became reclusive and detached. He was restrained in sharing his experience and knowledge of the Indigenous people and gave the impression that there was more to his experience than he was willing to say.

There are others who spent time living among Indigenous groups along the east coast of Australia from settlement and throughout the colonial period. These included: John Wilson who came to Australia as a convict aboard one of the ships of the First Fleet. After his sentence had been served, he went to live with the Dharug people along the Hawkesbury. Thomas Pamphlett (also known as James Groom) along with Richard Parsons and John Finnegan were convict mariners who were blown off course and assisted by the Aboriginal people of Moreton Bay in 1823, only to be discovered some months later by a passing surveying ship.

There is also the intriguing story of Eliza Fraser who spent six weeks with the Aboriginal people of Fraser Island in 1836 though mystery surrounds her experience as it is not known how much of it has been sensationalised over time.

*

ONE OF BUCKLEY's strangest adventures took place on an afternoon when he was hunting along the banks of Lake Modewarre around Waurn Ponds (Jerringot). The water was perfectly still, and the sky was overcast with no shafts of sunlight. Suddenly something moved in the water.

The birds immediately fell silent, and whatever movement there had been in and around the lake and in the air stopped. Buckley noticed a hump that surged for a short distance through the water and then quickly submerged. It could have been a cormorant or a musk duck, but it was far too large and didn't dip in and out like a bird. It was also much too big to be a fish. This amphibious presence, which Buckley felt was about the size of a mature calf, had grey feathers on its back.

Buckley recounted that in this lake and in quite a few others inland, as well as in the deep rivers, the bunyip dwelt. It was an extraordinary animal, he claimed, but it was hard to discover: 'I could never see any part except the back, which appeared to be covered with feathers of a dusky grey colour.' The bunyip only appeared when the weather was particularly calm, and his clan had never seen the beast's head nor tail.

Buckley's bunyip experience may have been added into the memoir by Morgan to spice up the story – or maybe Buckley had become so tied to the Indigenous consciousness that he believed he had seen one. The bunyip was part of the Dreaming, and its name translated as 'evil being' in Kulin languages. He was said to have been cast down by Mindie the serpent, and condemned to lure tribespeople and their animals to their deaths. Some said the bunyip laid blue eggs, and had deadly claws, massive hind legs and a brightly coloured chest. Other descriptions are of a giant starfish-shaped creature, or one that had an emu-like head or resembled a crocodile.

An early settler was told by a Wadawurrung man that the bunyip inhabited the larger lakes and rivers in times past, and would frequently seize women and children, plunging headlong with its prey into the deep waters of Lake Purrumbete (three miles west of Lake Corangamite). The man made a drawing of the bunyip which resembled a giant mermaid, the whole of the body, however, being covered with scales, overlapped like armour plates, with the head and neck of a giraffe. It also had a thick flowing mane and two short powerful forelegs, each armed with four immense talons.

Some scholars believe the bunyip may have a scientific basis: it is possibly a folk memory of the diprotodon, the largest known marsupial to have ever lived. The diprotodon was one of the Australian megafauna that existed from about 1.6 million years ago and became extinct about forty-six thousand years ago. There is no doubt the ancestors of the Kulin would have been there to see it. The stories that were brought down through hundreds of generations may have changed drastically in the telling, but many have some basis in fact.

The Djargurd Wurrung, the Wadawurrung's neighbours to the west, created an earthen sculpture in the shape of a bunyip about twenty feet long and similarly high. The sculpture was literally carved out of the earth. It was first noted in 1851 in an article in the magazine *Australasian* and was afterwards called 'The Bunyip of Challicum'. Sometime in the past, it was said among the Djargurd Wurrung, a bunyip had dwelt in one of three local waterholes.

Aboriginal water spirit beings throughout south-eastern Australia have generally been called 'bunyips'. Aboriginal studies expert Professor Ian Clark writes: 'Some have been described as animal-like, and others as aquatic humanoid creatures. Generally, they are taken as a symbol of danger in inland waters and they often contain the theme of posing a threat to children who have strayed too close to the water's edge'.

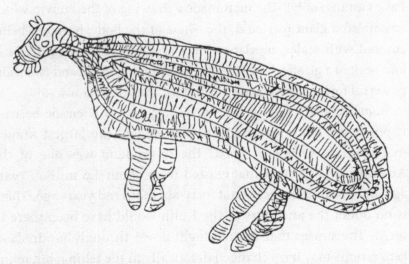

A picture of a bunyip drawn by an Aboriginal man of the Murray River. First published in *The Aborigines of Victoria* by R. Brough Smyth, 1878.

Clark writes that the word bunyip is believed to derive from *banib*, the word used by a number of tribes, including the Djab Wurrung and Wadawurrung peoples, but Murray River language groups knew them as *katenpai* (Wiradjuri) and *kyenprate* (Wadi Wadi). In the Melbourne district they were called *tooroodun* (Boonwurrung) and in Gippsland *tanutbun* (Ganai/Kurnai).

Clark notes that many white colonists in the nineteenth century believed – just as much as the Indigenous people did – that the bunyip's existence was 'incontrovertible'. Anthropologist Philip Clarke analysed accounts of bunyips in Victoria and discerned that the bunyip appeared to be an amalgam of several known creatures, with the emu being prominent. An example of this is the description by one colonist that it was 'a fearsome beast, as big as a bullock, with an emu's head and neck, a horse's mane and tail, and seal's flippers, which laid turtle's eggs in a platypus's nest, and ate blackfellows when it tired of a crayfish diet'.

The emu/feather theme is found in Buckley's account and in Boonwurrung accounts of the 'tooroodun' in Western Port. Others such as Associate Professor Fred Cahir, say that the seals were often believed to venture inland, trapped in watercourses and that with the strange noise and features – the existence of this mysterious animal was ascribed to bunyips.

'They would come in and out of the water – but were mostly in the water. I wouldn't describe it as Dreamtime folklore. It wasn't considered necessarily as a myth. I think it was highly likely an animal that people actually saw.'

*

ONE INCIDENT HAD consequences that affected Buckley's behaviour for many years.

It started with a man being bitten by a snake while walking over a fallen tree. He died almost instantly. This man was likely a highly ranked song maker or hunter because he was given the honour of a burial in the treetops. Buckley described the funeral in some detail. The clan selected a strong tree, and about twelve feet up they placed some logs and bark sheets; on these they laid the body face upwards, inclined towards the setting sun as the man's soul would wander in this direction. Over the body they placed more bark and boughs, as heavy as the branches would bear to protect the body from the birds of prey. This solemn exercise caused great lamentations among the women. A fire was set to smoulder around the tree, intended to cheer the dead man with its warmth. 'One word was uttered,' Buckley wrote. 'Animadiate' which means he is gone to be made a white man, but not forever.'

Buckley recorded that over time he was separated from most of his tribe, and that it was then just him, his family and a few others living on the Barwon. One day a large party of unknown people came past and began to paint themselves for war; they looked as though they were preparing to commit violence. Buckley said he and his small band were virtually defenceless and hoped this might weigh in their favour.

They soon found themselves facing sixty men painted in full war regalia, shaking their spears from across the river. Yelling and gesticulating, the men crossed over in force. Most of Buckley's band escaped, but his brother-in law was mortally wounded by a spear. After this the men hunted down his wife and one of their two sons –

whom Buckley had come to see as a beloved nephew – and killed them both instantly.

The reason for these killings, Buckley later found out, was that the man who had died from the snakebite was a relative of this tribe. They believed that Buckley's brother-in-law had 'carried with him something that had occasioned his death'. This form of payback wasn't unknown in Kulin culture. In the 1840s, a white settler recounted the story of Gennin (also known as Jack Weatherly) who was bitten by a snake in the Narre Warren area south-east of Melbourne. Gennin was an influential man among the Woiwurrung and the Boonwurrung, and his people tried every possible remedy to save him. As he was dying, he told his friends that a man from the north – whose country he was able to describe in some detail – had entered the snake and, in biting him, extracted his kidney fat. This meant the man had used the snake to steal Gennin's source of strength – and the dying man had no compunction about seeking vengeance upon this distant northern perpetrator.

Buckley was distraught and couldn't stop the tears 'flowing in torrents'. His assigned family had always looked out for him and kept him safe from trouble. 'Nothing had ever exceeded their kindness,' he wrote.

The killers of Buckley's family tried to insist that he join them. But he wouldn't relinquish his brother-in-law's spears, as the victors normally demanded of the vanquished. One of the killers said he wished Buckley the best, and that if he waited for the killer's wife and family to arrive they would show him similar kindness. Buckley was no doubt incredulous that the very man who assassinated his brother-in-law would now offer him some form of help. A scene of carnage was followed by a gesture of generosity. It's how Buckley described it, but it made no sense.

After bundling up his possessions Buckley fled the scene, putting himself 'in light marching order'. He headed for the bush as far as possible from the murders. Not long afterwards, he happened upon a friendly group who, greatly alarmed at the news, set off to take their revenge. Three of the killers' group were subsequently killed by his friends, who also took the time to burn the corpses of Buckley's family so that no part of them could be taken by the killers' tribe and presumably used as a sacrament to make themselves stronger. A few days later, Buckley returned to the scene of the massacre and performed his own private ceremony: 'Finding the ashes and bones of my late friends, I scraped them up together, and covered them over with turf, burying them in the best manner I could, that being the only return I could make for their many kindnesses.'

This was a turning point in Buckley's life with the Barrabool Hills clan. While he still respected the ways of his tribe, he had lost the family who had loved and nurtured him. He had been right there when they were brutally killed. In his state of desperate melancholy, he had no desire for company and spurned his new friends' offer for him to live with them. Inconsolable, he wandered aimlessly until he reached Mangowak, the area now known as Aireys Inlet.

Chapter 15

B Y THE LATE 1820s, John Batman's district in the north-eastern part of Van Diemen's Land had suffered seventeen Palawa attacks. In July 1829 a war party plundered a stock hut belonging to Batman, and in August some of his men were speared and a stonemason in his employ was killed.

Batman was now called upon by the government to act. And, just as he'd once turned on his employer back on the mainland, he now turned on his neighbours, the Plangermaireener clan. He must have realised that success here would give him the leverage and respectability he needed, so he was enthusiastically employed in the Black Line: the formation of a human chain across the island to drive the Palawa from their lands into a so-called manageable area. The Oyster Bay, Big River, North Midlands and Ben Lomond people were to be physically driven like cattle southwards and eventually surrounded. This farcical plan was easily evaded by the local people.

Batman believed that the only way to beat the canny guerrilla fighters was to bring in the equivalent – to all intents and purposes,

Indigenous mercenaries. He requested and was granted men from southern New South Wales. The once conciliatory pastoralist, who had dealt fairly with the local people, was now a semi-sanctioned government bounty hunter. He took to rounding up the Plangermaireener with the help of his 'Sydney blacks' (none were actually from that region). His first two recruits were John Pigeon, a Warrora man from Shoalhaven, and Tommy (who would later be known as John Crook) from the Wollongong area. Pigeon had been in the Bass Strait Islands with sealers and knew something of the local language. Later other Indigenous men would join: Quanmurner (aka Joe the Marine), Bill Bulletts, Joe Bungett (aka John Stewart), Old Bull and Macher (aka Mackey).

That year, Batman wrote to British Colonial Secretary John Burnett about his difficulty in capturing the local people. In his explanation he asked if he could 'follow known [Aboriginal] offenders once they had made it to their own ground'. He wanted to pursue them outside the settled areas, as he was confident he could beat them in their own territory. One of his neighbours, the artist John Glover, hardly flinched when asked what he thought of Batman. 'A rogue, thief, cheat and liar, a murderer of blacks and the vilest man I have ever known,' he said, having seen at close quarters what Batman was capable of to serve his own cause. Glover captioned one of his Tasmanian paintings *Batman's Lookout, Benn Lomond (1835)* '... on account of Mr Batman frequenting this spot to entrap the Natives'. Batman fervently harassed the locals, driving them from place to place within their formerly safe retreats.

There were others who made their feelings clear.

While Arthur insisted his policy was to treat captured Palawa with humanity and kindness, he armed the roving parties. He also encouraged their efforts by augmenting the military along the settlement frontiers in order to hem in the local people. Batman correctly took this to mean the government had a laissez-faire attitude to the consequences. The grazier reported all of his murders to Arthur in the full knowledge that the lieutenant-governor would turn a blind eye to his activities.

Once Batman was given a licence to capture (and kill if he felt it necessary), he wasn't given to compromise. Always conscious of his lowly standing in society, he did everything possible to counter it – including murdering people in order to become the best bounty hunter in the land. He may have naively believed that working so diligently for the authorities would somehow remove the stigma associated with being a currency lad.

*

IN SEPTEMBER 1829, Batman and his posse attacked an encampment of about sixty to seventy Plangermaireener. There were also people present from the Oyster Bay, Ben Lomond, Campbell Town and Stoney Creek tribes.

Batman, using the skills of Crook and Pigeon, had followed this party after finding a number of hastily built huts that had been abandoned as they travelled. At the east side of Ben Lomond, Batman and his men could hear the Palawa not far off. Batman's group nudged forward as quietly as possible, then halted when they had come to about twenty paces from the assembled tribes. He ordered men on his right flank into position so they would rush the congregation with such speed that the Indigenous people wouldn't have time to defend themselves and would surrender immediately.

But in the jostling of positions, two muskets struck against each other. The dogs gave off the alarm, and pandemonium ensued. According to Batman:

> [The Palawa] Were in the act of running away into the thick scrub, when I ordered the men to fire upon them, which was done, and a rush by the party immediately followed, we only captured that Night one woman and a male child about Two years old, the party was in search of them the remainder of the Night, but without success, the next morning we found one man very badly wounded in his ankle and knee, shortly after we found another 10 buckshot had entered his Body, he was alive but very bad, there was a great number of traces of blood in various directions and learned from those we took that 10 men were wounded in the Body which they gave us to understand were dead or would die, and two women in the same state had crawled away.

Of the sixty or seventy people present, about fifteen were either dead or would die of their wounds. Batman paid no heed to those said to be dying and concentrated on a woman, a child and two men who were still alive. He reported later to Arthur that he tried to take the two men to his farm, but they couldn't walk. After trying everything he could think of to make them move, he found he could 'not get them on'. He didn't mince words: 'I was obliged therefore to shoot them.' When Arthur read this, he made the note that Batman 'shoots wounded natives because they could not keep up'. But Arthur never reproved Batman to his face. He later wrote that Batman 'whose sympathy for the much injured and unfortunate race of beings was second only to that of George Augustus Robertson, had much slaughter to account for'. It was clear that Batman was quite capable of murder under any circumstances.

For his own reasons he took into his fold the woman, Luggenemenener, and her two-year-old son, Rolepana. He doted on the boy and asked Arthur for a special dispensation to rear him, which was against protocol: Aboriginal people were to be rounded up and sent elsewhere for 'protection'. By taking in a child he was openly defying both Arthur and the man Arthur had by now charged with corralling the Indigenous people into so-called safe harbours, George Augustus Robinson.

Robinson had established a settlement where he could 'civilise' the Aborigines on Bruny Island, on the south coast. In 1829, he was asked by Arthur to 'bring them in' – that is, all the Palawa. Robinson realised that to do this, he needed to understand their customs and language. He would mount six expeditions in all over five years, accompanied by Indigenous people, informing the Palawa of the governor's 'humane intentions'.

Those he persuaded into captivity were sent to live at a permanent settlement at Wybalenna on Flinders Island. By 1839, due to his experience in Van Diemen's Land and knowledge of Indigenous culture, he was appointed Chief Protector of Aborigines at Port Phillip.

Despite Robinson's so-called 'friendly mission' to remove all Palawa (and their children) to Flinders Island, it seemed that Batman was rendering such a magnificent service that he got his way – he could keep the children who should have been sent to Flinders Island. Rolepana would later become one of his most steadfast followers, renamed Ben Lomond. Luggenemenener, of less use to Batman, was sent to Campbell Town Gaol and separated from her son; she died in March 1837, an inmate at the Flinders Island Settlement. Robinson, no doubt piqued that Batman could 'keep' the people he was trying to take into so-called safety, would later write an unpleasant character assessment: 'This is a bad and dangerous character,' he would write later in his journal about Batman. 'He married a prison woman. He has recently lost part of his nose from the bad disease. Recently turned his wife out of doors because the prisoner servants said they saw the cook in the bedroom with his wife. He took her back.'

In October 1829, Batman captured a party of eleven Indigenous people, but six men escaped. Batman personally retained a young man named Mungo and an infant boy he christened John Allen. Both were reportedly sons of the Oyster Bay chief, Mannalargenna. Batman claimed these boys were at his homestead with the consent of their parents, and that they were 'as much his property as his farm and that he had as much right to keep them as the government'. Later observers have said that Batman abducted all three of the Indigenous children he took in that year. And while there's no doubt he fed and nurtured them, there is also no doubt that he would use them for their bush skills whenever he could.

Batman used clandestine methods for capturing Palawa in line with their own hit-and-run tactics. Some of these methods involved using Aboriginal women as bait. In all of this, he had the help of his Aboriginal mercenaries. All seven of these so-called Sydney blacks were repatriated to New South Wales after the Black War, but they all eventually came back to work for Batman. He once praised them to the *Launceston Advertiser*: 'No possible means could ensure the desired effect better than the Sydney blacks. They had their dexterity in the use of the spear, their quickness in guarding themselves from any spear wound by means of their shield, (made of the iron bark tree) ... and their usefulness in providing themselves and company with game.' He failed to mention that Crook and Pigeon had been issued with muskets.

Through Batman's auspices, the Indigenous men who worked for him were classified as 'semi-civilised' by contemporary whites. They were held up as examples of well-behaved Indigenous people who were useful and practical for the invaders' mostly acquisitive purposes. These mercenaries did Batman's will in exchange for food, arms and goods, and yet they were never totally disenfranchised from their own culture – because Batman wanted them to place at his disposal all their bush skills.

In all, Batman and his men, with the help of Robinson, are said to have brought in for 'protection' well over 350 local people. James Backhouse, a Quaker missionary who recorded much of the violence in Van Diemen's Land, visited Batman in 1833 and reported that he had murdered at least thirty Palawa.

But back in 1831, only a year after his successful raiding and bounty-hunting exploits, Batman had made efforts to transform himself into a conciliator. In Launceston that year he helped Arthur to strike a deal with the Palawa who hadn't been killed or moved on: they could stay in their districts and be given flour, tea and sugar, in exchange for 'a good white man' (Batman of course), being allowed to dwell among them. Batman also insisted that two of his senior Indigenous men, John Pigeon and John Crook, should receive a hundred acres of land for their efforts.

It has been estimated about 700 Palawa were murdered in the Black War, but this number can't be substantiated. It is thought that about 170 Europeans died too. The Palawa, of course, were far less numerous than the Europeans on the island. There may have been no more than 2000 to 3000 Palawa in Van Diemen's Land before the Europeans came. The Black War wreaked far greater havoc on their social fabric than on the Europeans on the island. They never recovered.

At the time, many Europeans claimed to believe that the removal of the Indigenous people was a necessary evil. 'Our right, is derived, as most rights are, from might,' thundered the Launceston *Independent* in 1831. 'That this is a good title, every page of history, both sacred and profane, affords abundant precedent.' The Tasmanian historian John West said much the same thing a few decades later, but his words seem laced with guilt: 'That law, which gives strength the control of weakness, prevails everywhere: it may be either malignant or benevolent, but it is irresistible. At length the secret comes out. The tribe that welcomed the first settler with shouts and dancing, or at worst looked on with indifference, has ceased to live.'

Chapter 16

AFTER THE DEATHS of his family members, Buckley stayed alone at Mangowak for several months, desiring peaceful contemplation. It was summer so the pickings were relatively easy – the fruit and shellfish that had sustained him when he first entered the country many years earlier were as abundant as ever. He now knew exactly where to find water, what berries could be eaten and which roots were edible. Behind the coastal sandbar, a creek and a billabong abounded with fish, and on the coast he relished the long expanses of golden sand.

Once the winter winds set in, he decided to move about twenty miles up the coast to Karaaf, where his clan had found him many years earlier. There he built a *wuurn*. Oddly for a man who claimed to want to be alone, he had relocated only a few miles from his tribe's main camp at the mouth of the Barwon. But for now he remained undisturbed.

This serenely beautiful campsite would become Buckley's favourite, partly because food was readily available. Mudflats abounded in worms, crabs and prawns, attracting fish and birds. The area was also replete with murnong, the daisy yam. Buckley rued just one thing – having no dog beside him, he couldn't catch kangaroo.

By now he was adept in all local methods. He knew how to make a *torrong*, a water trough, from a sheet of bark stripped from the bend of a gum tree. This trough ran to about five feet long and a foot wide. It was a way of keeping water close by, suspended on posts so animals couldn't get to it. He sweetened it with banksia cones.

To make fire, he would put a piece of dry grass-tree cane, lightly bored in the middle, between his feet. He would then place some dry stringybark fibre onto the bored part and vigorously twirl a piece of sharpened soft wood onto the grass cane until it combusted.

He used a small hooked wand to prise out grubs, the best of which were often found at the bases of wattle trees. He knew they could easily be extracted from trees and dead timber and eaten alive, but his Wadawurrung family had shown him that they tasted best roasted on embers. He also knew that large fat grubs would be found in marshes around the Karaaf, many of them drowned out of their holes by the tides.

He knew that he could get sugar from a substance called *buumbull*, a manna resembling small pieces of loaf sugar that was exuded by the leaves and small branches of certain gum trees, and which could be mixed with acacia gum and dissolved in hot water to create a very pleasant sweet drink.

There was also the gum of the acacia that could be consumed as food or used as a glue. He knew that in his clan each man had an exclusive right to a certain number of these trees, but he had the right to all of them at the Karaaf as none had ever been claimed. At the end of summer, notches were cut in these trees, allowing the gum to exude so that it could be gathered in large lumps and stored.

But Buckley's biggest break was his fishing technique. He noticed that the bream would swim up the creek, making their way to feed at a certain branch of the river. When the tide turned they would all come down again and re-enter the sea. 'It occurred to me that if by any means I could stop them in their retreat by a sort of wear [weir] I should have a great supply of food, this placed at my command, as it would seem, by Providence.' But providence had nothing to do with it: clan techniques were his guide. He set about making faggots from rushes and the boughs of trees, then selected a shallow and narrow part of the watercourse away from the beach. He fastened a barrier across that part of the stream with sharp stakes rooted deep into the sand. When the fish came down at low tide, they would meet the barrier, go back and then try again to come down; as more did the same thing, the area would start to boil with traffic. He'd wait for the tide to drop – by then the weir would be above water, and the crowded, half-suffocating fish could be easily plucked out. He knew, of course, that the ebb and flow of fish depended on the tides, which depended on the moon, so he began to consult the moon for tidal movements. He may have made his own variations to these techniques, but he had learnt about all of this from his tribe.

The full moon brought thousands of fish up the creek. He caught countless numbers, so many that he spent much of his time preserving them for more fallow periods, just as his tribe would have treated their surplus catch. He dried them in the sun by spreading them across the roof of his hut and bringing them in when the weather worsened.

Buckley was cultivating a place he could live in for years. 'With feelings of comparative content, I set about improving my habitation, making it more substantial and comfortable, by getting some logs and making the roof better able to resist the cold and rains.' He used branches as a frame for his hut and added turf for insulation, then from this he constructed a chimney so he could enjoy an indoor fire: 'After a few day's labour, I found myself more at home in my solitary abode, having from the doorway a long view over the plain, and out to sea.'

*

BUCKLEY'S IDYLLIC SOLITARY existence couldn't last forever, and he didn't seem to mind when he was eventually found. From a distance someone called out to him, *'Amadiate!'* – white man. His initial instinct was to conceal himself, but he had already been spied by two men and two women who came with their children. They were members of his clan, old friends of his sister and brother-in-law. It was a joyous reunion. 'On seeing me, the women began to cry with joy at finding me safe. It was more than a year – perhaps nearly two, since I had met them, or any human being – they had supposed me to have been killed long since.'

His friends swapped their kangaroo for his dried fish and expressed great delight, he wrote, when he explained his method of entrapping them. 'They could not contain themselves for joy, patting me on the back, and saying I deserved three or four wives for my invention.' Word spread to the tribe that Murrangurk had found a prime fishing spot, and people simply invited themselves to live with him. The land, of course, was everyone's, and everything in it was theirs. They brought meat to supplement his fish, and the Karaaf soon became an established hamlet.

They were at some point joined by Boonwurrung men, who erected huts just outside Buckley's camp perimeter. According to Buckley, they kept their distance and remained 'peaceable enough for several days'. Everybody seemed to be enjoying themselves when, seemingly without provocation or warning, the Boonwurrung surrounded Buckley and his band, and speared a young man – he had been promised a girl whom his assailant desired, Buckley said. When the intruders heard that warriors had assembled to fight them, they fled.

The murdered boy was given a treetop burial. After a few days, according to Buckley in his account with Morgan, the tribe brought away the lower part of the boy's body, leaving his torso hanging in the tree. 'Lamentation succeeded lamentation, burning with firesticks and the rest of it,' Buckley related. 'At length the mangled remains were roasted between stones, shared out and greedily devoured by these savages.' Buckley said he turned away in a state of 'indignation and disgust'.

The above is clearly another case of Morgan's sensationalising events, but it seems there may be some elements of truth in the description. The Morgan–Buckley account also mentions that the eating and then carrying of body parts was 'performed out of what they consider respect for the deceased': 'The cap bones of the knees, in this instance, after being carefully cleaned, were tied up in a sort of net of hair and twisted bark. Under such circumstances, these relics are carried by the mothers, tied around their necks by day, and placed under their heads by night, as affectionate remembrances of the dead.'

European settlers in later years recorded that they witnessed Indigenous people hanging desiccated human hands around their necks. The existence of such practices has been corroborated by anthropologists, although it seems they weren't widespread. Tasting or carrying body parts was a way to bring the bereaved closer to the deceased person, a way of guiding the souls of the dead into the bodies of living. This is often referred to as endocannibalism or ritual cannibalism.

In the Langhorne account there were no savages lustily devouring human flesh but people 'who eat small portions of the flesh of their adversaries slain in battle': 'They appear to do this not from any particular partiality to human flesh, but from the impression that by eating their enemies they would themselves become more able warriors.' He added: '... many of them are disgusted with this ceremony and refusing to eat, merely rub their bodies with a small portion of fat as a charm equally efficient.'

It is known that the Wadawurrung – and other Kulin – believed that the kidney – not the heart – was the true life force of a human. They didn't eat their enemies, as Morgan would have us think, but would exact revenge with a practice known as *marmbula*: they would cut out and remove the kidney, and afterwards smear its fat on their bodies or even taste it. In this way they believed they would appropriate the 'essence' of their enemies, their strength and prowess for themselves.

In 1841 George Augustus Robinson was presented with a parepole, a charm or amulet, by a man from the Djabwurrung clan. A parepole consisted of the flan or fat of a human subject from the kidney or near the heart tied up in a piece of skin or rug. The fat is procured from a victim of an enemy tribe and by possessing it, that enemy would die. It could also be used by the owner to direct his own form of revenge on his enemies. Robinson believed this was why the fat was sometimes taken from white men when they were killed by Indigenous people.

Weighing up the evidence, it seems that the Langhorne account is closer to the truth than the greedy savages scene offered by Morgan. There was likely a ritual among the Kulin of tasting or rubbing the kidney fat against the skin, as a means of appropriating a person's strength. In the case of the death of a child, the removal of body parts and possibly the tasting of flesh was an act by the grieving person to keep a part of that child with them. In both cases it seems, it was all about appropriating the spirit, not the flesh.

Among the Kulin, or indeed throughout Aboriginal Australia, there are no documented forms of non-ritual cannibalism – that is there is no proven case of people eating people for the sake of it. It was considered abhorrent and practised – they believed – only by some particularly backwards tribes in far-off areas. Buckley mentions in the Morgan account a people he called the Pallidurgbarrans – people notorious for their cannibal practices and whose women were renowned for killing their infants. These people were barbarous, ugly and lived deep in the forests. It sounded very much like the peripheral 'other' here – yet another far-off tribe that was the source of all evil. If the Wadawurrung had believed this, there's every chance Buckley was just repeating the story as it was told to him.

The Kulin weren't the only society to practise what is sometimes termed either mortuary or ritual cannibalism. The consumption of the dead during funeral rites wasn't uncommon in the Eastern Highlands Province of Papua New Guinea, and in the Brazilian and Peruvian Amazon. It was considered in these societies to be an act of affection and respect for the dead, and even as a means of helping survivors to cope with their grief.

Some Western scholars have argued that the practice isn't so different to the Catholic Eucharist, in which the offerings of bread and wine are transubstantiated into the body and blood of Christ. As Langhorne said in a slightly Biblical style (he was, after all, a missionary): 'They eat also of the flesh of their own children, on whom they have been much attached should they die a natural death.'

Chapter 17

Buckley had again retreated to a private enclave on the Karaaf, fearing that he would be besieged by people. Much to his surprise, his privacy was respected for several months. By the time the quiet was broken, he was relieved to see his friends again. Among them were the two remaining children of his slain sister and brother-in-law, a girl and boy aged around nine and ten; the boy had somehow been rendered blind.

Likely wanting Buckley to return from his isolation, the tribe pronounced him able to marry. He was being offered a woman of about twenty years of age who was already a widow, having lost her husband in a fight. She was, he remarked, 'tolerably good-looking' and 'apparently very mild tempered'. He joked that 'the marriage feast, the ring, the fees for the ceremony, the bride's dress, my own, and all the rest of it did not cost much … I was not obliged to run in debt or fork out every shilling.'

Whatever relationship they had, it didn't last long – neither party, it seems, was overly fond of the other. 'My dearly beloved played me most abominably false, for at the end of the honeymoon, one evening when we were alone in our hut, enjoying our domestic felicity, several men came and took her away from me in force, she, however, going very willingly.' He said that others cajoled him to take revenge on her and the man she had left him to live with, but Buckley, hardly heartbroken, tried his best to calm all parties down. It was to no avail, as she later cheated on her new partner. She was speared – and Buckley believed her to have been killed – for her sins. An imbroglio ensued, and some even threatened Buckley for no stated reason. Buckley, for the first time ever, told them in no uncertain terms that anyone trying to fight him would be met with a show of force; he believed he was just as capable with spear and boomerang as they were. The big man had never shown this kind of aggression before, and the threat of his wrath seemed to end the affair.

In the Buckley–Langhorne account, we get a slightly different version of events. In this, Buckley said he willingly gave up his wife to make sure that no jealousies would occur from other men. He had seen enough trouble over the possession of women and didn't want to become embroiled. Whatever really took place, Buckley said from that moment 'he was no longer apprehensive of danger from them' – meaning, we would surmise, that he was no longer under threat from other jealous men.

After his failed marriage, the clan again tried their best to make him happy, this time by giving him guardianship of the children perceived to be his niece and nephew. He was effectively asked to become their surrogate father. This was an intelligent and far-sighted way to keep him attached to the tribe. It shows the depth of love between the clan and Buckley, and that they valued his presence.

Buckley's participation in the community and his guardianship of the children lasted for many months before an outsider intruded into their group. This young man had taken ill and needed succour, and he eventually died of an unspecified malady. After the burial, Buckley and his friends left the area, wanting a change of scene.

Unfortunately they soon fell in with the deceased man's tribe, who may have been looking for him. When informed of his death, they pointed the finger at Buckley's little blind nephew. The boy had spent time in the *wuurn* of the deceased man, and so it was argued that he had somehow caused the death.

Buckley's nephew was prised from his arms and killed on the spot. This death was avenged with the killing of two children in the enemy tribe. Buckley was again left disconsolate.

*

BUCKLEY WENT OFF alone to wander the Port Phillip area, neither wondering nor caring where his footsteps would take him. It was around this time, probably the mid to late 1820s, that he felt a desire to return to white society as a possible way of delivering himself from his troubles. But he remained torn. He realised his mind hadn't retained a single word of English – after his twenty-plus years with the Wadawurrung, he remembered no other language than theirs. He even dreamt in this tongue.

In the first twenty to twenty-five years since Collins's failed colony had packed up, white intruders hadn't stopped coming, they just hadn't arrived in force or stayed for any significant period. The Wadawurrung had seen them and been visited by them many times, but it seems Buckley either avoided or ignored them.

In November 1824, an expedition led by William Hovell and Hamilton Hume had set off from Lake George, New South Wales, and entered Wadawurrung country. This was the expedition that would fire up John Batman and his friends, but Buckley never mentioned it and perhaps never knew of it.

The relationship between the Wadawurrung and the explorers started haltingly but soon became amicable. The British men realised the clan was intensely interested in European goods – so interested, in fact, that they were among the best thieves the explorers had ever encountered. After spoons, pocketknives, tin cans and other small items went missing from his and fellow explorers' tents, Hume made a jocular aside: 'These ancient Australians are admirable adepts in the art of thieving.' In one technique – observed by the explorers with a great deal of humour – locals would tread softly on a desired article and clench it between the toes, then pass it up their back or between their arms and side to conceal it in the armpit or between the beard and throat.

Hovell was only able to negotiate the countryside in the Geelong region by following numerous paths with the help of a guide. These routes frequently led to clusters of *wuurns* that were well located on dry land and near water. At one camp, he found the men in possession of iron made into tomahawks, a steel pot and some pieces of cloth. These items could have been obtained from escaped convicts or sealers encroaching on Kulin lands, or perhaps they had been salvaged from shipwrecks.

Hume and Hovell may not have fully recognised the integral role that axes played in the Kulin nation – and far beyond. Hovell deduced that they were used to procure important foodstuffs such as insects, possums and honey, but they were also essential as weapons and ceremonial objects, and for the butchering of meat and the construction of weirs, houses and canoes. The sometimes audacious and fearless behaviour displayed by the Kulin in obtaining metal axe heads from the white intruders indicates the high value placed on these items.

Around this time in the 1820s, Buckley discovered the wreck of a whaleboat, with its eight oars still intact but half-buried in the sand. The boat had obviously been hastily and badly rigged, the sails made of coarse blankets. Its ropes, mast and some other articles were still intact, and Buckley recognised that the blankets at least had value. He had clearly acquired the local people's sense of thrift: they rarely let anything of value, no matter how small, slip from their grasp – everything had its uses. Buckley knew of people nearby who would cherish the blankets, so he cut them into equal portions and that afternoon offered these squares to each of the local families he knew. They were ecstatic to see him, as he didn't often come to visit.

They told Buckley that, some weeks earlier, two men had stepped from the beached boat. The locals had looked after them, feeding them kangaroo and fish, and had tried to tell them about Murrangurk, whom they knew was wandering in the area. But the men hadn't understood, and when they had recovered well enough they'd headed off to view the lie of the land from the You Yangs. Buckley knew their likely fate. Not much later, he heard that after scaling the hills they had moved east towards the Yarra. Somewhere on the shores of the great river they had been surrounded by suspicious Woiwurrung men who took them to be white intruders and speared them.

Buckley also wrote about how he found a barrel of beer partly hidden in sand that had washed ashore from a wrecked ship. He didn't care about the contents, he said, but he knew the local value of the iron hoops that strengthened the lower part of the barrel. He dug around it until he struck these hoops at the bottom. When he finally prised open the top, the contents spilt out and 'disgusted him'. After his years in the bush, any love of alcohol had long dissipated – he found its smell abhorrent. He managed to break the iron hoops and divided the precious metal among his closest friends. 'It added greatly to the influence I had already acquired over them,' he wrote.

It seems Buckley was flummoxed as to how he should handle the growing number of white people in the region. Although he implied that the Wadawurrung regularly visited sealers' camps, he claimed to have never gone there. 'I always avoided going to Western Port to fall in with the sealers who often came over,' he wrote in his account with Morgan. 'During thirty years' residence among the natives I had become so reconciled to my condition that although opportunities offered, [of leaving his Wadawurrung family] and I sometimes thought of availing myself of them, I never could make up my mind to it.' When speaking to Langhorne, Buckley was seemingly more direct: he said that he'd avoided Western Port mainly out of self-preservation. He had also declined throwing in his lot with the sealers, he told Langhorne, because these men 'ill-treated the blacks and were attacked and ill-treated in their turn'.

The presence of the sealers and whalers on the coast was seasonal. Some capital was needed to conduct whaling, and parties were often sent out from bases in Sydney, Launceston or Hobart Town in April, the month when whales started migrating northwards along the Australian coast and did so for the next five months. Around that time the sealers, too, would arrive en masse in Western Port, their quarry's breeding grounds in the summer months.

There is little on the historical record concerning sealers' and whalers' activities until the 1830s. However, the available evidence strongly suggests that they participated in killings and even massacres of Kulin people, and that the sexual exploitation of local women was rife. Women were removed by barter or force, then imprisoned under enormous duress. Most women living with sealers and whalers on the Bass Strait islands, where there was no government, were thought to have been abducted from Boonwurrung clans in both Port Phillip and Western Port. In 1833, nine women (and a young boy) were captured by sealers and taken as 'wives' to the islands, according to Derrimut, a highly regarded Boonwurrung man.

One well-known incident occurred around 1833 or 1834 when a harpooned whale broke free near the Portland area and beached itself on the coast. The Kilkarer gundidj clan, who were accustomed to eating beached whale, claimed the catch just as the white whalers arrived to retrieve the huge mammal. As reported by settler Edward Henty to George Robinson, the whalers become enraged, telling the Kilkarer that they would 'convince' them by any means necessary that the spoils were theirs. The local people were slaughtered by the whalers' guns. This incident was later dubbed 'The Convincing Ground', the place where the Kilkarer were made to be convinced of their mistake by the whalers. It caused such trauma among the Kilkarer that for years they never returned to the site.

Considering what Buckley told Langhorne, it seems stories like this help explain why he didn't make contact with white people. He may also have felt it best to avoid them because his identity might have been discerned, and the authorities could have returned him – a convict bolter – to custody. And if he went back, he must have wondered, could he re-adapt to European ways? His native language had been lost. There was also his loyalty to the Barrabool Hills clan, who had fed, clothed and initiated him into their ways – he couldn't just part from his friends to join a motley crew of whalers or sealers.

His alleged wife, Purranmurnin Tallarwurnin, told James Dawson that Buckley simply didn't want to meet any white people.

His clan no doubt sensed his constant restlessness and by this time may have implicitly understood that he didn't fit in with them. They may have even guessed that he was feeling the draw of his fellow white people. As the knowledge and sightings of white people became more common in Kulin lands, Buckley must have known that eventually he would encounter them somehow.

My theory is that he may have surmised that new colonists would arrive at some point. The land would be annexed, and his Indigenous friends would be in serious danger. He may have recollected what had been done to his own family so many years ago in Marton. For this reason, I believe, he felt he had to stay: he could be a useful go-between when the invasion came, doing his best to guarantee both his own safety and that of his adopted people. Only he had the ability to engage the white men on their terms. How to handle this situation would become one of William Buckley's most difficult dilemmas.

Chapter 18

Buckley was wandering south towards the Otway Ranges when out of the coastal banksias stepped a beautiful girl. For weeks he had been living frugally on shellfish, acacia gum and roots, and he was feeling alone and miserable. The girl was perhaps no more than fifteen years old and quite obviously alone and far from home. It is generally believed that she was Purranmurnin Tallarwurnin (Buckley doesn't give her name), and that she'd left the Keyeet Balug, a clan who lived around Mount Buninyong south of Ballarat.

Buckley claimed that he and this girl appeared to be in similar circumstances. He believed that she'd left her tribe, as he had left his, due to the frequent violence. Whether she had been the object of a revenge fight or a disputed marriage isn't known, but he would have immediately understood the ramifications of a single Indigenous woman on the run – someone, somewhere, would be seeking her. He took her in immediately.

There is an interesting scene in the Morgan–Buckley account: 'I was successful in procuring an abundance of food; amongst other kinds was a large sea animal, one of that sort that the natives call

Koorman ... we found the flesh very good eating, and my female friend enjoyed the repast with great gusto: greasing herself all over with the fat, after we had made the most of the carcass, which might well be compared to bacon.' This is Buckley's version of a love scene, feasting on seal with his paramour, the closest we have to a sexual allusion. Further details would probably have been too risqué for Victorian readers, perhaps doubly so when the couple were unmarried by Christian standards and the girl was Aboriginal.

To our contemporary eyes, Buckley was a much older man behaving inappropriately with an underage girl, but Purranmurnin Tallarwurnin – if indeed this is who she was – wouldn't have been considered underage by Europeans at this point in history. Indeed, the *Offences Against the Person Act* raised the age of consent from twelve to thirteen in Great Britain and Ireland as late as 1875. Ten years later, through the *Criminal Law Amendment Act* of 1885, it was raised to sixteen years of age.

Of course, we only have the Morgan–Buckley account to go on. We aren't told of any marriage ceremony, nor can we be sure her feelings were reciprocated.

Buckley wrote that his 'amiable young lady friend' made all sorts of excuses not to return to her tribe. The two of them decided to move to Danawa (Spring Creek, around Torquay), which may have been their joint attempt to get as far as possible from their tribes and seek sanctuary in an alternative hunting and fishing spot. Here, Buckley told us, there was a considerable river flowing from high mountains way off in the interior.

But Danawa must not have fulfilled the needs of the runaways, and Buckley persuaded his new love to come with him to his old hamlet on the Karaaf. They made their way along the shore as best

Waran-drenin
Warrencep Tribe

Watercolour drawing by William Strutt of Waran-drenin, wife of Morum-morum-been, from the Ballarat region, wearing a possum skin cloak. (British Museum).

they could as the weather cooled, surviving precariously, sleeping in caves and crevices in the rocks. It was a miserable existence in a style Buckley had come to know well, and he was now hardened to it. By some time in midwinter they were back in 'his old fishing castle' at Thompsons Creek.

An experience of love that must have been of huge value to Buckley is given relatively short shrift in his memoirs – Morgan may have judged that readers would consider it a tawdry episode. We hear no more of Buckley's life with this girl other than that she was eventually found by men of her clan and returned to her people unwillingly. Buckley was back to being alone, the Crusoe-type figure that Morgan preferred to cultivate. The big man must have been desperately unhappy without her, but all that is said of this time in his life is that members of his tribe would visit him periodically.

When James Dawson interviewed Purranmurnin Tallarwurnin, she confirmed that she was around fifteen when she first met Buckley.

It is likely that Dawson's daughter, Isabella Park Taylor, was the individual had interviewed Tallarwurnin probably in the late 1870s at Framlingham Mission station. She wrote a great deal of Dawson's seminal book *Australian Aborigines*, which was the first ever volume to publish the voices of Indigenous women. That comes mostly down to Taylor, although her father only gave her some credit and no by-line. She was known to be rigorous in her research, not allowing anything to be published that hadn't been approved by all respondents, including Tallarwurnin. Back then, for Dawson (or Taylor) to document the views of Tallarwurnin and credit her Indigenous name was almost unheard of. It was an unusual act of empowerment, especially because Tallarwurnin contradicted

Morgan's account about her clan's discovery of Buckley. Taylor must have deemed her version of events highly creditable.

Exactly what progeny Buckley may have produced has never been substantiated. It has been commonly said that Buckley had a daughter but if so, she was never mentioned by either Morgan or Langhorne, perhaps at Buckley's request. Nor did Tallarwurnin ever speak of a daughter, which leads one to think that she and Buckley had no children.

George Augustus Robinson stated in April 1841 that a native woman, Cunderwondeek, (who lived around Lake Colac, which adjoins Wadawurrung Country) claimed she was Buckley's daughter. 'One woman who was of lighter cast than the rest said she was Buckley's daughter,' wrote Robinson. 'But this is I believe fudge. Some person may have told her so and she may have continued it.'

Indigenous people were known to be extremely knowledgeable and protective about their parentage – as it prescribes which country they belong to and whose kin they are. In a culture which places kinship at the core, Robinson may have been overly dismissive. He never explained why he didn't believe the woman.

Buckley is silent on names and descriptions of people who were close to him. Some have even suggested that the niece he had left behind with her anointed husband's family before returning to his wanderings – was actually his daughter by an unknown woman.

One of the most difficult aspects of Buckley research has been to pinpoint his descendants, and while we cannot even identify the mother(s) of his children, there have been snatches of information that have come through over the years.

The journal of William Thomas has some intriguing snippets of information. Thomas, writing in the late 1850s, said that he met two of Buckley's sons, the result of Buckley's relations with a woman of his tribe known as Pikururuck. She gave him two sons, Mumba and Mewarreun. By the late 1850s, Thomas says the boys were thirty-three and thirty-four.

'They were not strikingly of the half-caste ... but in personal features and appearance were decidedly different from pure Aborigines,' Thomas noted. We know that Buckley told both the Reverend Joseph Orton and the missionary George Langhorne that he had once had a child while living among his tribe in the Barrabools, but this is the only reference to a second child.

There is another snippet in Thomas's journals. Thomas states that he met with the granddaughter of William Buckley. The journal entry is simple: '31 Oct 1855: find a fine Lubra [colonial vernacular for Aboriginal woman] is the Grand Daughter of the celebrated Buckley. She is in great trouble and states that her father [Buckley's son] is in the jail ...'

We may never know how many children Buckley sired, and even back then, it was a bit of a joke – among the Indigenous people as well. Robinson in his tours throughout Victoria listed quite a number of Aboriginal people giving their names as Billy Buckley. As Robinson put it, Buckley's presence/notoriety in Victorian Aboriginal circles had indeed spread far and wide.

As one writer in the 1860s, George Thomas Lloyd, wrote: 'Many of the sable sons of Victoria, to this day, claim immediate descent from the colossal white man, and exhibit considerable pride in their self-assumed title. "Picanninny Buckley me; my fader big one white fella Buckley."'

*

IT WAS AROUND THIS TIME, in 1833, that John Batman was diagnosed with syphilis. It isn't known whether he contracted it from his wife or from his many other dalliances.

Few knew that he was suffering from the bacterium until New Year's Day 1835, when he took a large party to the summit of Ben Lomond, including his wife and seven daughters. Also present were the seven 'Sydney blacks' and some very prominent Van Diemonians, including John Wedge and George Arthur's nephew Henry, by now the collector of customs on Van Diemen's Land. The occasion was meant to be auspicious, but for Batman it was humbling when many guests first saw how the disease had struck. His cankered nose was covered by a handkerchief. The once great bushman was now struggling to make the precipitous walk to the top of the mountain, at one point doubling up in pain and refusing to go further. He couldn't make the summit.

In the nineteenth century, syphilis wasn't as virulent for Europeans as it had been in previous centuries, when it had first struck their populations. It now moved more slowly through their bodies. In the infection's early stages, Batman would have experienced genital sores or 'pocks', also often called chancres. After these had healed, there would have been a more generalised rash, often accompanied by fevers, aches and what doctors referred to as the 'night bone pains'.

After this stage, the patient would often appear to go into remission, sometimes for several years. Eventually, however, ulcers would erupt that could eat into bones and destroy the nose, lips and eyes. Batman developed destructive ulceration of the nose around January 1834. By 1835, his nose was always covered but he hadn't yet entered into the worst and most disfiguring stage of the disease: what doctors in those days referred to as 'the gumma', featuring a pus that flows from sores and hardens into scabs like resin. This stage often ended with severe debility, madness or death, and as the most feared part of the disease it often caused social ostracism. Syphilis was still viewed by society as the wages of sin, its symptoms considered a reason to shun and spurn the sufferer.

But Batman was still vibrant enough to carry out his plans in early 1835. He was assisted to the top of Ben Lomond, and when recovered he told those assembled that Hamilton Hume's descriptions of the pasture land on the Bellarine Peninsula had 'dwelt in his mind'. Ten years had passed since he'd first heard of these Edenic pastures, but only now had he decided to act upon his desire to own them. Why he waited so long is unclear, but he now knew very well he was dying of syphilis – if he didn't go ahead, he would never get another chance. He had named his effort the Port Phillip Association when unsuccessfully applying for land on the mainland in 1826, but whereas then it was nothing more than a name, now it was a reality. Here he was now looking for investment and with some of those present he would form a syndicate. The idea was to spread the risk and ensure no single investor carried too much financial weight. All men present on the hill agreed to the idea.

The Port Phillip Association had firm intellectual support; now all it needed was money. Batman, Wedge and Gellibrand took founder stakes, and other prominent men followed. Other than Wedge, Gellibrand and Henry Arthur (the governor's nephew, who also had significant landholdings), the most salubrious member of the syndicate was Charles Swanston who ran the Derwent Bank. He could tap into huge amounts of overseas capital for investment, charging borrowers exorbitant rates of interest. He would become, like George Arthur before him, the most prominent lender on the island. Everyone owed Swanston money.

The association knew there would be decent profits in wool, but the real purpose of their land grab was property speculation. Once the wool runs were established, the land would soar in value, and Swanston and company knew it. Some members, like Gellibrand, believed somewhat naively that the association had genuine altruistic aims to profit from the land and yet maintain mutually beneficial relations with its Indigenous inhabitants. Others were clearly in it for the end result. In this, Swanston described Batman as 'a useful pawn'. Men like Swanston watched social inferiors such as Batman do all the hard work, only stepping in at the pivotal profit points.

There is little doubt that George Arthur was an investor in the venture. Wedge reportedly said that Arthur was 'favourable' to colonising Port Phillip and 'doing all he can to support it'. The lieutenant-governor was never known to pass up a good land deal, and in his case, as per usual for him in business matters, his investment would be silent. But everybody knew it was there.

Batman was by no means the first to talk of colonising Port Phillip. Indeed, this was the dream of many of the landed gentry in Van Diemen's Land, most of whom would jump in after Batman's daring deal and become the (mostly) absentee landholders of Melbourne. In May 1835, no other man in the colony had the drive, determination and backwoods experience to pull off the land grab of the century. He might have been dying, but nobody could hold Batman back.

Chapter 19

William Buckley was well into middle age when he began waxing philosophical about how he had become more than just a clan member: he was now considered to be an elder of significance, known as a *ngurungaeta*. 'I had seen a race of children grow up into women and men, and many of the old people die away, and by harmless and peaceable manner amongst them, had acquired great influence in settling their disputes,' he wrote. 'Numbers of murderous fights I had prevented by my interference, which was received by them as well meant; so much so, that they would often allow me to go amongst them previous to a battle and take away their spears and waddies and boomerangs.'

Buckley's unique status as resuscitated kin, which had prevented him from taking part in warfare, now gave him special consideration as an elderly peacemaker. And this doesn't seem like an empty boast. According to Tallarwurnin, the famous *waygerie* Weeratt Kuyuut had heard that Buckley was a chief and had 'died and jumped up white fellow'. Weeratt said that Buckley was treated with great respect and consideration. Buckley, Weeratt said, had influence and sway over the people with whom he mingled.

By the early 1830s he had lived for three decades with Indigenous people. We don't know if at this point he was living with his band – it seems that he wasn't, as he recounted that there were visits to-and-fro. But he said they always welcomed and provided for him: 'They assured me … of the interest they had in my welfare.'

Now the tribe was being affected by something far too destructive for Buckley to counter. Around the late 1820s, smallpox spread down the east coast of the continent. Victims would at first experience raging headaches and a high fever. Symptoms would progress to rashes and then pustules that covered the body, especially the face, hands and feet. These pustules would burst, and not long afterwards the sufferer would die.

This wasn't the first time the disease had come to these shores – it had ravaged Indigenous populations in 1789 just after the First Fleet arrived. There has been debate among scholars over the arrival of smallpox in the early colony, with some speculating that spores were deliberately released onto clothing that was handed to the Eora people in and around Sydney as presents.

The second smallpox epidemic, which occurred from 1829 to 1831, is thought to have originated with the arrival of a convict ship, the *Bussorah Merchant*, at Sydney Cove in August 1828. After embarkation of a new crew member who subsequently came down with the disease, others on board became infected. The quarantine procedures were poor in those days, and Eora people on the North Shore of Sydney were soon infected. On 15 August 1828, the *Sydney Gazette* reported: '*Smallpox epidemic strikes Aboriginal people*'. This epidemic, forty years after the first, caused around 150,000 deaths. It was a catastrophe for Indigenous people living on the east coast.

In a matter of months, the disease wreaked havoc among the Kulin tribes. Buckley recalled a complaint 'which spread through the country, occasioning the loss of many lives, attacking generally the healthiest and strongest, whom it appeared to fix upon in preference to the more weakly ... It was a dreadful swelling of the feet, so that they were unable to move about, being afflicted with ulcers of a very painful kind.' This is almost certainly a description of the effects of smallpox on the Wadawurrung people.

The Gippsland people known as the Gurnai were reportedly unaffected, as they had little business or social intercourse with the Kulin.

In the 1840s, an elderly Murray River man told the pastoralist Peter Beveridge that locals believed the pestilence had been sent down the Murray River by sorcerers from the north. Beveridge wrote:

> ... in speaking of the scourge which has so indelibly left the marks of its foul presence they say that it came with the waters, that is, it followed down the rivers in the early flood season (about July or August), laying its death clutch on every tribe in its progress until the whole country became perfectly decimated by the fell scourge.
>
> During the earlier stages of its ravages, the natives gave proper sepulchre to its victims. At last however, the death rate assumed such immense proportions, and the panic grew so great, that burying the bodies was no longer attempted, the survivors who were strong enough merely moved their camps daily.

The man also told Beveridge that the dead would have to fester in the sun 'or as food for the wild dogs and carrion birds, which fattened to their hearts content thereon'.

The problem, of course, was that the more people fled, the faster the contagion spread. Some may have believed that northern sorcery was behind the outbreak, but William Thomas, an Aboriginal protector, was told in the 1840s that most people put the blame on Mindie, the great rainbow snake and archenemy of Bunjil. According to this belief, Mindie was wreaking vengeance on the people by hissing and spitting white particles of disease from its mouth. People set the bush on fire as they fled, trying to stop Mindie advancing. Many died in flight, and the survivors could only keep running.

Economic historians have estimated that the Aboriginal population of Victoria as a whole was around sixty thousand in 1788 before the first smallpox outbreak, which killed about half of these people. The second outbreak would have halved the population once again – and that meant there were just eleven to fifteen thousand Indigenous people left. In and around the area of Port Phillip, the population was a mere two thousand. This rendered the locals even more vulnerable to European invasion.

The *ngurungaeta* and other leaders would have felt desperately challenged. Buckley, however, mentioned the disease only in passing and gave no sense of the widespread fear and loathing that must have accompanied it.

*

AROUND THIS TIME, the Kulin received a portent of doom. Buckley related this story, which many believe offers some insight into the thinking of the local people in the early to mid-1830s. He told Langhorne that just before the coming of settlers to Port Phillip in 1835, a supernatural being had sent a message to the Wadawurrung that they needed to give him a certain number of axes (*murring/kulbullineruk*) to enable him to cut new props for the sky. What these props were was never discussed, but the entity said that the present props were getting rotten.

The Wadawurrung saw this as a potential calamity of the worst kind – if the props broke the sky would burst open, and all the people would be drowned. In order to supply the axes as speedily as possible, some of the men rushed off to Western Port and stole the ironwork from carts owned by sealers.

Buckley cynically wondered if an enterprising local had been amassing these valuable axes, profiting from his kinspeople's belief that the end was nigh.

The greenstone quarry from which the native axes were derived by all tribes in the region – and by many further afield – was almost certainly Mount William (William-i-Murring), about a hundred miles to the north-west of Geelong.

A Wurundjeri elder, William Barak, told much the same story about the sky props to a settler a few years later. He also confirmed that the Wadawurrung obtained their axes from the greenstone quarry of Mount William, often by theft. It therefore seems clear that the sky props story wasn't just prevalent among Buckley's adopted people but had been widely transmitted and taken seriously by other tribes in the region, including Barak's in the Yarra catchment area.

Of course, the sky wasn't about to fall in – or was it?

*

AT AROUND 9 a.m. on 29 May 1835, the *Rebecca*, a thirty-ton sloop, sailed through the heads and cast anchor just outside what would one day become the town of St Leonards. On board was John Batman, who recorded that his ship had slipped between the heads with the tide running out, through a heavy surf and a volatile wind. It hadn't been an easy entry, but they were unscathed. 'We succeeded, however, in entering one of the finest bays, or basins of water, well sheltered, that we remember to have seen,' Batman recorded in his diaries. 'Within the bay, the water was, compared to our late tossing in the boiling and foaming waters outside, as smooth as a mill pond; and our little bark floated gently along like a sleeping gull.'

Batman knew that Edward Henty and his brother Stephen had landed the year previously in Portland, where they'd set themselves up as whalers and graziers. Nobody had tried to stop them, and Batman believed that if he didn't strike now, others would beat him to the big prize.

Batman didn't have the breeding of a gentleman, but he was a self-made man with many wealthy men backing his outrageous ambition. However, he had never been on equal terms with the older, more established squatter families in Van Diemen's Land. He was always going to be the son of a convict who had married a runaway felon. He was blessed with all the right chips on his shoulders to drive him to success, and no doubt his syphilis affliction also made him a man in a hurry. By late May 1835, as he looked upon the bounteous green plains of the Bellarine Peninsula, he knew time was running out.

He came ashore along with Shipmaster John Harwood and five of the 'Sydney blacks' whom Batman had worked with since the early 1830s. Three of Batman's white employees were also on the expedition: James Gumm, William Todd and Alexander Thompson. As the expedition party proceeded to move to slightly higher ground, Batman was only interested in the quality and quantity of the grass.

His eyes stretched across the land from Swan Bay in the south all the way to its rise at Mount Bellarine. He proclaimed the land perfect.

On the coast they encountered what he described as 'marine villas' around which were mounds of mussels and periwinkles, the shell middens. From there they walked inland for about four miles. It was a little sandy in parts, but the more Batman saw, the better it looked to him. He now decided to take his entire team with him, which included three of his hired men and all seven of his Aboriginal contingent.

They kept walking, and it wasn't long before the great Werribee Plains stretched out before them, a region the Wadawurrung called the Iramoo. Other than the prominent You Yangs rising to the north-west, it was flat and utterly green, with just a few large and thick trees seemingly planted in poetic isolation. These blue gum and ironbark trees had been recently scorched by firestick burning. 'I was never so astonished in my life,' Batman wrote in his journals. It was an infinity of green, the place of his dreams. It was 'of the finest description for grazing purposes', he wrote. 'Nearly all parts of its surface covered with kangaroo and other grasses of the most nutritive character ... and as green as a field of wheat ... We found it to open around into softly undulating hills and plains, with as before, the richest grass and verdure, so delightful to the eyes of a sheep farmer. As a relief to the landscape, the rising eminences were adorned with wattle, banksia, native honeysuckle and the she-oak, whose short, straight, stubby butts and round heads resembled a number of pins sticking in a lady's pincushion.'

Batman wasn't wandering aimlessly: he had in his hand a copy of a map made by Hamilton Hume, who had crossed this land in 1824. They were schoolboy friends, and the explorer's journey had been published in the *Sydney Morning Herald* in 1833. After reading the article, Batman had corresponded with Hume, and now Batman knew where he and his party were heading.

It was here at Iramoo that he put his plan into action. He called upon two of his Sydney blacks to find the locals and offer them small presents. They were to go ahead naked, without any Western accoutrements. The plan was for these two men to fall in with them and gain their trust and confidence. The next phase of Batman's plan was to locate the 'chief men' of the Kulin and achieve something that had never been done on Australian soil.

The expedition was now travelling through Buckley's country and encountered explicit signs of Wadawurrung land tenure: recently used trails, marks on trees to indicate ownership of food resources, and domesticated dingoes. Batman's entourage then came to a permanent village comprised of substantial huts. Near the Werribee River, the party came across seven large huts. There they came upon a group of twenty women and twenty-four children. Batman observed that all of the women except one had a child on her back. There were four native dogs, and every woman had a heavy load on her back which consisted of two or three baskets and net bags in which were stone tomahawks and bones.

He noted that 'they had obtained and innovatively modified some European implements'. 'I found in one of the net bags a part of a tire of a cartwheel, which had two nail holes in it,' Batman noted. 'They had ground it down to a sharp edge, and put it in a stick to cut with as a tomahawk. They had also several pieces of iron hoop, ground sharp to cut with; several wooden buckets to carry water in.'

Batman thought that the children were good-looking and had a healthy appearance. He speculated that they might not have heard reports of guns or seen one, as they all 'dropped down immediately' when his men shot at a large number of wild turkeys in their presence. Of course, it may have been that they were well informed of a gun's potential to harm, rather than ignorant.

Venturing further, Batman saw substantial weirs on Hovells Creek 'in about ten or twelve places'. He reported finding, on several occasions, an intricately engineered fish-farming system that incorporated interconnected walls spanning a width of 'fifty or sixty yards'. In one part of his journey, he wrote: 'We passed many dams of stones across the creek, made by the natives [Wadawurrung] for the purpose of catching fish during the summer months. These dams were from four to five feet high, and excellently contrived. Three or four of these stone walls were built in succession, with floodgates formed of sticks and bushes.' On another occasion, he repeated his findings: 'We found at least a dozen of these dams or weirs in different parts of the creek built of stones about four feet high, and well done and well placed out. Two or three of these places following [sic] each other down the stream with gates to them, which they appear to stop with a bundle of rushes.' He seemed surprised that these weren't exactly the hunting-and-gathering people he'd expected to meet – they had ingeniously wrought farming techniques.

Walking towards the Yarra River across an increasingly boggy landscape, the party moved into Woiwurrung country.

Everyone then marched another seven miles to a much larger settlement thought to have been around the Merri Creek area, north of present-day Melbourne. There Batman's party distributed knives and tomahawks amid friendly discourse. The Sydney blacks performed their own corroborees to the delight of the locals.

A Wadawurrung woman 'Queen Mary' (true name unknown) photographed by
Fred Kruger in 1877. She is wearing a possum skin cloak and holds a boomerang,
spears and a digging stick. Woven baskets sit at her feet. (National Library of Australia)

Batman then asked for the 'chiefs' of the area to be summoned, as he had an important proposal for them. There has long been conjecture as to how the Sydney blacks parlayed with the Kulin, as their languages would have presumably been unintelligible to each other. It's surprising, as well, that the Sydney blacks were never treated as 'evil foreigners' – by all accounts they were charismatic, charming the locals, and corroboreeing with them.

What is clear is that the Sydney blacks were Batman's cross-cultural diplomats, the true mediators between him and the Kulin. Among them was John Pigeon, Batman's most senior Indigenous guide and helper, who is thought to have lived with sealers in the region and because of this may have been able to communicate with the Kulin in some form.

By deploying the Sydney blacks, Batman was practising a well-worn method of rapprochement. When Aboriginal Protector George Augustus Robinson had sought out Indigenous people in Van Diemen's Land, he'd been careful never to go anywhere without Indigenous helpers in tow. Batman was likewise trying to show he was a friend to the locals. Somehow, his Indigenous workers were able to convey his intentions: 'I fully explained to them that the object of my visit was to purchase from them a tract of their country; that I intended to settle amongst them with my wife and seven daughters; and that I intended to bring to their country sheep and cattle. I also explained my wish to protect them in every way, to employ them the same as my own natives, and also to clothe and feed them; and I also proposed to pay them an annual tribute in necessaries as a compensation for the enjoyment of their land.'

*

ON 6 JUNE, Batman met eight tribal elders, the local *ngurungaeta*, who purportedly represented all four of the Woiwurrung clans that lived around the Yarra. There by the side of a stream, most likely Merri Creek, the local people gathered. Two of the elders lit bark in their hands as a sign that they were purifying the air. Women and children of the host tribe sat on one side, men and boys on the other. Batman and his 'clan' were ushered in – in total silence.

In a few minutes the Woiwurrung got up and gathered twigs, branches and leaves from nearby trees, ensuring that every species was selected and brought into the ceremony. From these they built raised bowers on which sat all the principal players, including the elders and their wives and children. Amid them, Batman and his 'clan' were being attended on and weren't allowed to do anything for themselves. Fresh water was brought to them, which a man stirred carefully with a reed before they were summoned to drink. Food was then laid at their feet consisting of all the bush tucker the country offered. Still nobody spoke. The fact that the boughs on which they sat came from various trees was a sign that Batman and his coterie were welcome to every tree in the forest. The water stirred with a reed signified that no weapon should ever be raised against them. The ceremony also involved the formal presentation of tokens such as soils, plants, water and food. When it was over – according to William Todd, a member of Batman's party – Batman asked Billibellary, the most senior elder of the Wurundjeri-willam clan and perhaps the most important of all the elders, to make 'a signature of the country and tribe – on the bark of a tree'.

Batman and his men had been inducted into a *tanderrum*: a ceremony used by a number of Victorian tribes which gave those who had been inducted 'the freedom of the bush'. But the formal deal hadn't yet been signed. With the ceremony over, the whole party progressed to the river's edge, where Batman spread out the treaty and presented it to the eight elders.

There were, in fact, two separate deeds to sign. The first was entitled 'Grant of the Territory called Dutigalla, with livery of Seisin endorsed, Dated 6th June, 1835'. It covered an area of 500,000 acres, and is commonly referred to as the Melbourne Treaty. The second deed ceded 100,000 acres of the Geelong–Indented Head area. How this one was negotiated is anybody's guess: it wasn't Woiwurrung land but that of the Wadawurrung – and no elder of that tribe was present.

We don't know if the wavy marks used by the eight signees were authentic 'tribal marks' or forged by Batman. Three of the elders were given the same name – Jaga Jaga. There was also Cooloolock, Bungarie, Yanyan, Moowhip and Mommarnalar. In the Geelong deed, (which seemed to be little more than an afterthought purchase),

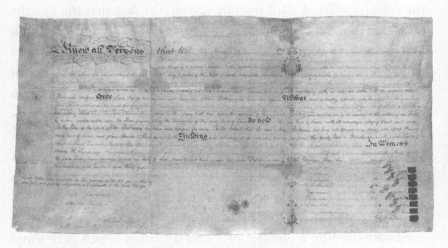

Batman's deed to the 'Territory called Dutigalla.' (State Library of Victoria).

the same chiefs allegedly signed over the Bellarine Peninsula called by the natives 'Geelong'.

Billibellary, a Wurundjeri-willam song maker and man of great knowledge, would become a vital Aboriginal voice during the first years of Melbourne. He and his three brothers all signed with the name 'Jaga Jaga'. Another who signed was Bebejan, whose son Beruk (now better known as William Barak, the man who later spoke to Europeans of the 'poles' holding up the Earth) would become known as an important leader in the post-European contact period. In years to come, Barak would also find fame as one of the most celebrated artists among the Kulin nation.

The final act that day was symbolic: Bebejan was said to have poured soil into Batman's hands.

Batman now believed he was being delivered, for his use, the great wealth of the land. With the treaties allegedly signed, he proceeded to attend to his part of the bargain – offering paraphernalia worth roughly £200, including twenty blankets, one hundred knives, one hundred pounds of flour, six shirts, thirty looking glasses, thirty tomahawks, two hundred handkerchiefs and fifty pairs of scissors. He also agreed to a further annual rent of more blankets, knives, axes, suits of clothing, scissors and flour. It was one of the most lopsided property deals in colonial history.

Chapter 20

EVER SINCE BATMAN'S treaty was 'signed', there has been plenty of talk about its illegitimacy. To wit, Batman declared that he had signed a treaty for the land with eight chiefs from a family group of about forty-five Indigenous people. They didn't actually have chiefs, and thus none of them were entitled to sell land. The land Batman said the treaty covered wasn't held solely by the tribe of the eight alleged signees – but by five different tribes that he never met, let alone negotiated with. Batman probably never marked out the boundaries, as this would have taken him days and brought him to areas he couldn't possibly have seen, let alone marked. And there are questions concerning the signatures that the eight men used. Were they fabricated? What of the tribal marks? Most have said these were totally inauthentic. The names of some of the elders on the treaty document didn't correspondent with their known names. Three supposedly had the same name.

Even so, it seems some kind of understanding arose between Batman and the elders. They may have believed they had done well: Batman had promised that only a few white men would be coming –

only he and his 'clan' (his family and men) would be granted access. The elders may have even believed that through signing they could contain the growing number of incursions by Europeans, by keeping numbers low. The elders weren't uninformed, nor were they fully duped. It was well known how Indigenous people had been treated by colonists to the north, and by sealers and many others nearby. These men would have been keen to minimise the white man's well-known desecration of country.

Batman claimed he wouldn't prevent the locals from remaining on the land. For the Indigenous people involved, this treaty wasn't about ceding land but about peaceful coexistence, along with the promise of a supply of highly coveted European goods and Batman's solemn guarantee to be their protector. They appeared agreeable to – or at least resigned to – the fact they would be living with the *ngamadjidj*.

The alleged signees, of course, believed they were granting Batman access to the land, not handing over ownership. The concept of selling land was completely alien to the Woiwurrung.

Interestingly, the treaty, which presented separate deeds to both Woiwurrung and Wadawurrung lands, was drawn up by Batman's lawyer Joseph Gellibrand. Gellibrand describes the conveyance as a 'feoffment' – an archaic, rarely used legal notion of freehold dating back to early Norman times. Both the *tanderrum* and feoffment involved strangely similar rites: both required soil or parts of trees to be handed over to the new users of the land. The feoffment conferred rights over the land, but not ownership of it. The *tanderrum* similarly conferred rights of use and access. Gellibrand had managed to dovetail two entirely alien legal systems into the one treaty, and make both appear intelligible to those on both sides. In describing the land conveyance as a feoffment, he may have been attempting to show that he wasn't annexing terra nullius (which was deemed Crown land) but simply arranging the right of use. He must have believed that this would make the treaty seem more legitimate to British authorities.

But was the treaty actually signed by Woiwurrung elders? William Barak confirmed that some kind of marking did occur – that the runic-like wavy marks on the deed were indeed those of clan elders, or at least marked their agreement.

Of course, the elders couldn't have known the exact nature of what they were signing. Any document could have been given to them, and it's highly unlikely its terms were read out in detail and explained. Of course, they had no idea what use would be made of the land and the ramifications on the environment of thousands of sheep and cattle pouring into their territory. This was certainly never explained to them.

*

ON 7 JUNE, the day after he claimed to have enacted his treaty, Batman wrote that 'the two principal chiefs came and brought their two cloaks, or royal mantles, and laid them at my feet'. They then 'placed them round my neck, and even my shoulders, and seemed quite pleased to see me walk about with them on'. They also 'made me a present of native tomahawks, some spears, woomeras, boomerangs, etc'. It all sounded as though Batman was being anointed as a new king.

He would later boast that he owned the land, which even by his own treaty wasn't correct. He claimed he had been granted the use of 600,000 acres, over nine hundred square miles, of some of the best-yielding grazing pastures on Earth. But the treaty, in the end, was never legitimate from either a British or Kulin standpoint. Still, it was a crafty means to take a seemingly benign foothold in the Port Phillip area, uncontested by the locals. The colonial authorities, of course, knew a land grab when they saw one. When the treaty was later presented to Governor Richard Bourke in New South Wales a few months later, it was vehemently rejected.

To the British, Batman had done the unthinkable by entering into a treaty that inherently legitimised Aboriginal ownership and control of the land. To the Empire this was Crown land, even if the British had never physically claimed it. It wasn't part of the Nineteen Counties deemed fit for settlement, but in this case that was irrelevant: Batman's deal both denied British sovereignty and asserted native title. The colonial authorities saw this state of affairs as unconscionable.

My view is that an illegitimate treaty was the founding instrument upon which Europeans obtained free and unfettered access to the region. The only alternative would have been for them to forcibly take over the land – something which no settler, Batman included, had the physical or material means to do.

Just two days later, Batman's party reconnoitred 'his' new land when they took a whaleboat up the Yarra. The boat reached a wide basin that featured a low waterfall. This was to be the site of the Queens Bridge, where those coming upriver would first hit fresh water. Batman recorded in his diaries: 'I am glad to state about six miles up, found the River all good water and very deep. This will be the place for a village.' He named the imagined village Batmania – a name that would change even before he settled there. For a while the place was called Bearbrass, which is said to be a mangling of the local name

Birrarung that meant 'river of mists' among the Woiwurrung. All the same, it sounds much more like a misrendering of the Boonwurrung word for the Batman's Hill area: *'Barebeerip'* or *'Bareberp'*

It's unclear what the Kulin thought of Batman and his fellow settlers. Did they still see white people as bona fide *ngamadjidj*, or had the illusion shattered after thirty years' experience? Nobody has ever answered this question completely. What is often said is that whether Europeans were considered former kinsmen or not, many clans tried to embed them into their own kinship system, from which both parties could benefit. Even if the perception of reincarnation was long gone – or only believed by some – the new arrivals could be considered like kin through place of residence, intermixing and mutual gift giving. Others say this kind of misconception was a big part of the problem to come; that by welcoming Batman and so many others, the locals allowed Europeans – at least initially – to gain a foothold and from there to usurp Kulin lands.

Batman, I think, always understood this. He had some understanding of Indigenous culture and was happy to use that against them. The *tanderrum* had been little more than a device to manipulate the tribes, because there was no other way in.

Even if Batman had somehow obtained the manpower and the means to wrest control of the area, aggressive invasion was at that time politically impossible. The zeitgeist in Britain had changed radically since George Arthur had tacitly financed the Black War five years earlier. The long struggle by British philanthropists against slavery in the colonies had also revealed wide-ranging abuse and ill-treatment of Indigenous people, and the colonies in Sydney and Van Diemen's Land were no exception. Usurpation by any means was no longer in vogue.

In 1833, two years before Batman's treaty, the *Bill for the Abolition of Slavery* had been passed by the reformed Parliament, a bill successfully fought and won by William Wilberforce and his circle of 'saints'. Now the Anti-Slavery Society and the 'Exeter Hall' humanitarians – a lobby group made up of philanthropic foreign missionary societies – turned their attention to improving the conditions of all the indigenous people subjugated by the British colonies. One of the most prominent anti-slavery campaigners in Britain, Thomas Buxton, would later write that 'the native inhabitants of any land have an incontrovertible right to their own soil'.

Even Arthur, who had instigated the Black War, knew that the colonial mood had tempered dramatically. That year, Quaker missionaries had been in Hobart Town counselling the governor that he and others had to find better solutions in dealing with the local inhabitants. There were members of the Port Phillip Association who also felt this way. One was Thomas Bannister, a soldier and explorer said to be obsessive about the need to maintain harmonious relations between the Kulin and the association. Gellibrand, too, who had drafted the all-encompassing treaty, was passionate about Indigenous rights.

The takeover of the Port Phillip District, Batman declared, would be different – it would be peaceable – but nobody on the European side was under any misapprehension as to what it really was. His association was a commercial enterprise posing rather badly as a philanthropic cause. Nevertheless, he knew that a number of factors were working in his favour. The NSW government had neither the will nor the ability to prevent the trade, nor could they 'stop the boats', an ironic notion given the present-day usage of the term in Australia. Batman was also backed by well-resourced interests and had the tacit approval of George Arthur – the most powerful man in Van Diemen's Land was privately in favour of a treaty, but as a government official he couldn't publicly sanction it.

It had only taken about a week for the syphilitic son of a convict to become the de facto 'largest landholder on earth' – it was mostly Batman himself who declared this – and he now proceeded at lightning pace. He made sure that the treaty was drawn up in triplicate and, without further ado, returned to Launceston on the *Rebecca*. Back in town, he would load up more provisions and bring his sheep to graze. There would be no subterfuge, either: he would send a copy of the signed treaty documents directly to Governor Bourke in New South Wales, in an attempt to convince him of its validity. Batman played his cards both ways, knowing full well that if Bourke rejected the treaty, it would be far too late. By then Batman's sheep and cattle would be spread out across his beloved Werribee Plains, munching on kangaroo grass and murnong.

Occupying the St Leonards beach while he was making these preparations would be three white men: the two ex-convicts, James Gumm and Alex Thompson, and the Irish freeman, William Todd, who would write a journal of the early days of the settlement. There would be five of the seven Sydney blacks, two of whom had been instrumental in making the deal; there was Joe the Marine, Bullet, Bull and Bungett, and their de facto leader, John Pigeon. Batman left his men well armed and with what he thought would be sufficient provisions until his return. He also left a further supply of gifts for the locals: handkerchiefs, knives, tomahawks, scissors and shirts, as well as looking glasses and tin pots. He set up two tents and planted a British flag.

*

WILLIAM BUCKLEY WAS out gathering roots with an old man when two young boys came walking through the marshes towards him, 'each having a coloured cotton handkerchief fastened to the end of his spear'.

The boys told Buckley they had met three white men and five black men, none of whom they had encountered before. The strangest thing was, they added, that the men had made a camp but their ship had gone. They had erected two white tents at a beach south of Indented Head and were extremely well provisioned, but had only offered the local people knives, scissors and a few other trinkets. They hadn't offered any of their treasured tomahawks, the boys reported, which had caused offence. The boys were on their way to rally round other men of the tribe to raid the camp, kill these intruders and hopefully take some of the booty for themselves.

In a flash, Buckley realised that this time he had to act. These weren't men coming ashore for wood and water, but settlers here for the long term. He couldn't ignore them or be a passive bystander. 'That night was one of great anxiety,' he recalled, 'for I knew not how, without danger, to apprise the strangers of their perilous situation.' Buckley wrote that in warning these settlers that they were about to be murdered, he felt he would be betraying his own people, but he also felt something had to be done – after all, he was now known as a peacemaker. 'My reflections were very painful. I was, of course, aware of having long since forgotten the language of my youth. I was at a loss of what to do for the best, but at length determined on hazarding my life by going to them at the earliest opportunity, for their protection.'

Buckley made his way towards Indented Head, around twenty miles from where he'd heard the news. A few days later he spied a beach with tents erected just a few yards off the shore, and a massive post with a large red, white and blue flag fluttering riotously and rudely above. Buckley knew it wasn't the pole holding up the firmament, but he might have guessed it was the beginning of the end.

Chapter 21

B UCKLEY'S ARRIVAL AT John Batman's camp caused an enormous stir. Nobody knew quite where he fitted into the scheme of things, but it was clear that this man knew the territory and the people within it. It was just as clear that he would be an invaluable asset to the small group. He spoke only the local tongue, but with a little time he could be coaxed back into English; his vocabulary improved, and over the next week he could reply with increasing fluency. He was given a tent and offered European clothes – how they had clothes big enough for his size was never explained.

Before Buckley there had been Indigenous visitors who had made Batman's overseer, the Irishman William Todd, extremely nervous. He and his fellows had given these visitors as much as they thought they could spare – everything from trinkets to damper – but the locals kept coming. Todd recorded all the events of his time at Indented Head in his journal. The Sydney blacks would take the locals hunting; the locals showed their love of the camp's bread; and, all the while, Todd was expressing anxiety that these people, who seemed to want everything they had, would not leave. His journal states that not long after Buckley arrived, an alarm went up that they were about to be raided by the Wadawurrung. It was false, and on 7 July Todd reported that the Sydney blacks had gone 'Cangarooing with the natives'.

The strong reception the foreign Aboriginal men received from the local clans was extraordinary given that it was known that Aboriginal people from different language groups were generally considered to be *mainmait* (undesirable foreigners considered untrustworthy) and were often killed.

It may be that the Sydney blacks entered into a reciprocal relationship with the Wadawurrung by regularly hunting with guns and English hunting dogs with the local clans and supplying kangaroo meat for them. They also gave a local clan two of their hunting dogs and distributed large amounts of flour and other Western supplies.

When Buckley felt he was sufficiently capable in English, he told Todd a fairly plausible story about his past. He explained that he had been a soldier, one of four shipwreck survivors from a convict transport that had been heading towards Van Diemen's Land about twenty years ago. The captain had walked into the wilderness alone, and the two others had died. Buckley said he walked for forty days until he was 'discovered' and looked after by the local people.

Buckley's acceptance by the Europeans was well known by the Wadawurrung and by other groups. In 1865, William Barak would recall: 'Captain Cook [here he was probably referring to Lieutenant Collins] landed at Western Port. Then Batman came looking in for the country. Looking around the sea he found a lot of blacks other side of Gealong; and found Buckley in the camp. Know [no] trousers, all raggety; he wore oppussum rugs, and he fetch him back to Batman's house.' Was this a mild way of saying that Buckley had decided to forsake the people who had looked after him for so long? It seems to comment on this without any form of rebuke.

At the time, Buckley had other concerns. It was clear to him that Batman's party of eight were in some danger, and he told them so. They were on Wadawurrung land, and no elder of this land had made a contract or ceded land of any form whatsoever.

The locals kept coming and asking for more provisions, and Buckley kept repelling their advances. Todd wrote that only three days after Buckley's arrival, around ninety locals were milling around and about the camp. Buckley would say the same thing to anybody who nosed about: they must retire to the bush until the next ship came. The locals kept asking, and Buckley kept politely explaining the situation – but he couldn't contain them forever. Todd wrote that Buckley's presence was 'invaluable'. 'He was a complete terror to the natives,' he wrote.

In the Morgan account, Buckley said that to keep the peace he had to play a double game. In broken English he informed the settlers of their danger, but to the locals he played the spy within.

Buckley: 'We could kill them now, but what about the next cargo from the next ship. Do you think these new white spirits would give you anything after you slaughtered their people?'

The Wadawurrung men's response: 'They have not been asked on our land. They have not shared their axes. They have not shared their food. There is so much they are not giving us.'

Buckley: 'I understand, but when the next ship comes in – and they see how many of us are here, they will give us so much more.'

This argument seemed to work. Buckley claimed that his strategy was 'to fall in line with their views'. The one fault with his type of diplomatic doublespeak was that the more he heightened expectations of great booty, the more the local people kept coming. But he managed, throughout the following weeks, to keep the peace.

Meanwhile Gumm, Thompson and Todd were employed cutting rafters to make a house for Batman, but supplies were running short. On 3 August, Todd reported that the camp was now without flour or meat. They were mainly eating what the Sydney blacks brought back from hunting kangaroos, fishing and mussel-gathering with the locals. As time wore on and less food was offered to the locals, suspicions mounted. These *ngamadjidj* were invaders, honour-bound to pay tribute. Tools, including knives and tomahawks as well as shirts and potatoes, were being regularly taken.

But Pigeon and his men still seemed to be ingratiating themselves nicely with the locals. They hunted together and performed corroborees by night. The whites thought the corroborees were simply performances, but these ceremonies had a much more important role: the locals were using them to cement relationships with the Sydney blacks – and vice versa. Todd remarked on their diplomatic value; he wrote that Pigeon and others were able to defuse tense situations not just by sharing out food but also by performing their own corroborees, and that the Wadawurrung men were astonished by the ceremonial brilliance of the foreigners. The two groups were establishing trade and friendly relations, and there is also evidence that the spiritual knowledge of language groups increased when they were learning a corroboree from an outside group.

Normally outsiders of all kinds were treated with great suspicion, but not the Sydney blacks. Wherever they went in Kulin territory, they were feted. Todd wrote that they were all being offered wives, which may have been a slight euphemism for the fact that women were being made available to Pigeon and his men.

There was an underlying tension as both parties waited for what the other would do, but no overtly hostile actions. Batman's men desperately needed the relief boat for provisions and to keep the local people at bay, while the locals were highly impatient for the great gifts promised to them from over the sea. Buckley knew that the mutual goodwill could change to animosity in an instant if there were any contretemps.

The locals expressed surprise that Buckley was dressed in English garb – some were taken aback to see Murrangurk in these clothes. He knew very well some among them suspected he was betraying them. It's not known if any directly threatened him, but his control of the situation gives the strong impression he had the confidence of an elder who knew the people and their ways. He believed they were angry but not about to commit hostilities, and he also knew that they still held him in high esteem.

Over the following two to three weeks, the locals became more demanding, and Buckley eventually snapped: 'I threatened, in strong language, the life of the first native who raised a hostile hand against the strangers, telling them that on arrival of the vessel they should have presents in abundance.' Todd wrote of this moment: 'After they were quiet Buckley explained everything to them. It was most astonishing to see how amazed and pleased they were.'

On 6 August, salvation came in the form of a sloop whose great white sails could be seen fluttering and billowing towards the peninsula on that blustery winter morning. As the sloop made its way towards the neck, Buckley's heart leapt. It touched at a sandbank a few miles offshore and, in due course, he noted a smaller boat coming towards the shore. He quickly related the intelligence to both sides.

On board was Batman's brother Henry and his wife, their four children, John Batman's two remaining Sydney blacks, and a number of people involved with the association. The most important of the arrivals was the surveyor John Helder Wedge, who, with Gellibrand, was John Batman's most trusted partner in the syndicate.

Not long afterwards, Todd reported that with provisions aplenty, corroborees and merrymaking of all sorts were again the order of the day. '[The locals] are extremely quiet and well satisfied,' he wrote in his journal. 'Mr Batman allows them rations of potatoes and biscuits daily.'

A few months after this, John Batman would report to John Montagu, the colonial secretary, that on leaving his small party at Indented Head 'however sanguine I may previously have been as to the complete success of the undertaking, I feel now infinite reason to be much more so'. Much of this, if not all, was down to Buckley. Without him, Batman's weak toehold on a strip of beach on the Bellarine Peninsula would almost certainly have been lost. There had been no treaty here. The Wadawurrung knew it, Buckley knew it, and Wedge clearly knew it too. Buckley the mediator, the go-between and the man torn between two worlds was born.

*

THERE IS A STORY, most likely apocryphal, which tells of John Batman's triumphant return to Van Diemen's Land. It's all about the prodigal son, the conqueror of vast lands. Batman stepped off the *Rebecca* and was said to have walked straight to John Pascoe Fawkner's ale house, the Cornwall Hotel. He strode into the centre of the pub and looked directly at Fawkner. Batman said it was his shout. He knew Fawkner was a teetotaller, so he proposed the man drink tea.

Batman's next sentence was like cold water on Fawkner's face. 'I am the greatest landowner in the world,' he proclaimed. There was a stunned silence from patrons. Fawkner, too, was lost for words: Batman had beaten him to the prize.

Whatever really happened that day at the Cornwall, at this point Batman may not have yet realised that Fawkner was a rival, harbouring his own ideas about how to take over land in Port Phillip. But apparently they would soon discuss Fawkner's ambitions: he wished to return to the area of Sorrento where he had years earlier been part of the first failed settlement. Fawkner was an entrepreneur, a man who had tried just about everything in business, and had never asked for permission or help. He had a bakery and a newspaper, and this ale house where for years Batman, Gellibrand and Wedge had been discussing their dreams of mainland acquisition.

Fawkner wasn't the only Van Diemonian subjected to Batman's boasts – in fact, this happened to anybody he came across. Batman now claimed to be the rightful owner of 600,000 acres of the best sheep paddocks in New Holland, if not in the world. From his arrival on 11 June in Launceston, he had been in full-blown publicity mode, believing all would listen in wonder while the great man explained how he was going to start a new colony and govern it single-handedly from his lofty seat in the capital of Batmania.

Boasts aside, it couldn't be denied that Batman had cracked the mainland. The *Cornwall Chronicle* of Launceston was the first to publish the news only two days after Batman's arrival:

... Mr. Batman, arrived yesterday from Port Phillip, and reached his own home from thence within little more than forty-eight hours. We are informed that he has purchased from a tribe of natives about 500,000 acres of land, taking his boundaries from a short distance in the rear of Port Phillip. Almost immediately after landing Mr. Batman fell in with a tribe of forty, who at first evinced a disposition to oppose him, but after a short parley the natives he had with him effected an understanding, and he was received by them with open arms, and every manifestation of good feeling.

The *Chronicle* also spoke of the

... peaceable disposition shown on the part of the holders of the new country which enabled Mr. Batman to execute the object of his visit effectually and speedily ... A fine, athletic fellow – the chief of the tribe – after being made acquainted with Mr. Batman's wish to purchase land, and his means to pay for it, proceeded with him and his party, accompanied by his tribe, to measure it off. At each corner boundary the chief marked a tree, and tabooed it, and at the same time explained to his tribe the nature of the treaty, and the positive necessity on their part to observe it inviolable.

The paper had no doubts about the brilliance of the deal: 'A horse might run away with a gig for twenty miles on end without fear of upsetting from irregularity of the ground.'

If Batman needed any more reassurance, he would receive it from just about everyone. On 26 June, the *Hobart Town Courier* described how he had induced 'above a dozen of our wealthy and influential capitalists' from both Hobart Town and Launceston to be part of the venture. All of these men were spirited individuals 'willing not only to explore and bring out the resources of a hitherto almost unknown country' but were capable of creating 'an amicable discourse between the graziers and their black associates'. 'Happy had it been for Van Diemen's Land if the same step had been taken with the aborigines on its first settlement by the English,' the paper pronounced.

Some immediately concluded that this was all no more than typical Batman bravado, but there's no doubt the news had charged the normally stilted atmosphere of Hobart Town and Launceston with electricity. The Reverend John Dunmore Lang, a prominent politician, educationist and writer in the colony, wrote to the *Hobart Town Courier* saying that throughout his travels in Van Diemen's Land he had never seen anything like the reaction to Batman's bold move across the water. 'I found almost every respectable person I met with – either individually or in the person of some near relative or confidential agent – anxious to occupy the Australian El Dorado.'

Batman's lofty ambitions were brought down to earth by his now very noticeable illness. A canker was eating away at his face, and his body was beginning to fall apart. He would work hard on his dreams in the morning, only to collapse semi-depressed and disconsolate for the rest of the day. He was losing his famed stamina, but his brain was still working at breakneck speed. There was so much to do. He needed to apprise all the appropriate government authorities of his land deal and organise stock to populate the land. His family would have to remove itself from Kingston in the north-east and resettle in Port Phillip. His partners also had to be ready to bring their stock over so that grazing allotments could be organised.

People throughout Van Diemen's Land and in New South Wales were hearing the name Batman. He was being hailed as the local version of William Penn, the founder of Pennsylvania, who had been granted around 45,000 square miles of territory west and south of New Jersey by the English monarch, Charles II. In reality Batman's deal was more reminiscent of that negotiated between the Dutch and the Canarsie Indians to buy up the island of Manhattan in 1624 – prime New York real estate acquired for about $24 worth of trinkets and beads.

Charles Swanston was busy praising Batman's efforts while acquiring capital from his group of investors. It was the opportunity of the century, and men were told to roll up and be part of the association's membership – even better, put all your money with us as investors!

Gellibrand, meanwhile, was busy on the lobbying front formulating formal letters to persuade the authorities on Batman's behalf. He sent a report of Batman's trip to both George Arthur and the colonial secretary in Hobart Town, John Montagu. The Secretary of State for War and the Colonies, Lord Glenelg, was also sent a copy – he was a humanitarian and Whig, someone whom they believed could be amenable to the treaty and who might conceivably lobby for it on their behalf. Gellibrand emphasised the treaty's humanitarian status, barely mentioning the commercial enterprise. The treaty was equitable, he wrote, and not just to those people who owned the soil; there would even be statutes and by-laws that stated clearly how the Kulin would be compensated on a yearly basis. It would therefore be madness, he argued, for the British government not to ratify this treaty.

The Port Phillip Association said its aim was to create a nucleus 'for a free and useful colony, founded on the principle of conciliation, of philanthropy, morality and temperance ... calculated to ensure the comfort and well being of the natives'. The association, in other words, claimed that it would be bringing decent British morals and principles to a supposedly backward people, as well as the restriction of those things (notably alcohol) 'which might have a baneful effect on them'.

Everyone who wanted to believe in the association reassured themselves that this colony wouldn't be like Sydney or Hobart Town, both of which had been established with rough convicts and enforced by military brutality. This would be on a higher plane, a colony of free settlers only. And that idea was what would drive white people to Kulin lands – the idea of freedom, the kind that populated the American West, the kind where men could assert their status as freeborn Britons, unshackled by the intervention of metropolitan authorities. This was the dream of settler self-rule, unfettered by intrusive big government and driven by respectable intentions. Batman had done it all on his own, in defiance of the law and the authorities, and in the face of incredible odds. Others felt they could do this too – and chief among them was the man who resented Batman's success more than any other, John Fawkner.

And so the lie was spread: that in taking away an entire nation's land and freedom, the association would be giving back most liberally and kindly. Nobody would be uprooting the local people but rather embracing them, offering them the delights of reason and education and Christianity. First in line to offer such gifts would be the generously minded landed gentry of Van Diemen's Land, quickly followed by the altruistic and selfless local experts in business, politics and the law. What more could anyone want, and what more could they be offering the people they dispossessed? A better class of people was coming to Port Phillip. This time it was going to be different.

Chapter 22

WHEN WILLIAM BUCKLEY met the surveyor John Wedge, they had an almost immediate empathy despite the vast chasm separating their backgrounds. Wedge was an Enlightenment man who prided himself on his knowledge of science, but he also had a love of whatever he saw as exotic. He was that ever-curious type that the nineteenth century produced so often – akin to a taxonomist, he collected samples from his wanderings. His great love was Indigenous artefacts including weapons, utensils and tools.

Like so many of his fellow squatters in Van Diemen's Land, Wedge had been involved in the war with the Palawa and had taken in one of their children under dubious circumstances. He had appropriated this boy, Wheete, from the Peerapper people after a skirmish in northern Van Diemen's Land. Wedge then took on Wheete, who had been trying to flee, and in the course of several years 'acquired' more Aboriginal children. It was rumoured that his interest in children was disquieting, but nothing could ever be proved of an illicit nature. Many Palawa children were taken in by white settlers following attacks on their parents. Men like Batman and Wedge treated 'their' children as no less their rightful property than the land they had been granted. This wasn't considered abnormal, and most British colonists believed it would help engender a civilising influence on the captured. Wedge would later say that his experiences with Wheete had 'completely falsified' the belief that the Palawa were 'little more than brutes', and had proved it was possible to train them to become 'useful'. He also talked about a scheme to transform all the local people in a similar way.

Wedge probably viewed William Buckley in a similar spirit. Here was yet another curiosity: a white man turned native, the opposite of Wedge's experiment with Wheete. Wedge would be the first highly educated British man to meet Buckley and the first to give a considered view on his character. Wedge realised that the giant convict would be an asset. The association needed someone who understood the language and culture of the locals.

Wedge described Buckley in his diary: 'Height, 6'5 7/8', age fifty-three, trade bricklayer, brown complexion, round head, dark brown hair and whiskers, visage round and marked with smallpox, forehead low, eyebrows bushy, hazel eyes: nose pointed and turned up, well proportioned with an erect military gait; mermaid on upper part of right arm, sun, half moon, seven stars, monkey and W.B on lower part of right arm.'

At first Wedge, like Henry Batman and his children, was intimidated by the huge man whose demeanour seemed to them quite basic and simple. Although Buckley was extremely helpful, in Wedge's sketches he looks withdrawn and alienated. He had an air of despondency; he said little and didn't always respond to everything that was said to him. Wedge may have been the first to realise that culture shock might be involved – from Wedge's perspective, Buckley was a Wadawurrung man with a white folk memory, a unique specimen who was understandably confused and consternated.

Wedge made a point of never questioning Buckley too sharply. The surveyor's style was to engage him in slow and casual conversation, teasing out information as it came. Wedge must have said the right things in the right way, because within a few days Buckley had told him the entire truth about being an escaped convict. There are no records of this conversation, but we can gather that Wedge was the first to explain to Buckley all that had transpired after the camp at Sorrento had been abandoned.

Henry Batman, on the other hand, would fire questions at Buckley repeatedly. As Henry saw it, they were on his family's land. The Batmans knew they would have competition in the near future, and Henry, who had none of his older brother's intellectual talents (and was often inebriated), was naturally suspicious. But within a few days he softened and became reliant on Buckley's advice. When Buckley explained that the local people couldn't get enough bread, Henry sent for a big load of biscuit to be despatched from the ship and handed it out at a great corroboree that night. Henry then put the locals on a daily diet of wheat and potatoes.

Buckley took Wedge on walks around the bush and along the coast, showing him the areas he knew best and the ways in which the land was used. All of this was Wadawurrung land that had been included in Batman's treaty without their consent. As a surveyor and draftsman, Wedge consumed as much geographical intelligence as he could. With Buckley's help he quickly began to understand the landscape around the Bellarine Peninsula and what could be expected further afield. The men travelled with two of the Sydney blacks, as well as two Wadawurrung youths whose names Wedge recorded as 'Diabering' and 'Joan Joan'. Wedge was among the first white men to utilise local guides and was unequivocal about their usefulness whenever he set out exploring and mapping: 'The reason why we proposed taking them [Indigenous guides] was that in the event of our provisions failing we might avail ourselves of their forest habits and skill in procuring food.'

Their party travelled up the Barwon River until they reached Lake Connewarre (Kulib a Gurrk) on the first night. On the second day they moved up to higher ground, a place Buckley called Booneewang (present-day Fyansford) from which Wedge could see the land for many miles around. Buckley later wrote that Wedge was 'surprised and delighted with the magnificence of its pastoral and agricultural resources'. In time, Buckley would show Wedge where he had lived, including his beloved Karaaf.

Buckley would provide the place names, and Wedge would duly anglicise them onto his map. We owe it to Wedge that as the first surveyor, he kept the names of the places he saw – the best known, of course, being *jillong*, the Wadawurrung word for 'bay', and *carayo*, their word for the tongue of land leading to it. But in later surveys these words were mistakenly swapped, with Corio becoming the bay and Geelong the township. In this way Moorabool, Gheringhap, Malop, Moolap, Barwon, You Yangs, Colac, Beeac and Birregurra were all noted down and anglicised.

Wedge's party came to a picturesque point west of Geelong on the Barwon River, which he named Buckley Falls. It wasn't a great gushing waterfall, but rather a set of low stepped rocks of an ochre colour through which the river teased its way. It then trickled quietly into what appeared to be a deep waterhole bordered by steep banks of gently leaning eucalypts. By naming this peaceful place after Buckley, Wedge was making it clear to him that he was of vital importance.

The going was all very peaceful. When they met with some of Buckley's Wadawurrung friends, Wedge wrote that he pitched his tent between two families, and the party of eleven local men remained 'sitting around my fire' until he went to bed. Wedge appeared fascinated by the people and, with Buckley as translator, set down useful words as well as the names of the people he met. His portraits of individuals are sympathetic and give the impression he was studying them while listening carefully. His field book includes many words and phrases that seem to reflect his good intentions and his interest in collecting: 'I am your friend – *banwadejaie*'; 'will you give me this – *gunathianic*'; 'hand spear – *carp*'; 'shield – *geramb*'; 'Spear for kangaroo – *daire*'.

One of the more interesting observations Wedge made was that 'the above families belong to this Ground where we are on'. This was hardly official phrasing – the 'natives', as the British saw them, had no rights to Crown land – and Wedge, the surveyor, would have known this. Wedge, the human, would have also known that it was their land.

Although Wedge showed a lot of interest in the locals, he wasn't always approving towards them. He said they were – as he put it – 'slaves' to the food search and treated their women as 'drudges', and he mentioned the usual colonial fear that they practised cannibalism (but, he added, only against those they had fought in war). He also claimed that the women practised infanticide if they gave birth while breastfeeding another – he could hardly have found any proof of this and this information, we must surmise, came from Buckley.

It was probably around this time when Buckley began to feel a mild unease that was growing stronger by the day. When he and Wedge toured Wadawurrung lands, the surveyor told the locals that he would supply them with all sorts of gifts, a glib offer that was never honoured. This made Buckley, as translator, the mouthpiece of promises he knew he couldn't keep.

In a letter to a friend, Wedge wrote that Buckley had told him there was no such thing as 'chief' in the tribe. In other words, he and Buckley must have been discussing the land deal, and Buckley explained why it wouldn't pass muster even among the locals: the elders who'd signed the deal weren't chiefs and had no relationship with Wadawurrung lands, and thus no authority in this legal context. Indeed, nobody had this authority, as the land didn't have an owner. Wedge wrote to his friend: 'This is a secret that must, I suppose, be kept to ourselves or it may affect the deed of conveyance.' Even then Wedge knew the treaty was false, yet he held out hope that it would be accepted by British authorities.

It's worth noting that Buckley needed Wedge too – perhaps even more acutely than Wedge needed him. Wedge had promised to petition Governor Arthur for a pardon, and Buckley hoped this would be his ticket to freedom from further incarceration. There's little doubt that the two men liked and appreciated each other, but this was the unspoken deal: Buckley's local expertise in exchange for Wedge's submission for a pardon.

In a few days, the *Rebecca* had departed again carrying vital letters from Wedge. The most important was his missive asking Arthur to grant Buckley a pardon on the basis of his help in the initial encampment, his part in stalling potential aggression from the locals, and his work fostering good relations. Wedge added that Buckley hadn't infringed in thirty-two years, and that a free pardon should be granted. Wedge had also written to John Batman explaining why he should agitate on Buckley's behalf.

For Buckley, the *Rebecca* carried hope. If the lieutenant-governor granted his wish, he would henceforth feel safe in going to Van Diemen's Land: 'For I was resolved not to go there as a prisoner.' We don't know whether at this point Buckley actually wanted to go to Van Diemen's Land or if he simply wanted the option.

While waiting for Arthur's response, Buckley had much to do – he was now acting as a freelance guide and interpreter for the association. Not long afterwards the *Rebecca* returned, not with news on Buckley's freedom but with the intelligence that the party of settlers was to move to the area designated as Batmania on the Yarra. Buckley would be needed for this settlement as a vital component of the association. John Batman, it was presumed, would be arriving soon.

Unbeknown to the settlers, others were on the move. The Batmans had 'taken' the land and Wedge surveyed it, but they hadn't counted on another party of settlers leaving from Launceston.

*

JOHN PASCOE FAWKNER was no stranger to Port Phillip. When the Sorrento encampment had been abruptly abandoned when he was a boy, he had been plainly upset. Since then, it seems, his heartfelt ambition had been to return.

When Batman had arrived in Launceston with the news that he had done a deal with the Woiwurrung, Fawkner must have realised he had little time to reach his goal. His great rival had won the first battle, but in Fawkner's mind this was a full-blown territorial war. Batman had miscalculated – caught up in his own braggadocio, he'd never considered that anyone would seriously challenge his new-found hegemony over the mainland. Fawkner not only eschewed the deal with the Indigenous people, but he also eschewed Batman's right to invoke it.

Their rivalry went back several years. Fawkner once described Batman as one of Arthur's 'toadies', who had 'gotten a large grant or two of land prior to this'. The clear implication was that Batman was 'in thick' with the government, doing Arthur's private bidding in return for favours. It was also rumoured that Fawkner had applied to be part of the association and been rejected by Batman. Fawkner was evidently not their kind of man – he had too much of the commoner and the convict about him – and probably had nothing to offer that Batman didn't already have.

When Batman's treaty was unveiled, Fawkner would tell anyone who would listen that it was a joke. He also rubbished Batman's talk that he and the locals had walked the entire course of the land he had bought, marking the trees along the way. 'These falsehoods,' Fawkner wrote, 'were too transparent to blind an old colonist on the spot.' He would later write that Batman's treaty wasn't even read to the Woiwurrung elders, nor was it interpreted or explained. 'Not one of the Sydney blacks knew the language of the men of the colony, not one of the Sydney blacks could read, except Bullett ... any man of sense must know that to translate a deed to anyone of a different tongue requires a real knowledge of both languages, and these Sydney blacks could not read, much less translate writing.'

If Batman's treaty was seen as a fraud, this would be to Fawkner's advantage: a fraudulent treaty would in no way preclude his own attempt to settle in the new lands. Fawkner, the teetotaller who didn't drink with the right people, wasn't suggestible and took no heed of others' opinions. Van Diemonians with far more wealth and access to power dithered on the Batman claim, adopting a wait-and-see approach. Fawkner didn't ask or wait for government sanction – he simply set about going there.

Fawkner was his own man, and was said by some to have a 'partiality towards disputation and argument'. In recent years he had become what was loosely termed an 'agent': a bush lawyer with no official legal qualifications at a time when there were virtually no real barristers or solicitors on the island. 'Fawkner was glib of tongue, choleric in disposition; and it is therefore, not much wonder to hear of his having practised as an advocate in the old public Court of Launceston,' the historian James Bonwick wrote in 1883. Fawkner clearly saw himself as a defender of the oppressed, representing convicts as their agent and pleading their causes.

Fawkner had once known the other side of the dock. In his early twenties he'd been accused of aiding and abetting a convict to escape. When sentenced in 1814, he was handed five hundred lashes and three years' gaol time in Newcastle, but he somehow managed to get released in 1816. From then on he hated the powers that be and convictism.

A few years later he'd taken a cart from Hobart Town to Launceston and started afresh with his convict wife, Eliza Cobb. They married in 1822 and together established a bakery, timber business and bookshop. In 1826 his reputation as a teetotaller didn't stop him from becoming the proprietor of the Cornwall Hotel. Three years later he launched the *Launceston Advertiser*. In 1830 his newspaper criticised Governor Arthur's Black Line by exposing the waste of £30,000 of government funds on this failed attempt to round up and incarcerate all the Palawa on the island. Batman, by contrast, had ardently taken to the Black Line.

Fawkner was said to relish his role as the common people's champion. He was no Batman, even if their ends were practically identical. Fawkner was less a bushman, more a businessman; an outsider, not an insider. Both were the sons of convicts, but Fawkner, who had experienced penal servitude himself, felt the stain keener than Batman. And there was another difference: Fawkner wasn't interested in sheep runs – he wanted to grow wheat.

In the mid-1830s Fawkner had trouble chartering a boat to emigrate to the mainland. He finally purchased the *Enterprize*, a topsail schooner of fifty tons, in April 1835, but couldn't take possession of it until June. Then his plans to reach the mainland were thwarted by legal entanglements. At around the time Batman's *Rebecca* was anchored off Indented Head in early June, Fawkner was in court accused of assault and was forced to plead his case for the next two months. By the time he was ready to take the schooner north, he was in trouble again, this time presented with a restraining order for a debt claim.

But Fawkner didn't wait any longer, even though he couldn't go personally. On 21 July he sent out a party to prepare the way, the *Enterprize* setting off from George Town. He hadn't yet decided on where he would make his settlement, and he told his man, Captain John Lancey, to have an open mind. The *Enterprize* would reconnoitre Western Port seeking suitable landfalls; if none were satisfactory, Lancey would move on to Port Phillip Bay.

Only a few days after Henry Batman had docked with his wife and children at Indented Head, Lancey's ship entered Port Phillip Bay. It was 15 August, and on board with Lancey were George Evans, builder; William Jackson and Robert Marr, carpenters; Evan Evans, servant to George Evans; and Fawkner's servants, Charles

Wyse, ploughman, Thomas Morgan, general servant, James Gilbert, blacksmith and his pregnant wife, Mary. The boat was under the command of Captain Peter Hunter.

The *Enterprize* was close to today's Queenscliff and had just passed Shortland Bluff, the little outcrop to the south of the Bellarine Peninsula, when Hunter spied a whaleboat coming towards them out of nowhere. As it drew closer he saw it was manned by one white man and two Indigenous men. 'What is your news?' the white man hollered as the boat came close to port side. 'Where are you from and where are you going to?' When Hunter told them they were settlers, there was some hesitation from the boat. The man then declared, 'Mr John Batman is the King of Port Phillip. He has desired all trespassers to keep aloof.' Lancey no doubt ignored this piece of information, and when the three men came aboard, they were friendly. The Indigenous men were two Sydney blacks, Pigeon and Bungett, who handed over fish as a gesture of welcome. There were reportedly no hard words or contretemps.

The *Enterprize* spent the next few days examining the bay. While exploring its eastern side, some of the men took the whaleboat up the Saltwater River (now today's Maribyrnong). With no fresh water in sight, they deemed it not worth following and soon returned. On the way there, however, they'd seen the junction of the Yarra, and on 22 August they pushed up the river. Within an hour of rowing, they came to what was unanimously agreed to be perfection: the Yarra's basin, an area of deeper water that Batman had encountered and declared to be the future site of Batmania. To the eyes of the colonists, this was an Eden they had never expected. The water was entirely fresh, and the surrounding grass was velvety and light green, decked with flowers of many hues and spread liberally across the banks. This was lowland country of the most idyllic kind, with picturesque knolls around a number of lagoons. They saw ducks and swans and all manner of birds.

There was no debate: they had reached their goal. A few days later the *Enterprize* was taken up to the junction of the Saltwater River and then hauled by the whaleboat up the Yarra. The captain reported the river at about three fathoms as they progressed and nearly eight fathoms at its deepest around the basin. On 29 August the schooner docked in an area where the Queens Bridge now stands between present-day William and Market streets. The next day, planks were brought out to assist the colonists' landfall. With the arrival of the party on this turf, a hamlet was born.

Four days after the *Enterprize*'s docking, John Wedge had crossed over the Werribee River from Indented Head, forded the Saltwater River and was now in a party being guided by Wadawurrung up the Yarra. He came to the basin – known later as the turning basin – and expected to look on the falls, a ledge of rocks strung across the river, known by the local Woiwurrung as the *yarro yarro*, which physically divided the salt water from the fresh. The falls were the highest point a ship could reach – and there, just before the rocks, was a decidedly European encampment. Wedge happened upon a large schooner; evidently, with the help of Woiwurrung workers, the *Enterprize* had been winched up the river against the prevailing winds and currents by men pulling on ropes attached to trees.

Wedge noted a number of white men milling around a small camp that consisted mostly of calico tents and timber piles. Fawkner's party had set up directly on Batman's most treasured site. The surveyor, who had already sketched out a proposed town for Batman, was rudely shocked. The land he wanted to plan was already being cleared for vegetable gardens, and the settlers were laying the foundations of a store for provisions and equipment.

Wedge was said to have spoken with Lancey and iterated Batman's claim, trying to deliver it not as a threat but more as advice. Lancey took this in with relatively good cheer. There were no more troubled words between the two men, and Wedge stayed a night with the party. But his heart must have sunk: this would be heavy tidings for Batman, who had known of Fawkner's ambitions for some time.

The self-proclaimed king of the Yarra had been unseated before even taking his seat. The tiny village that would one day be a major metropolis was at this point being contested by two absent landlords. Melbourne was definitely going to be different.

Chapter 23

SOME HISTORIANS CLAIM that when the members of the Port Phillip Association were naming its lands, they had a disguised agenda – that Wedge adopted Indigenous names wherever he went so that the association identified itself with their interests. For example, the Fawkner party had christened the main river the Hunter, but Wedge called it the Yarra when his Wadawurrung guides seemed to call out 'Yarra, Yarra' on their approach. They were actually calling out '*yarro*', referring to the falls; only afterwards did Wedge learn this was a term meaning 'rapids' or 'waterfall'.

It's debatable whether Wedge was truly sympathetic – he had shown some interest in the language – or simply disguising his colonial intent by adopting local place names. The issue was symptomatic of the problems this newly 'acquired' land would throw up intellectually. Was the land meant, as the association proffered, to be worked in sympathetic cooperation with its local inhabitants or to be seized, cultivated, revamped and Christianised? From the start, the British authorities had tried to mix together two ideas that were logically inconsistent. The association had couched its treaty as a humanitarian effort in order to sell it to senior members of the Colonial Office, many of whom were evangelical Christians. But British government policy told its subjects to go forth and carry their way of life throughout the colonies, with many thousands of free settlers being encouraged to take up land across the Empire. All the while prospective settlers were being told to do this, their government officials were being told that aggressive invasion was clearly politically impossible.

Nobody knew this paradox better than George Arthur, and he played the double game of deracination clothed in Indigenous welfare better than anyone. He had done it all before, sending Palawa people to Flinders Island supposedly for their own welfare and the higher advantages of a Christian education, but really to clear the land for profitable use. When Arthur received the news that Batman had 'acquired' land at Port Phillip, he was the closest political leader to the scene. The astute governor knew the treaty wouldn't be considered politically acceptable by either NSW Governor Sir Richard Bourke or the even higher authority of the Colonial Office in London. But Bourke was a known Whig (liberal), and Arthur believed he could play on Bourke's liberal views.

Bourke was hardworking and incorruptible. He had been instrumental in New South Wales in improving the lot of convicts while introducing a number of legal, educational and religious reforms. He was adamant (against much opposition) that there should be no official Christian denomination in New South Wales, even if it was dominated by Anglicans; he had seen the sectarianism of his native Ireland and didn't want that repeated in the colony. He proposed the extension of trial by jury and the substitution of civil for military juries in criminal cases, and successfully brought about the end of military courts in New South Wales. He was, in all, attempting to reduce the military component of governance and increase the civil component. He allowed emancipists to serve on juries and ended the power of local magistrates, many of whom tended to pronounce judgement based on a convict's former record. In all, he was nothing like Arthur – and he was his superior.

By August 1835 Arthur was stalling. A month earlier he had informed London of the association's move, but he hadn't yet told Bourke. Arthur would have known that the association was on Crown land under Bourke's immediate jurisdiction, but he went over Bourke's head and straight to the Secretary of State for War and the Colonies, Lord Glenelg. Arthur knew the official response would take more than twelve months. By that time, there could be thousands of settlers.

Arthur didn't write to Glenelg asking whether he should take action, but only to seek advice. He argued that the settlement would be highly advantageous to Van Diemen's Land: 'Its extensive plains and rich pastures are capable of supporting large herds of cattle and sheep, and given the short distance between the two coasts it might be very rapidly covered with flocks and herds from this colony.' What Arthur wanted, of course, was to bring Port Phillip into his gubernatorial fold. When he finally wrote to Bourke informing him of the association's land deal, two months had elapsed since Batman and the Kulin had signed the treaty.

Bourke's reply ensured there was no misunderstanding. On 1 September he wrote through his colonial secretary that any bargain or contract made with the Indigenous people would be held to be null and void. While the letter said the government had respect for Batman's association and approved of their regard for the welfare of the Indigenous people 'it has nevertheless been deemed necessary to announce in the most formal and public manner the right of the

Crown of England to the territory in question, and the absolute nullity of any grant for its possession made by any other party'.

The proclamation itself read:

> ... *any such treaty, bargain and contract with the aboriginal*
> *natives for the possession, title or claim to any lands lying and*
> *being within the limits of the Government of the Colony of New*
> *South Wales ... extending from the Northern Cape or extremity of*
> *the coast called Cape York, in the latitude of 10 degrees 37 minutes*
> *south, to the southern extremity of the said Territory of New*
> *South Wales, or Wilsons Promontory in the latitude of 39 degrees*
> *12 minutes south, and embracing all the country inland to the*
> *westward, as far as the 129th degree of east longitude ... is void*
> *and of no effect against the rights of the Crown.*

In other words, New South Wales from all points north, south, east and west was Crown land, and anyone making a deal with Indigenous people that led to leasing or acquiring it was defrauding the Crown and trespassing.

Batman's treaty had forced Bourke into a proclamation that while repudiating Batman's false treaty, he was intimating another longstanding fraud. This would become known as the doctrine of terra nullius, an assertion that Indigenous Australians couldn't sell or assign land, nor could an individual person acquire it other than through distribution by the Crown. Bourke had no real choice in this matter. It would have been unconscionable for any government to officially recognise Batman's treaty. If Bourke had done so, this would have repudiated Governor Phillip's settlement in Sydney in 1788, where there had been no dealings with the local populations at all – and certainly nothing that approximated a treaty. The government couldn't even say that the treaty Batman had negotiated was unfair or lopsided to the Indigenous people, because doing so would have presumed that a fairer one could have been enacted by government-approved conquerors – including James Cook.

But the proclamation was probably a bit of a laugh to Batman and Arthur, who by now were regularly talking and strategising. One of Batman's business partners, Charles Swanston, thumbed his nose at the proclamation, saying, 'It will not deter us in our operations.' They had expected this, so to them it was now mainly a matter of making the best of a fraudulent deal.

After the publication of the proclamation, Batman realised it would be best if he hunkered down in Van Diemen's Land for a little while longer, reassuring his investors and privately building further support for his association's venture. The understanding was that with a little push here and there, it would all work out. Batman knew that Bourke's unerring position would throw immediate doubt on his plans in the public eye, and he now accepted that there had to be some changes to his monopoly of the land. He and Arthur passed on a message to Bourke: perhaps Batman and the government could do a deal, if Bourke could offer help in the form of a controlling authority. In effect, Batman was telling Bourke that he was saving Port Phillip from the depredations of other settlers who might not share his association's enlightened principles. What was needed now, Batman argued, was a competent authority to intervene and ensure there was propriety and law in the new settlement.

The hand of Arthur was very strong here in Batman's plea. This was a done deal whether the NSW government agreed with it or not, so Batman was arguing that they should do it in the correct way, with the power of government behind them. In the message to Bourke there was also a clear implication that the closest governor to the scene, a man with the highest credentials on dealing with Indigenous people, a man of high instruction and impeccable Christian beliefs should be there to manage the whole thing – who else but Lieutenant-Governor George Arthur? Arthur may have realised that this probably wouldn't happen, but it was worth a try. And so he played games with everybody, including Bourke.

When it suited him he could happily rubbish Batman's claims and he could do that fairly convincingly as well. He wrote to Bourke saying that of course the treaty was false, and laughed at the association's expressed intent to civilise the locals. 'This, of course, is all stuff,' he wrote, 'and it is better for all parties to be sincere, and plainly state the occupation of a good run for sheep, has been the primary consideration – if not the only one.'

Bourke knew that a heavy-handed and unequivocal proclamation – that every grain of sand in New Holland was British – wouldn't do very much to stop the squatters' boats, nor hinder them from bringing sheep and cattle over. In October, he wrote to Glenelg advising him to grant the settlement official recognition. If this didn't happen, he warned, there would be the same old evils of uncontrolled squatting, a nightmare for a government that needed to be seen as both philanthropic to the Indigenous people and firm in its control. Later, Bourke confessed in other correspondence that he had been as keen as Arthur to have the area colonised. They were all playing a game of professing to be against the idea of unauthorised colonisation while privately supporting it.

Bourke's letter to Glenelg would take many months to be received in London. In the meantime, Port Phillip would be a kind of illegal halfway house, a place where squatters could break the law and set up runs while governments looked on haplessly, professing to be unable to intervene.

Perhaps nobody knew this better than John Fawkner, another man who wasn't afraid to take on the government. He couldn't have cared less. On 13 October, the very day Bourke sent his letter asking Glenelg to recognise the colony, Fawkner finally landed on the Yarra along with his first stock. His great rival, John Batman, would not be far behind.

*

THE CRACK OF Henry Batman's musket was the sweetest sound William Buckley had heard in years. 'Fire a shot if there is good news for me,' he'd asked Batman as he had pushed the launch onto the beach to meet the incoming *Mary Ann*. 'I need to know if I am free.'

It was 13 September, and Buckley had been setting his eyes seawards for several days, watching intently for a ship. Then the *Mary Ann* arrived and had set anchor about two miles from the shore. When the gunshot came, it was one of Buckley's proudest moments: he had been reprieved. This ship had brought a pardon, his deliverance from penury and thirty-two years as an exile.

Wedge later showed him the letter he couldn't read. Arthur had written that Buckley was a 'fit object for an absolute remission of his sentence'. He was overjoyed and obviously felt honoured. 'Wedge showed me a free pardon from Governor Arthur,' he recalled. 'And a very flattering thanks for my services he wrote.'

But there was a flipside. The *Mary Ann* also brought notice that the camp would be moved to the Yarra. In two days Buckley would depart Indented Head with a heavy heart, sailing across the bay to the mouth of the Yarra while wondering if he'd done the right thing. 'My sable friends were not at all pleased with our leaving,' he wrote. 'Thinking we might be going away altogether.' His adopted friends, the Wadawurrung, now realised that the goods that were flowing to them, might soon cease as the party moved away. As Buckley said of the cargo they were enjoying 'They did not by any means like the idea of its probable escape'. Buckley may have also known this would be his last time living with the Wadawurrung.

We don't know how his friends took his departure. They likely felt that they were losing not only the man who had arranged excellent booty, but also a respected elder who had made a final choice – not in their favour. There may have been a mixture of sadness and resentment. The *ngamadjidj* were here to stay and Murrangurk, one of their number, had made his choice.

Buckley's writing gives the impression that he felt extremely guilty to be leaving them in a very confused environment. He may have told himself that his best work would be done among the settlers as long as he put Kulin interests at the heart of his actions. If he was to influence events and ensure there was no bloodshed between the races, he would have to do it from the colonists' side.

The trip to the Yarra wasn't easy – in severe wind conditions 'they had to beat about the bay for two days'. When the ship arrived at the basin, Buckley described their reception as complete mayhem. There were around two hundred people in the vicinity, with more arriving by the hour. He also noted with trepidation that no women and children were about, a sign that if the locals didn't get what they wanted, there could be trouble.

The Morgan–Buckley account gives a sense of the colonists' exposure at this very early part of the settlement. As the ship's goods were discharged the party set up armed guards who were seriously outnumbered. But Buckley reported that the locals were partially mollified by gifts. 'This devilry, was, however, neutralised by the gentlemen in charge of the settlement making them more presents of blankets, bread, knives, scissors, and such like useful articles.' When more ships came, the locals would be promised more gifts. The immediate threat was dispersed.

The birth of Melbourne involved a lot of give and take. The Woiwurrung and Boonwurrung both claimed parts of the area we now know as Melbourne and expected to be heavily compensated – by their standards – for the use of the land. They didn't appear willing to wait a full year for Batman's annual gift giving, as promised by the treaty.

The two camps now eyed each other off, with Fawkner's party occupying Batman's intended campsite on the north bank, and Batman's party creating one on the south bank instead. Both sides of the river echoed each other, but Fawkner's was more advanced, by this time ploughing fields and sowing crops. Batman's people were setting out to build dwellings and workshops.

It wasn't Melbourne yet. The village was now named Bearbrass.

*

WHEN JOHN FAWKNER arrived in mid-October, he noted in his diary that there was no ill will against him from any of the local people. Some helped him to unload and erect his house, in return for biscuits, potatoes and clothing. But underneath the apparent calm, there was reportedly a rift among the locals as to what to do with him. It was well known throughout the Batman camp that this wasn't the man with whom they had done a deal – Fawkner was a transgressor.

Fawkner told the Batman camp that he, too, had done a deal with the Indigenous people, and he told them in no uncertain terms what he thought of their leader's treaty. Without any government or legal body able to officiate between the claims, who could say that Fawkner was wrong or lying? He claimed he had as much right as Batman to be there, and he had brought his wife, servants and household stock. There seemed to be good relations between his Indigenous workman William Watkins and the locals.

Fawkner and Batman appear to have clashed over their respective Wadawurrung and Woiwurrung guides in order to obtain exclusivity to the trading networks of local clans. As Fawkner wrote in his diary: 'Mr Hy [Henry] Batman sent blacks out to get parrots, got Buckley to abuse William Watkins [Fawkner's servant] for buying squirrel skins for me and I found him [Batman] forbidding the natives to sell us any skins or birds. He wants them all himself ... About 20 blacks here now ... more blacks came in ... About 30 blacks about this settlement ... A number of blacks came in this day and their wives, got 3 kangaroo from them and two fine baskets'.

Fawkner allowed Kulin (including Wadawurrung) people free access to his huts and regularly employed two Wadawurrung clan heads; Baitbainger and Ballyan and two other Boonwurrung clan heads, Derrimut and Benbow, as labourers, guides, and hunters. Fawkner observed they 'worked well' at fencing, obtaining bark, guiding the whites to water, warping Fawkner's vessel up the Yarra River, building huts, acting as messengers as well as providing fish, birds and large game.

But a few weeks later Fawkner noted in his diary: 'The Blacks we learnt intended to murder us for our goods.' This message had been delivered to Fawkner by the Boonwurrung man Derrimut, the head of the Yalukit-willam clan, whose land extended from the mouth of the Yarra to what would become the districts of St Kilda and South Melbourne. He said that a large number of men of the Wadawurrung and Taungurong (from the Goulburn River area) were threatening to kill the Fawkner party. Why did Derrimut sound the alarm? It is believed that the Wurundjeri elder Billibellary, a clan head and one of the supposed signatories of Batman treaty, gave him permission to warn Fawkner. After Fawkner heard about the intended attack, his party readied themselves, and the threat of their firepower 'chased [the attackers] away'.

Within a couple of months, Fawkner would again be under attack – and again Derrimut warned him that some Kulin from the north were contemplating a raid. This time he chose to hit out before he was hit, hunting any Indigenous people encroaching on his property. At one point he and a few others were chasing men on horseback with swords and pistols in hand. 'We came upon them quite unawares and put them into great fear,' he wrote in his diary. Derrimut was working with him by then, and the two men were said to have 'exchanged names', a ritual of brotherly friendship that would last both their lifetimes.

Unlike Batman, Fawkner hadn't shown due respect to the Kulin via the *tanderrum*. Nor had he paid tribute. He had been sparing in his gifts, not offering the highly coveted metal blades – not surprisingly, in the months that followed many of these were stolen from his property.

Fawkner believed Buckley was partly responsible for stirring up the locals. The former publican claimed that Buckley was so incensed that Derrimut had given away the plot that he threatened to 'spear Derrimut for his giving the information'. But this accusation was preposterous, part of the propaganda Fawkner spread to taint the man he believed was 'more than half a savage'. The smear that Buckley was somehow behind the attacks would never go away.

Fawkner may have also suspected that Batman's camp was agitating behind the scenes. Although John Batman hadn't yet arrived, he and Wedge were corresponding regularly, and Batman wanted Fawkner gone. It was he who had an alliance with the local people, and in a letter to Wedge he said he seriously considered using them to drive Fawkner's party from what was 'rightfully theirs'. Wedge baulked at the idea, arguing that if the association used Indigenous people to start a war 'it will at once open the eyes of the natives, and teach them their power, they will not fail to use it against us'. There were other considerations. If Fawkner and Batman had a turf war, how would that appear to the powers that be who were supposedly assessing the rights of the squatters? Wedge was far-sighted enough to realise that any form of violence – be that between Indigenous people and Europeans or Europeans among themselves – would have a detrimental effect on their aspirations for official settlement. Batman took Wedge's sage advice and never threatened Fawkner, although he did at one point say that he might let his sheep loose on his rival's crops. There was never a good feeling between the two archenemies, but at the same time never any evidence of a direct confrontation between them or their parties.

Fawkner and Henry Batman were known to have serious arguments, but they never escalated beyond a legal dispute – with Buckley, however, it was more personal. He was by now famous as Batman's interpreter and go-between, the only white man who spoke the local language fluently. It seems Fawkner took Derrimut's messages as veiled threats from his rivals and promptly laid the blame on Buckley, the man with the greatest influence among them. Fawkner held two contradictory ideas: that Buckley was a brainless lump of lard and, at the same time, a deadly enemy, a mastermind plotting the colony's demise. When asked why Fawkner so disliked him, Buckley wrote that he could never understand it: 'From some cause or another, and although not knowing much of me, he represented me to be a dangerous character.'

'He stood six foot five inches in his stockings,' Fawkner wrote of Buckley. 'Was not very bulky, nor overburdened with nous. He fell to the level of the blacks, he did not by any means elevate or raise them, or instruct them in any manner.' Fawkner made his resentment clear when he said Buckley refused 'to give any part of his local knowledge to those persons not belonging to his co-partners'. Buckley was Batman's man, and he wasn't shared out – and it seems Fawkner had great trouble accepting this. 'Alas the lump of matter was too mindless to yield any useful information,' he wrote in later years. Buckley, according to Fawkner, was always at ease, and 'cheerfully supported' by 'two gins' (two Aboriginal women). Fawkner later made an incredible assertion that would plague Buckley's reputation for years afterwards: 'He refused or was unable to account for the fate of the two men [McAllenan and Pye] that left the camp with him in 1803.' This clearly implied that Buckley was a degenerate who had descended into the supposed savagery of the Indigenous people and cannibalised his fellow convicts. And it was nothing more than slander, given that McAllenan had returned to the Sorrento camp with no ill reports about Buckley. Whatever Fawkner's feelings about Buckley were, he was not the power in this tiny colony. That man had yet to arrive.

Chapter 24

AT THE STATE LIBRARY OF VICTORIA there hangs a painting by Frederick William Woodhouse, in which a very handsome John Batman in a bright red coat leans casually on his rifle as the possum-skin clad Buckley, trailed by a number of Wadawurrung, approaches gingerly as if he is about to meet a king. In this 1861 painting, *The First Settlers Discover Buckley*, Batman, the deliverer of justice, freedom and civilisation is at the centre, brightly lit. He and Buckley are supposedly meeting for the first time at Indented Head, and Batman gestures magnanimously for the big man to come forward. The painting is an allegory of Batman 'returning' Buckley to civilisation. He's being welcomed in from the wild by the guidance, love and strength of the great Batman. This is, of course, how the Victorians of 1861 wished Batman to be seen – guiding the Indigenous people, Buckley included, into a new light.

There are many renderings of Buckley's arrival. There is O.R Campbell's *The finding of Buckley* (1869) which shows the stark surprise of John Batman's cohort at St Leonards as the giant man arrives, hovering at the edge of their camp. Then there is the Samuel

Calvert picture, which featured in James Bonwick's *The Wild White Man and the Blacks of Victoria*. Here Buckley is depicted as a peace-giving, almost Jesus-like figure in robes. He is seated with his hand outstretched to welcome the white visitors. Behind him are a crowd of belligerent native men, but Buckley is depicted as the calming influence between the angry natives and the curious white men. He is the gateway ushering in the new age.

There was only one artist who ever captured the dilemma that was Buckley. Indigenous artist Tommy McRae's drawings of Buckley have become famous for their naïve brilliance *Buckley run away from Ship* (1870) and *Ceremony with Buckley and Sailing Ship* (1890) are the best known, and in the first McRae makes it clear that Buckley is obviously European. McRae does not depict Buckley running into the arms of Europeans, but quite the opposite. In his drawings Buckley is a member of a line of men painted and posed for ceremony. He is just like them except for his white skin, hat, and clearly drawn bristly body hair.

McRae is showing Buckley fully immersed, mirroring the stance and appearance of the Wadawurrung men. A line of ten men is drawn diagonally across the page. Fourth from the right is Buckley, who is interlocking his legs in lock-step with the others. It's a brilliantly simple image of Buckley being accepted and integrated – despite his difference. Behind him is a three-masted ship that appears to be suspended and shrinking back into the horizon – a sign that he has left one life behind and is starting another. Europeans are nearly always depicted as smaller, less significant figures in McRae's work. Buckley is the only exception to this.

*

DISCOVERY OF BUCKLEY.

(top) 'Discovery of Buckley', illustration from *The Wild White Man and the Blacks of Victoria*. (HathiTrust Digital Library)
(below) 'Buckley run away from Ship' by Tommy McRae. (Koorie Heritage Trust)

THE TRUTH OF Buckley's meeting with Batman was far more prosaic than any painting. On 9 November 1835 the enfeebled John Batman, whose strength was waning and whose face was visibly decaying, arrived at the Yarra in his chartered barque the *Norval*. He had to be helped onto land from the whaleboat and at some point came face to face with a giant, ruddy-faced Englishman, badly clad in the colonial garb. It was no great meeting. Buckley never even mentioned it in his memoirs.

Batman had come with various servants and his solicitor, Joseph Gellibrand – and five hundred sheep. Within a few days, Gellibrand had offered Buckley an official role as interpreter on the salary of £50 a year, plus rations. For the first time in thirty-two years, he was officially employed. The role wasn't just linguistic but more that of a roving ambassador or public relations person. When Batman needed to ensure there was no disquiet among the Indigenous people, Buckley was the man to keep the calm.

Not long afterwards, Buckley was asked to gather Indigenous people to Batman's camp for a great meeting. About three hundred Kulin from at least three tribes would form the welcome party for 'King John'. The event was later recalled by William Barak, then a youth who would become a great Woiwurrung elder.

I was about eleven years old when Batman visited Port Phillip Bay. I never forgot it. All the blacks camp at Muddy Creek. Next morning they all went to see Batman, old man and women and children, and they all went to Batman's house for rations, and killed some sheep by Batman's order. Buckley told the blacks to look at Batman's face. He looks very white. Any man that you see out in bush not to touch him. When you see an empty hut not to touch the

bread in it. Make a camp outside and wait till the man comes home
and finds everything safe in the house. If you kill one white man,
white fellow will shoot you down like a kangaroo.

Barak's memory may have been a little selective. Batman also allegedly said that 'any ill treatment on the part of the white men towards them, if reported to the heads of the establishment, would meet with its proper punishment'. Batman knew that in this fledgling stage of the colony he must be fair and be seen to be fair.

Of course, all Europeans would have been oblivious to the effect that Buckley's 'pacifying' speech must have had on its speaker. He was now becoming the bearer of passive-aggressive threats to the locals, saying Batman could shoot them like animals.

Soon after Batman's arrival, he and Fawkner parlayed and came to some sort of territorial arrangement. Fawkner set off from his camp to a new settlement across the river but stayed only very briefly, relocating he and his family and workers a little further upriver overlooking the basin and creating a house that doubled as a hotel.

Batman's house was built at the base of a hump of land that extended up the north bank of the Yarra, a hillock unsurprisingly named Batman's Hill that was sited not far from where Docklands Stadium now stands. The house was substantial, built of logs and mud, and finished with a lime whitewash.

Fawkner's house-hotel above the basin was far more crudely made and, it was noted by many, had a defective chimney that smoked out the building. One visitor described it as a six-roomed hotel 'of a very primitive order'. Fawkner didn't seem to care. The front of the house was dedicated to well-heeled customers, the back area allotted to drinkers at his inn. It was the only place in town for visitors, and the only public house. When one of the early pioneers, David Fisher, arrived in early 1836, he said Fawkner's house was 'a place of entertainment where we could not get entertained ... with nothing to eat nor a place to sleep in'. Much to Fisher's relief he decamped to Batman's house, which, while small, had a working fireplace – made by Buckley.

Bearbrass in its early stages was barely more than a few mud huts and a sprinkling of tents, settled in between she-oaks, the odd river gum and the ubiquitous tea-tree scrub. The settlers scythed the long green grass until there was barely any of it left; then, as men and carts trampled the ground, the remaining grass was destroyed. As time progressed the green hills became dust in summer, and when the winter rains came the entire area was beset with mud and waterholes. There were very few houses, and those who could afford this luxury had to import the wood from Van Diemen's Land as the local trees, few in number, were deemed unsuitable for construction.

When Batman employed Buckley to make chimneys for his residence, the big man admitted that his abilities were a little rusty – he'd been out of the trade for more than thirty years. Besides being employed in his old line of work, he was often engaged distributing food and desirable goods to the locals.

*

As the summer of 1835–36 approached, there was no doubt an appearance of harmony between the Indigenous people and Batman's camp, and there was no more trouble with Fawkner. Both men were intelligent enough to realise that war of any kind was rather bad for business, and that they were extremely vulnerable. The Fawkner and

Batman camps were, for the first year at least, very liberal in their gift giving to the Indigenous people. Batman knew to do this from experience, and Fawkner had no doubt belatedly realised – after two early threats of attack – that these tributes bought peace.

Bearbrass was still far more Aboriginal than it was colonial. The Kulin were, for a short time, treated almost as equals in the town. They hunted with the settlers and were constantly guiding them over country. And there was a strong trade in European foodstuffs for Indigenous implements: tea, bread and sugar were exchanged for skins, baskets and fish. On the Yarra's southern bank, which was virtually devoid of Europeans, there was a regular rendezvous for tribal gatherings. The great meeting place Tromgin was situated where the Royal Botanic Gardens now lie. Here the Kulin tribes transacted business, settled disputes and came together in corroborees.

Fawkner said that anywhere between four and twenty local men would often stay with him, the best known of whom was Derrimut. Fawkner would go hunting and fishing with them regularly, and he even took Derrimut and two others over to Van Diemen's Land, where the lieutenant-governor bestowed drummer boy uniforms on all of them.

Derrimut belonged to the Yalukit-willam clan, which roamed a three-mile wide strip at the top of Port Phillip Bay, including what would be Footscray and Williamstown. The clan had another elder, Eurernowel (also known as Benbow), whom the whites referred to as 'King Benbow', and he and his wife known as 'Kitty' built a hut on Batman's land. The Wurundjeri-willam elder Billibellary was also never far away, dividing his time between the town and his clan.

*

WHILE FAWKNER WAS one of the men besmirching Buckley, others quite simply had no idea what to make of him. From early on it was rumoured that he hadn't done the right thing as a white man.

After Buckley met the Wesleyan Methodist Joseph Orton in 1836, Orton wrote that during 'the whole period of his heathenish sojourning, he never forget to acknowledge one Supreme Being upon which he daily depended'. And yet it seemed strange to Orton that Buckley made no effort to instruct the Indigenous people on the one true God but 'had descended and conformed to all their barbarous habits without endeavouring to raise them to any degree'. Buckley responded by saying his life might have been in danger if he had attempted to convert the Wadawurrung to Christianity and ignore their customs and culture. He was again playing his double game, assuaging white fears when necessary. Orton took the view that Buckley's lack of education was behind his failure to proselytise.

There was no hiding Buckley's working-class origins, convict past and what some settlers suspected were his treacherous Indigenous ways. George Russell, who worked for the Clyde Company, described Buckley at this time: 'His looks were altogether not in his favour,' Russell wrote. 'He had a shaggy head of black hair, a low forehead, shaggy, overhanging eyebrows, which nearly shielded his small eyes, a short snub nose and his face very much marked by small pox and was just such a man as one would suppose fit to commit burglary or a murder.' Russell added that Buckley was expected to be of help in reconciling the Indigenous population to the settlers – 'but he was indolent, and never did much that way'.

Where Russell may have got his information from about the big man's indolence and inability to deal with Indigenous people is conjecture, but the influence of Fawkner was never too far away. Fawkner's propaganda reach was strong. His influence in these early days was far greater than that of Batman. Fawkner appeared to have far more clout. Batman was growing weaker by the day, while Fawkner, the kind of man who liked to throw his weight and opinions about, seemed to be gaining in stature and influence.

In a colony wracked with fear and loathing, which saw itself hanging on precariously in a sea of potential enemies, Fawkner's feisty opinions and pugnacious nature seemed to strike a chord. He was a natural leader and the people listened. There was the potential for all kinds of bogeymen to arise. First among them was William Buckley, the man none of them could quite come to terms with, a half savage who was neither understood nor trusted – and he was a giant, perfect fodder to engender fear.

All the same, we know from correspondence that Buckley's linguistic abilities and diplomatic nous were highly valued – at least by his own side. William Todd, who had described Buckley's work in preventing attacks at Indented Head, said that at the Yarra he was 'laying the foundations of good feeling between the Aborigines and the Europeans'. Wedge considered that the '[Wadawurrung] Tribe of natives were peacefully disposed due to Buckley's influence'. Captain Phillip Parker King, a visiting naval officer, also believed Buckley 'probably has been the principal cause of the friendly bearing displayed by them towards us'.

John Batman knew it too. He told John Montagu, the colonial secretary, that he considered Buckley's presence in Port Phillip extremely beneficial to the peaceful interracial relations experienced in the first few years of the colony:

The intercourse with the natives had gone on well. Once since our establishment as many as 400 natives were assembled for the purpose of settling some ancient quarrel; and, although so many different tribes were collected together, uniform goodwill was shown by all of them towards the white people ... Here, I cannot refrain expressing my thankfulness to that good Providence which threw 'Buckley' in our way, for certainly he has been the medium of successfully establishing between us and the natives an understanding, which without his assistance, could never have become effected to the extent it has been ...

While Buckley was working on Batman's chimneys, George Russell passed by and later reported that Buckley seemed very pleased with his work. 'He asked: "Did I not think it was pretty good for a man who had lived thirty years with the blacks?"' Buckley knew exactly what men like Russell thought about him – if he was such a savage, Buckley was saying, how was he capable of such artistry?

Some later said that it was Buckley who laid Melbourne's foundation stone by building these brick chimneys for Batman. In 1853 writer John Hepburn said the chimneys 'constituted the foundation of the capital of Victoria, which seems to have been entirely lost sight of, but nevertheless is true'. This was perhaps an exaggeration, but Buckley definitely had a hand in Melbourne's earliest construction.

*

IT IS OFTEN forgotten that not only was Buckley in a new and strange circumstance with the British after thirty years away, he also wasn't in Wadawurrung country any longer. Only one man showed an understanding of this. In January 1836, Joseph Gellibrand, who had described Buckley as being of 'nervous and irritable disposition', asked the big man to be his guide over Wadawurrung country in order to help him survey and claim the land he had requested from the association. Not surprisingly, Buckley jumped at the chance to go west.

Gellibrand was one of the few to witness the change that came over Buckley as they left the Yarra and headed west towards Geelong. The lawyer sat on a grey mare, while Buckley sat astride a large carthorse that had been borrowed from Fawkner. Once they passed the Maribyrnong River and headed towards Corio Bay, Gellibrand noted that having 'obtained a view of his own country, his countenance was much changed'. The nervous, quiet giant suddenly took command. They crossed over the swamps and marshland, and as they approached the great granite edifice of the You Yangs, Gellibrand saw a new light come into Buckley's eyes. He called out the names of places and greeted the land as the horses rushed past. Sometimes he was speaking English, at other times the local tongue. Buckley was now at a canter, and Gellibrand, surprised by the giant's determination to reach Geelong, was at pains to keep up.

They stopped somewhere near the edge of Corio Bay, where Buckley jumped off his horse. He was running towards a group of people, who, once they saw the unmistakable white giant, started running towards him. The children made for him first, screaming at the top of their voices. Gellibrand dismounted and looked on with incredulity. On one side, a leviathan; on the other, tiny children approaching him at top speed.

It was a collision of love. Buckley was picking up the children and throwing them gently on top of each other, wrestling with them in the grass, and singing to them in a language Gellibrand couldn't understand. The lawyer stood transfixed, watching Buckley being smothered in adoration. Last to the melee came a little old man and woman. The woman walked straight into Buckley's side and remained there, clinging to him as if her life depended on it. The old man was laughing and smiling, shaking Buckley's hands up and down, clearly saying something like 'you have come back to us'. Gellibrand finally understood: this was Buckley's country, and this must be close relatives or very old friends. It was his first meeting with his people in many months.

We don't know if Buckley was feeling a deep sense of unease about the future of Wadawurrung land as settlers continued to encroach. There he was, helping Gellibrand to stake out his future pastures and yet showing his unabashed love for friends he knew would be dispossessed. This was symptomatic of his difficult situation.

He had also realised that these friends hadn't been given the goods promised by Wedge some months earlier, and that they may have felt Buckley had let them down. Gellibrand handed Buckley a blanket to give to the old man, and made some assurances that the goods and provisions would at some point be delivered.

Buckley later told Gellibrand's party that some of the land they had passed was actually his, and that he would give it to Gellibrand's hardworking assistant, William Robertson. This may have been a wild exaggeration inspired by his buoyant mood, but it seems a confession of sorts that this land was as much his as anyone's. Buckley, for a short period, was home.

*

WHILE MUCH ATTENTION has always been placed on Batman's travails on the Yarra, he and Fawkner were part of a much larger group of settlers. Some were willing to fan out beyond the principal colony into areas where there was even less control – and no oversight. Others had disembarked on the *Norval* at Gellibrand Point, just south of the river mouth: John von Stieglitz, along with John Cowie and David Stead. They were among the first settlers to land stock at Port Phillip.

In March 1836, Cowie, Stead and von Stieglitz took up a run at what is now the suburb of Bell Post Hill in Geelong, seizing the land that ran down to the Moorabool River. By then another settler was already in the area: Dr Alexander Thomson had settled on the south bank of the Barwon around what is now the suburb of Belmont, Geelong. Thomson was the Port Phillip Association's surgeon and catechist, and had arrived in February 1836. By May that year, he had landed over a thousand sheep. These men took up vast tracts of land – Thomson, as an example, claimed all the land on the south bank of the Barwon River to Barwon Heads.

These men were the so-called pioneers, the early frontiersmen who wanted to stake early claims in the wilderness, but they were also clueless. They had no understanding of the people upon whose land they would so brusquely alight. All the dispossessors faced the same problem when they occupied Indigenous land: how best to negotiate relationships with individual clan members and their immediate families without loss of life or livelihood. Few if any colonists understood the nuances of Indigenous cultures – or the willingness of these people, if need be, to engage in guerrilla-style warfare.

For example, the squatters were mostly ignorant of the strict laws relating to all gift giving and exchange from a Kulin (and therefore

Wadawurrung) legal viewpoint. What they could never have known was that the Kulin applied these laws as much to themselves as they did to the settlers. Most squatters neither cared nor bothered to understand that both exchange and gift giving were part of the means of creating friendships. Trade was the thoroughfare for access to country, and access involved obligation – to fail in this was a very serious offence, and a cause of significant disputes. The majority of bloody internecine battles the colonists underwent were legal disputes because formal gift giving hadn't been correctly practised.

*

THE NUMERICAL BALANCE in early to mid-1836 was still very much in favour of the local people. In the first year of the colony, around two hundred whites would settle with livestock of around 25,500 sheep, fifty-seven horses and a hundred cattle. Others who desired land in Port Phillip were waiting in the wings for an official go-ahead from the NSW government. Arthur, of course, had his ear to the ground and was advising Batman accordingly. While the fate of the colony was formally in Lord Glenelg's hands, Arthur knew that the more colonists arrived, the more this colony was a fait accompli. Batman and Fawkner knew it too, and pressed on.

Buckley, the so-called indolent, was working busily at this time. In February 1836 he called on 150 Kulin from the Maribyrnong River to meet with Gellibrand about a serious grievance. A shepherd had captured a young, married Aboriginal woman, tied her up for the night in his hut and raped her. The tribe wanted some form of punishment meted out. Through Buckley, Gellibrand reassured them that the man would be removed from the district and punished. The man was sent back to Van Diemen's Land. Buckley attempted to comfort the rape survivor: 'I tied round her neck a red silk handkerchief, which delighted her exceedingly.'

By March, problems were arising in the areas where none of the local inhabitants had been party to Batman's treaty. Buckley had heard that a group of ex-convicts in Western Port who were employed in stripping mimosa trees of their bark (bark was sent over to England and used in the leather tanning process) had shot several Boonwurrung in a dawn raid on their camp. Buckley requested that they be sent to him and Wedge was one of the first to see their wounds. One young girl had been carried from Western Port directly to Buckley – around thirty miles away. She was one of four who had been shot. When Buckley asked Henry Batman to look into the matter, he refused to do anything.

In a separate incident that same month, two of Charles Swanston's shepherds from Van Diemen's Land were speared and killed, and a great number of his sheep killed. There were calls by men like Fawkner for a party to go out and find the murderers, but the prime reaction in the colony was fear. Some of Swanston's workers left the run and fled to town. Wedge wrote that perhaps the Van Diemonian solution of exiling the Indigenous people was worth considering, but this was probably just a fit of pique. Nothing was done to revenge the death of Swanston's men, and Swanston wasn't even there – he was still based in Hobart Town. There simply weren't the resources, the manpower or the will to do so. The colony just couldn't afford to antagonise the local people. Wedge advised Swanston not to 'take the law into our own hands'; such an action 'would only afford Bourke a pretext which he is most anxiously looking for, to interfere with our occupation of the land'.

In May, the first anniversary of the treaty, Batman kept to his word by distributing rice, flour and sugar to the locals. Fawkner would also give out food, but it was usually issued only after locals had worked for him. The local men demanded that he also offer sugar, and Fawkner obliged. But while the bonhomie was still there in the village, in the wider countryside tensions began to erupt.

In July 1836 the squatter Charles Franks and his shepherd Flinders were clubbed to death around Mount Cottrell, on the Werribee River. Franks and his shepherd had been driving a bullock through the land when they were joined by a party of Wadawurrung around the Corio Bay area. After these people had walked a short way with the two men, Flinders was invited to go with them in search of a kangaroo, and while searching was killed by a blow from a tomahawk. Franks, who had remained behind, was similarly killed.

It was a sign of the times that Flinders, a former convict whose first name nobody knew, was barely mourned. To the colonists, the real outrage had been done against Franks, whose wealth and position gave him a high status.

At first the problem appeared to be that Franks, who had only recently taken up a run in the area, had simply seized land and offered nothing to the local people in return. The settler story stated that unwilling to pay any form of tribute, Franks and his shepherd had been murdered for the few bags of flour on their bullock. Others, such as George Smith – Franks's business partner – said it was because Franks had a great aversion to the locals and wouldn't give them food, thinking this the best way to prevent them from frequenting the station. 'But seeing food in some considerable quantity in the tents, they no doubt resorted to the above act to obtain it,' Smith reportedly said.

The colony was on edge. This time, more than twenty vigilantes, led by John Batman's brother Henry, went on the hunt for the offenders. They rode down a group of about eighty Wadawurrung, firing indiscriminately. This massacre was largely hushed up. When Governor Bourke heard about it, he immediately appointed the police magistrate William Lonsdale to take charge of law and order in the colony.

The squatters all gave evidence on oath to Lonsdale that no Aboriginal person had been killed. As the testimony of all Indigenous people was considered invalid by the British legal system, Lonsdale had to take the settlers at their word. It has since been estimated that at least twelve Wadawurrung were killed by the revenge parties.

Henry Batman told Lonsdale that he and his party 'followed the tracks till we could hear voices'. They came upon a party of about seventy to eighty people living in nine huts. He claimed to have fired his gun over their heads in order to disperse them, and eventually came to the huts where some of Franks's belongings were found. Henry had heard guns being fired, but he said to Lonsdale: 'I do not know if any of the blacks were killed or hurt during this transaction. I did not see any that were.'

As Lonsdale kept asking questions, some sinister information came out. Franks's neighbouring squatter Robert von Stieglitz admitted that Franks had made 'blue pills' as a means of murdering the locals, and it started to seem as though Franks and his shepherd had been killed in revenge. Franks had told von Stieglitz that lead was 'excellent for making blue pills for the natives'. Was this a euphemism for lead bullets, or for the way squatters sometimes laced food with strychnine before offering it to the locals? Franks had only recently arrived, and this was allegedly his means of murdering Indigenous people. Even so, his fellow squatters saw his murder, which had put them all on alert, as unconscionable. In the press, he was spoken of as a man with a kind and gentle disposition, a worthy neighbour who had been highly feted in Van Diemen's Land, but the talk of blue pills suggested otherwise.

The press reports on this episode varied wildly. The *Cornwall Chronicle*, always sympathetic to pastoralists, argued that the incident was practically a reason to go to war: 'The annihilation of the whole body of Port Phillip natives, in our opinion, would afford an insufficient revenge for the murder of such a man.' Other press reports showed greater understanding of the tenuous state of relations between the races. It was well known that there had been a bloody reprisal led by Henry Batman. 'Men who stand up so pertinaciously for their own liberty of the subject, most barbarously annihilated a whole tribe, because three of its number were suspected of having destroyed two of their foreign intruders,' wrote the far more liberal *Colonial Times* in Hobart Town.

What did Buckley make of all this? Eyewitness reports say that when Franks's funeral procession passed by the line of mourners, Buckley, standing among Batman's men, laughed aloud. Buckley had refused to let Franks's coffin be placed in his hut and had similarly refused to join the Henry Batman-led search party for the killers. But laughing at a murdered colonist was inexcusable in the eyes of a society that was beginning to flex its muscles. 'Others saw the same indecorum,' reported James Bonwick, in his writings on Buckley. 'And a universal sentiment of disgust toward him took possession of the public mind.'

In July 1836, around the time of the Franks murder, it was rumoured in Van Diemen's Land that Buckley had taken to the bush where he was readying Indigenous people for war. As one settler, quoted in the *Cornwall Chronicle* said: 'He has threatened the lives of several of the principals of the establishment, and savage-like, will be as good as his word.'

A correspondent for the same newspaper had attended Franks's funeral and didn't mince his words about Buckley, who was by now – in the newspaper's eyes – an avowed enemy of all the liberty and prosperity the squatters stood for. 'It is generally believed by his best friends – namely the Company [the Port Phillip Association] that he is at the bottom of all the mischief that has taken place in the new colony,' the correspondent wrote. 'And unless he be speedily removed, I very much dread the results, he already having threatened to join the natives.'

And then there was Fawkner, who wrote later what many had been thinking at this time: 'He soon displayed a spirit of antagonism to the whites; and in fact stated one day, when hard pressed, that he should rejoice if the whites could be driven away, he did not care how, so that the Aborigines could have the country to themselves again.' It might have been a truer statement than Fawkner knew.

Why had Buckley laughed? The obvious reason was that a dozen Wadawurrung had been killed by Henry Batman's posse, possibly more. But none of the whites cared about them – instead the colonists gave all their sympathy to a dubious but rich white man, only recently arrived, whom barely any of the mourners had known. Or perhaps Buckley was simply laughing because what did they expect when they had dispossessed people of their land?

Whatever Buckley's reasons for mirth, here was all the evidence his detractors needed: this huge and unsightly man was by now an enemy of their people.

Chapter 25

I F THERE WAS a day that changed the fortunes of all those living in the new colony, it was 1 September 1836. On that day the convict ship *Moffatt*, carrying four hundred felons, narrowly missed being dashed on the rocks at North Head in Sydney. It also carried a letter from Lord Glenelg to NSW Governor Sir Richard Bourke. The colony at Port Phillip would go ahead, the letter stated, but all those who had decamped at the Yarra and around Geelong would now have to purchase the land from the Crown.

By this time, John Batman was living in a whitewashed house, his men cultivating the twenty acres around it with vegetables, pigs and cows. At the same time, he was grazing 3650 sheep on the block north of the Yarra along the Maribyrnong. Gellibrand had a man looking after his sheep, and Wedge at Werribee was establishing himself as stock agent for an association member, James Simpson, alongside the flocks that Charles Swanston and other partners had sent over.

The association had argued that it deserved its lands to be granted – not paid for – owing to its 'civilising and protecting' influence on the

Indigenous people. In return for a small quit-rent, it had expected free land. But Glenelg denied that any deal had been made and declared all land would have to be bought at auction, starting at the minimum price of five shillings per acre. The association men would be forced to contest their land grabs.

Glenelg had granted Governor Bourke the discretion to offer auctionable land at 'an upset price' of less than five shillings per acre, but this was meaningless: an auction meant any price could be offered for the best land. Bourke decided, however, that he would recompense any expense that a pastoralist had incurred *before* its members were declared trespassers – as in, before his proclamation of September 1835. That meant only Batman and Fawkner might receive something they had obtained before officially breaking the law. To them it wasn't much, but it was the best concession the association was going to receive.

The Port Phillip Association had little future now. John Batman was just another settler, as were his cohorts Wedge, Gellibrand, Simpson and Swanston. It seemed a big setback for them, but they could comfort themselves with the knowledge that as they had been the first to lay their claims, their stations were well advanced. By the end of 1836, Geelong and its environs were becoming clogged with sheep.

Of all the Kulin people, the Wadawurrung had been the most heavily encroached upon. Now that the colony was officially recognised, there was talk of a new El Dorado. Men and beasts were preparing to come in their thousands.

There were, of course, some logistical difficulties. Livestock might be lost in a storm over Bass Strait, and many of the animals arriving at Port Phillip killed themselves by drinking salt water. Sheep that had been herded in hot pens below decks died of shock when they hit the cold currents of Port Phillip. Wedge had done well, only losing fifty of his first thousand sheep, Thomson had lost a quarter of his livestock, while Swanston the banker had fared a lot worse: he'd lost 1300 of his first 2000. A certain number of sheep would also be lost to Indigenous hunters.

Generally, however, there was nothing but optimism. The sums were all working in the pioneers' favour. People could sell their properties in Van Diemen's Land, use the proceeds to buy more stock and take themselves – or their managing agents – to the new settlements. Batman himself had sold five thousand of his acres in Van Diemen's Land for £10,000, while Wedge had sold three thousand acres for £11,000. The costs of carriage weren't high either: only around £500 to bring a thousand sheep over the water. Being forced to pay for the land by the government, it turned out, was a trifle compared to the profits earned in a wool industry enjoying enormous demand.

*

By early 1837, Bearbrass was bustling. William Lonsdale, the police magistrate, had been in office for several months, and now the town would be given the services of a man of the cloth. George Langhorne had arrived to minister to his Anglican flock, and everybody believed he would be at the forefront in the effort to 'civilise' the Aborigines. He had a great deal on his plate. When he opened the colony's first school, it was said that around seven hundred Kulin – men, women and children – arrived, all expecting handouts.

That year Langhorne interviewed Buckley as the basis of a small book that would only see the light of day some seventy-five years later.

Langhorne's task as a ghostwriter wasn't easy: all he received from Buckley was a long statement of unconnected thoughts, but at least it was considered a fair and balanced narrative of the man's life. 'I found the undertaking an extremely irksome one,' Langhorne wrote. 'I frequently had to frame my queries in the most simple form, his knowledge of his mother tongue being very imperfect at the time.' Nor did Langhorne find Buckley easy to work with: 'He appeared to be always discontented and dissatisfied. I believe it would have been a great relief to him had the settlement been abandoned, and he left alone with his sable friends,' Langhorne commented. In truth, Buckley was apparently having trouble in his dealings with the Woiwurrung – he was, of course, not kin, and this land wasn't his home.

March was the month everybody had been waiting for: a chance for the town to demonstrate its potential. This was the month Governor Bourke was arriving to make the colony official – Melbourne's official naming day. By this time, the Bearbrass population was about five hundred, and in the entire Western District there were about a hundred thousand sheep at pasture. Bourke christened the port at the river mouth Williamstown (after the reigning King William) and the township Melbourne after the prime minister of the day: William Lamb, 2nd Viscount Melbourne.

Buckley had left Batman's employ and was now working for Lonsdale as a constable, so he was present when Bourke arrived with great fanfare on 7 March. There were boats of all kinds lining the Yarra, with people cheering and guns being sounded at the NSW governor's arrival. Buckley was placed in charge of about a hundred Indigenous people ranked up in line, soldier-like, for the official reception. 'They saluted him by putting their hands to their foreheads as I directed,' Buckley stated in the Morgan account. Bourke handed out blankets and clothing and a few brass, crescent-shaped neck plates for the senior Kulin. In return, Bourke was given kangaroo meat and, on 8 March, he witnessed a great corroboree.

Buckley's duties included guiding the governor and the surveyor-general, Robert Hoddle, to the outer provinces. It was a successful sojourn with all the usual promises made by officials: 'The natives we met with in these excursions, were, through me, assured by the governor that if they came to the settlement and avoided committing any offences against the white people, they should receive presents of all kinds of articles.'

While Port Phillip was waxing, Hobart Town and Van Diemen's Land were waning. Arthur had written to Bourke at the end of 1836: 'The rage for Port Phillip seems quite unabated.' In April 1837, there were fears that Van Diemen's Land would be drained of all its able-bodied men as they set off for the new colony. A newspaper stated that four vessels had sailed from Launceston in one week, and flocks of sheep were being daily driven into Launceston 'for exportation'. The consequences of the mass movement were also being keenly felt in Hobart Town: 'shops and houses in every part of Hobart Town are shut up; a death-blow has been given to building, and hundreds are being thrown out of employment. Capitalists prefer to invest in the settlement, where hundreds of acres of the finest soil in the world may be obtained for nothing, without paying any taxes or being in any wise molested.' Another article spoke of how 'our rich men will betake themselves there [to Port Phillip] and the withdrawal of capital will be keenly felt'. It urged those readers of the newspaper who might be infected with Port Phillip mania not to go there without capital. 'There will be only two classes of people,' it warned. 'The great wool growers and their shepherds.'

As Melbourne was being populated, it was also being planned. Bourke and Hoddle had traced out the bones of a city that would follow a standard rectilinear grid plan. Many have considered it to be the most poorly planned of all Australia's major cities, a case in which the topography was expected to fit the plan, not vice versa. While the streets were wide, there was no public square (those were thought to bring on congregations of the 'submerged classes'), and the grid was superimposed on a landscape which was naturally irregular, with its knolls, hills and swamps, and the curving riverbank. The plan ignored the fact that settlers' wattle and daub huts were already in situ, and it paid no heed to Indigenous landmarks. And yet it was the start of a great metropolis that would grow faster than any other English-speaking city in either hemisphere.

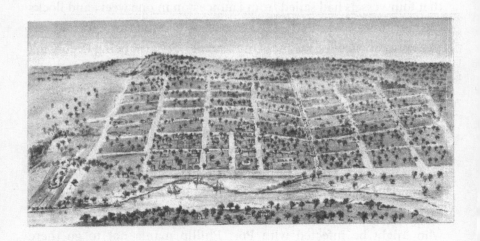

Melbourne, 1838. Illustrated by Clarence Woodhouse from a model in the Centennial Exhibition 1888. (State Library of Victoria)

By mid-1837, authorities were making plans to give Melbourne lawyers, courts and a military presence. That year there would be the first land auctions: one hundred lots between Flinders, King, Bourke and Swanston streets were going under the hammer. The streets hadn't even been properly levelled but demand for land was strong. The upset price was £5, but some lots went for as high as £95. John Batman bought up several of them. When Governor Bourke had visited, he'd told Batman not to expect too much in compensation and that he might even lose his house on Batman's Hill – it, too, was on Crown land. Batman managed to keep it.

As the town grew, the countryside was experiencing increasing ructions between settlers and the Indigenous people. This was where Melbourne's future wealth largely resided, in the health and productivity of increasing numbers of voracious sheep. The wealthy gentry, many of whom had yet to see their land, hired the toughest men it could find to manage their assets. Many were ex-felons or hard-bitten crofters from Britain, men who understood that the properties were best managed at the end of a gun. Buckley watched aghast as the white men became more aggressive, greedier and more demanding. Strength in numbers meant there was less desire to be beholden to any of the local people's claims and, after all, Batman's treaty was now officially defunct.

It was this year that Batman, who now virtually unable to move from his house, didn't honour his yearly tribute to the Kulin. We don't know his exact state, but he was probably entering the final, debilitating stages of syphilis. His body may have been wracked with pustules, and his face, once sunburnt and fair, would likely have been stricken with obscene-looking gumma.

Buckley must have realised that his task, though he was still acting as an interpreter, had subtly changed. He was no longer employed by Batman as a peacemaker and go-between, but as part of the fledgling police force whose values weren't appeasement but control. The association was no longer the power, and Buckley no longer an integral pivot point between the races; he was now more of a cog in an unstoppable, insatiable machine. Langhorne was correct when he said that Buckley wished the white man had never come, and Buckley said as much to anyone who would listen. But in a climate of rabid acquisition and dedication to profit, nobody was listening.

*

AFTER FRANKS HAD been killed a year earlier, a single posse of vengeful whites had massacred Indigenous people. In February 1837 when Joseph Gellibrand and his fellow lawyer George Hesse went missing in Wadawurrung country, four parties went out to find the 'murderers', although nobody had proved that foul play was at fault. The roving parties brought trackers and tribesmen with little allegiance to the Wadawurrung – the 'divide and conquer' strategy was alive and well in Port Phillip.

With time on their hands, Gellibrand and Hesse had decided to do some exploration around the Barwon River before journeying on to Melbourne for the arrival of Governor Bourke in early March. They engaged Robert Akers as guide and were expected to head north to Swanston's property at the river's junction with the Leigh, but somehow they went too far south towards the Otways. When Akers told them they must journey back, Gellibrand and

Hesse overruled him. Akers returned to his own station, leaving them with what he thought was sufficient food. When the lawyers missed their intended rendezvous at the Swanston station, the alarm went out.

The two men had disappeared into the trackless bush and mountains west of Colac. It was known that Gellibrand had no bush skills at all – a year earlier he had almost died on a walking trip to Melbourne, which he had undergone without guides. Party after party was issued out of town using local guides, and they all came up with nothing. One party was helped by Buckley, who knew that it would have been better to work alone. The Wadawurrung were becoming increasingly coy now when any white intruders approached. He needed the tribes he met en route to work for him, harnessing their own methods of intertribal communication.

Buckley was generally disgusted by the people with whom he was forced to journey – the Europeans were, according to Buckley, more interested in the pastoral prospects of the land than in finding the missing men. A farcical situation arose one evening when Buckley was talking to the Wadawurrung men and gaining their trust: one of his white companions thundered into the camp, thinking he could speak the local language. This act of stupidity destroyed all trust, and the quest got nowhere.

Buckley now pleaded with Captain Lonsdale to let him track the lawyers alone, unfettered by any whites who might cause consternation among the locals. Lonsdale agreed, but before Buckley set out, his horse was hamstrung: someone had cut the hind-leg tendons with a knife, and the animal bled to death. Buckley would never know if this was intended as a threat to his life or was simply a message that he wasn't wanted – or trusted – in the Gellibrand–

Hesse search. But Gellibrand had been his friend, one of the few colonists who had understood him, and he would keep trying. He set out by boat, and while travelling outside Geelong heard that a search party had shot and killed a local man and his daughter en route.

Buckley despaired – he couldn't get over the fact that these two people had been killed as a reprisal. He'd suspected all along that if white people were involved, Kulin would be killed. 'It was an inexcusable murder,' he wrote. 'For there was not the least reason to believe that the poor people who had been so mercifully sacrificed had had anything to do with the murder of Mr Gellibrand or Mr Hesse.' The entire affair had given him great pain and enormous effort. 'I thought such destruction of life anything but creditable to my countrymen; but on the contrary, that they were atrocious acts of oppression.' Lonsdale also regretted the killings and said, 'It would keep alive a spirit of ill-feeling and distrust, and identify our customs with theirs of revenge and retaliation.'

Some Cape Otway people later revealed that Gellibrand had been found half dead near the coast. They had tried to revive him, but he had died a few days later. Hesse had died in the hinterland.

It had taken very little time for Batman's colony, which at least had attempted a semblance of détente with the local tribes, to descend into an 'us and them' situation mired by fear, suspicion and reprisals. When the surveyor Robert Hoddle was in the country in July that year, he exemplified the white settlers' fear and loathing: 'I am obliged to go armed here, the Shepherds carry a firelock [gun]. The Blacks are not to be trusted. I do not allow any of them about my Tents. If they come after dark, they must expect some leaden Pills. I think I must have been crazy to have brought my single-barrelled-gun in lieu of a double one.'

The subtext of all this was fear – the fear of cannibalism foremost – which was stoked by false reports in the colonial press. One settler, Alfred Clarke, wrote around this time that he had received 'the distressing intelligence from Port Phillip that the natives had risen on the whites, and had murdered and devoured five women'. Fake news was very much alive in the fledgling colony in 1836–1837.

The conflict, particularly between whites and the Wadawurrung, was intensifying. Squatters spread out from Geelong to the north and west, and in June, William Yuille's station, Murghebaloak, was attacked by a large group of locals who dispersed the shepherds and ransacked the huts. In August the same group moved in to Thomas Rickett's home on the Barwon and were said to have taken from it every movable article. The squatters began to organise, and in the climate of hate that had been engendered by the loss of Gellibrand and Hesse, they sought out the band that was causing such havoc.

Later that year George Russell's Clyde Company, which ran a large pastoralist concern on the Leigh River, would be ambushed by several hundred Wadawurrung. A fierce fight ensued, and two of the Indigenous people were killed and a third wounded.

The Wadawurrung had clearly decided they wouldn't cede land without some form of compensation – and if that wasn't forthcoming, they were quite capable of guerrilla warfare. From 1837 onwards, many harboured a growing animosity towards the colonists who were invading the land and denying them the food and water – not to mention important spiritual sites – that had been their birthright for many, many thousands of years. The refusal of the colonists to enter into any kind of reciprocal relationship and share the sheep that wandered on their estates was bad enough.

A worse problem was that the livestock ate or trampled the locals' staple food. The survival of these people depended on the survival of murnong and other edible plants.

The newspapers of this time often described the rampant sheep stealing by Aborigines as 'outrages' without the slightest hint that the ubiquitous sheep were the only possible sustenance for a malnourished people whose land had been despoiled. From the Kulin point of view there was no question what the real outrage was: the uninvited presence on their land of the settlers and their sheep.

In the next few years, local resistance to white people intensified. There was a story around this time that when a drunken white man stole eels from a local man, it ended in straight fisticuffs. When the Kulin man regained his eels, the white man struck him and kicked him several times: 'the black justly aggrieved put down his eels and said "you too much hit me, now me fight you" and encouraged by some white people near the swamp where they were fishing, a regular fist fight was commenced which terminated in the white man being awfully beaten.'

*

As 1837 WORE ON, it was clear that Buckley, now aged fifty-seven, was coming to the end of his tether. A few months after the loss of Gellibrand, Captain Foster Fyans asked Buckley to accompany him to Geelong where Fyans would be taking up his new role as the area's police magistrate. In the aftermath of the Yuille attack, the squatters of the Western District had successfully petitioned Governor Bourke for protection. Fyans was ordered by Lonsdale to take on Buckley for help.

Fyans distrusted Buckley from the start, and it wasn't long before tempers flared. They set out on a wet night with Buckley describing himself as being in a state of extreme fatigue. When Buckley asked if they could rest en route, Fyans said no – he and his party of constables and twelve convicts had to press on. When Fyans ordered Buckley to eat, he refused the salt pork and damper that was offered to him. Buckley told Fyans he was quite capable of feeding himself, and before Fyans knew what was happening Buckley was hacking at an old tree and extracting grubs. He wasn't only being recalcitrant but also rejecting the white man's ways. When the time came to saddle up, Buckley simply baulked. As Fyans recorded:

'Well,' said Fyans, 'Are you ready?'

'For what?' asked Buckley.

'For Geelong.'

'No, no,' Buckley replied. 'It is too far for me to pull away there.'

'Why, Buckley, you must come on with me.'

Buckley refused. When he finally caught up with Fyans and his men, the new police magistrate was mustering the Indigenous people around the Moorabool River and distributing provisions including blankets and clothing supplied by Governor Bourke. Fyans counted just 275 people: already the numbers of Wadawurrung were thinning further, following their diminishment during the smallpox epidemic.

When it was discovered that there weren't enough blankets to go around, the locals reportedly became angry. 'I ordered my two constables to load, and my convicts to fall in close to my hut,' Fyans recorded. Yet again, a situation had disintegrated, and Buckley was ordered to deliver the usual threat of 'cooperate or be killed' to the locals, who later dispersed. He could no longer abide his role as mouthpiece of the aggressor, having to underlie every promise with a threat.

After two years in the employ of the colonists, Buckley had had enough. He was clearly defying Fyans, a tough policeman who brooked little dissension. Not long after the Fyans contretemps, Buckley quit his job. His role had become untenable, and he was clearly unfit for this kind of duty. He believed that both sides of the divide hated him. Perhaps melodramatically, he later wrote that his life was in danger at the time: 'Indeed, I could not calculate on one hour's personal safety from either one party or the other.' His resignation brought him a kind of relief.

Here was the clear problem. He could not be a friend of the natives and then pass messages that threatened them or heralded their doom. He could not be the man the white people depended on to communicate and still be widely distrusted.

Lonsdale never criticised Buckley in any of his letters, but he made it clear that the big man hadn't proved to be a very good policeman. Lonsdale was one of the few who understood Buckley's predicament, employing him more out of goodwill than necessity. He said privately that he could have hardly expected the man to be a model officer considering his circumstances.

Buckley's final act in Port Phillip took place in November 1837, when he petitioned Governor Bourke 'for a grant of land or such other assistance as your Excellency may seem fitting, in order that your petitioner may not in his old age be reduced to distress'. Buckley also asked for a pension of £100 per annum. Both requests were denied.

Thirty-four years after his escape from Collins's aborted settlement, Buckley found himself finally following the route Collins had intended for him long ago in 1803. It was 28 December 1837, and Buckley was aboard the *Yarra Yarra*, heading for Van Diemen's Land. The man once thought by Collins to have perished quietly in the woods had defied the odds and survived everything the alien landscape, the cultural demands of a new people and the distrust of an aggressive new colony had thrown at him. But this had all taken its toll. He had been there at the start of what came to be known as the killing times, and he didn't want any more of it. William Buckley was sick at heart.

Chapter 26

I N HOBART TOWN, William Buckley found he could do as he pleased. He was feted too: everybody knew of the wild white man, and nobody seemed to begrudge him his past. At the beginning of his time there, he seemed to be well liked and well regarded. As Buckley wrote, 'In my rambles about the town, I was frequently accosted by persons anxious for information about Port Phillip, with the extraordinary accounts of which all Van Diemen's Land had become, I may say, inflamed.'

Buckley described how vessels full of emigrants, with sheep and materials, were almost daily proceeding to the new colony. Any information he could give the so-called 'overstraiters' was considered valuable. Buckley was suddenly a minor celebrity whose opinions were keenly sought after.

Buckley at first lodged at the Duchess of Kent on Murray Street, then he moved for a time to live with a Mr Cutts who owned the Black Swan Inn on Argyle Street. A few days later he was accosted on the street by a man offering him a free ticket to the theatre. Buckley happily accepted, but when arriving at the show he found that there was no seat: he was expected to go on stage! Buckley had been advertised as the 'Anglo-Australian Giant' – he was the main attraction. A horrified Buckley gave his excuses and left. Perhaps the intentions of the Van Diemonians weren't as honest and amicable as he had thought.

Buckley also met an old friend from his days on the *Calcutta*. Joe Johnson, a man who was convicted for stealing horses, had become a highly respectable and wealthy settler. From here he was given an entrée to meet the governor, Sir John Franklin, who had replaced Arthur the previous year. Sir John and Lady Franklin were progressives who were equally interested to meet Buckley, throwing question after question at their slightly nervous guest. When they asked him what he might wish for, he said he'd like a small allotment of land. The governor couldn't offer him this, but he would find Buckley employment.

At first Buckley was appointed assistant storekeeper at the Hobart Town Immigrants' Home, a hostel where new arrivals to the colony could find their feet. But the appointment was only temporary, and several months later he had a job as the gatekeeper at the Cascades Female Factory (convict workhouse) in South Hobart.

Buckley had become acquainted with a widow, Julia Eagers, and her daughter at the Immigrants' Home, and in March 1840 they were married at New Town, in the local Episcopalian church. She was an Irish immigrant and free settler who had arrived with her husband Daniel and their three-year-old daughter Mary Ann aboard the *Bussorah Merchant*. They had reached Hobart Town on 11 December 1837, not long before Buckley. Eagers was a barely educated woman who had married a skilled stonecutter. But Daniel Eagers had died not long after the family's arrival, apparently speared by Indigenous men around the Murray River on a cattle drive from Sydney to Melbourne. She was said to be a tiny woman and just twenty-six years of age; Buckley was a giant and by this time fifty-eight. Despite the differences in age and size, the two became a well-known partnership around town. When they walked out together, she couldn't reach his arm, so he tied a handkerchief to his elbow, ensuring she would be attached.

Buckley settled down to lead a quiet life. But soon after getting married, he was struck by typhus fever and bedridden for many days. Only with the help of his wife and stepdaughter did he come through it – but, as he described it, he was never quite the same man again. He believed that as he'd aged, the privations and exposure he had experienced in the bush had 'materially damaged my naturally strong constitution'.

*

EIGHT YEARS LATER, Buckley's fame still hadn't been completely forgotten by the public. A fiction about his life was published in the *Geelong Advertiser* on 22 April 1848 entitled 'Waroon the Strong: a tale illustrative of the times of Buckley'. In it a fictionalised Buckley wielded a cutlass into battle against his savage foes. The real Buckley wrote to the *Geelong Advertiser* to complain about the inaccuracies, stating that a book telling his story would soon be forthcoming.

This may have been the catalyst that brought John Morgan and Buckley together. The two men first met sometime in the late 1840s, after many potential ghostwriters had tried to push Buckley for his memoirs. Morgan had persuaded William Robertson – the man to whom Buckley had offered land on their 1835 trip with Gellibrand –

to sponsor the publication and commissioned Archibald McDougall of Hobart Town to print it.

Morgan was one of those nineteenth-century wheeler-dealer types who had tried their hand at just about everything. He had been a marine who had served in Spain during the Napoleonic Wars. He'd spent time in Canada, then become a storekeeper on the Swan River in Western Australia. Through his connections there, he had become a magistrate in Richmond, Van Diemen's Land. At some point his debts from the Swan River came back to haunt him, and he was declared by the British Treasury to be £800 in debt – roughly the equivalent of $200,000 today. He took up journalism and became something of an outspoken writer, advocating colonial self-government and legal reforms, and denouncing the state of Van Diemonian gaols and lunatic asylums.

Buckley lost his job in 1850, when convict transportation came to an end. He was given the paltry pension of £12 per annum, on which he said he, his wife and stepdaughter could live 'humbly and honestly'.

Both Morgan and Buckley probably thought the book might provide their deliverance from penury. Buckley most likely also hoped that if his great travails at Port Phillip were publicised, the new self-governing government of Victoria might grant him the land he so desperately wanted. Morgan, who was still seriously in debt, was presumably in it simply for the money.

Either way, according to Morgan, writing a book with Buckley was a laborious task – just as it had been for Langhorne. Both ghostwriters had to deal with an introverted man who couldn't read. How Morgan finally elicited enough information from Buckley, we will never know.

WILLIAM BUCKLEY,
THE WILD WHITE MAN.

Portrait of William Buckley by Frederick Grosse published in 1857.
(National Library of Australia)

The Life and Adventures of William Buckley was published in 1852, and it would be Buckley's last hurrah. After its publication, the colony of Victoria added £40 to his annual pension. In the Victorian Legislative Council, elected representatives were asked to vote on the gratuity for William Buckley 'as the original founder of Port Phillip'. Batman and Fawkner were the men often cited as founders of Melbourne, but Buckley had arguably been given an even bigger accolade. However, the description never stuck. It was later excised from the record – the work of Legislative Council member John Pascoe Fawkner.

There was one last interaction between Port Phillip and Buckley. In 1855, the Legislative Council voted to raise his annuity to £88, but Fawkner desisted. Buckley, he said, had been a thief and had turned Port Phillip's Indigenous people against the white men. Fawkner also told the council that Buckley had eaten three of the men he had escaped with in 1803 – but then Fawkner was howled down by his fellow members. He had remained Buckley's archnemesis right until the very last. Buckley was granted the extra money – but it never reached him or his wife.

*

ONE MORNING IN December 1855, a two-horse cart was moving too quickly around a badly cobbled corner in the town of Green Ponds (present-day Kempton) when it lost traction and spun over to the side of the road. The driver, William Buckley, was thrown out of his seat, breaking his back. Buckley was doing what he normally did in those days, delivering messages and parcels, but old age had made him less sure of his movements and slowed his reactions. His driving had been erratic of late. He was taken to St Mary's Hospital to be treated. His case was deemed hopeless on 18 January 1856, and he was taken home to be with his wife.

Buckley died a few days later on 30 or 31 January 1856. He was buried at St George's Cemetery in an unmarked grave, which was later identified. He was seventy-six.

The only record we have of how his Wadawurrung friends felt about his departure from their country came from Purranmurnin Tallarwurnin, who was living at a mission in Framlingham in the 1860s. In a report from the superintendent of the station, William Goodall, she was said to be disconsolate when she heard that he had remarried. 'They had lost all hope of his return to them, and grieved accordingly,' Goodall reported. Buckley had been mocked and slandered by men like Fawkner, but he was always taken seriously by his Wadawurrung friends. Indeed, as events such as his warm reception during the Gellibrand trip make clear, he had been much loved among the Wadawurrung.

*

By 1838, John Batman was seriously crippled, his once solid frame now withered and frail. The mercury doses that had been prescribed to save his life were now probably doing just as much to end it. We don't know how this mercury was administered, but it could have been an ointment made from metallic mercury that was rubbed into the skin, or its vapours may have been inhaled as the sufferer bathed in its fumes. Many physicians doubted the efficacy of mercury, which had terrible side effects including neuropathies, kidney failure, and severe mouth ulcers and loss of teeth. Many died of mercurial poisoning rather than from syphilis itself.

Alcohol became Batman's only relief, and his legs were paralysed. The syphilis that had been destroying his nose now forced him to wear a bandage covering his entire face. He was said to have become unruly and difficult, often exploding in great outbursts of anger. Nobody came to see him except his old surveyor friend John Wedge, one of the few to keep faith with Batman in spite of his condition.

He was in the tertiary stage of the disease, in which the skin, bones, internal organs, nervous system and cardiovascular system would have been irreversibly damaged. He now moved around town on a creaking iron perambulator, a giant nineteenth-century wheelchair-chariot pushed by some of his Aboriginal servants.

He was no longer the wealthy landowner and scion of society he had once been. He had £5500 in assets and £6500 in debt. His wife, Eliza, had left him and, after much argument with the government, he was able to pay cheaply for his home on Batman's Hill. But, owing to his debts, it was sold for the paltry sum of £200. Batman's Hill would be razed in the 1860s to make way for train lines and the refuse used to fill in the beautiful saltwater lake that had been one of the most vibrant ecological sites of the area.

Batman died, aged just thirty-eight, in May 1839. For many years the people of Melbourne would remember him, mostly with great affection, as the man who had co-founded the city. There are avenues, lanes and alleyways named after him in both Melbourne and Sydney, along with a large bridge in Tasmania. His name also graces railway stations, parks and districts.

In the past few years there has been widespread reassessment of his historical contribution. At the time of writing in 2019, the electoral seat of Batman had only recently been renamed; the Melbourne electorate will now be called Cooper, after William Cooper, an

Indigenous activist. This isn't the first example of Batman's name being expunged. In May 2017 Victoria's Darebin Council changed Batman Park to Gumbri Park after the great niece of William Barak, who was the last Indigenous woman to be born at Coranderrk. The reasons for this are clear. There's no shortage of guilt concerning the way Melbourne was settled, even if Batman still has supporters who believe that his treaty was largely benign. But he undeniably had a very dark past. He was described, even in his own time, in egregious terms, and it's not uncommon for him to be described as a 'mass murderer' and 'child abductor' undeserving of public honour.

If you want to understand the dilemma, it's there for all to see. At the Queen Victoria Market site is the large bluestone monument to Batman. The original inscription refers to him as leader of an expedition launched from Launceston to form a settlement in 'unoccupied' land.

In 1992 a new bronze plaque was added: 'When the monument was erected in 1881, the colony considered that the Aboriginal people did not occupy land. It is now clear that prior to the colonisation of Victoria, the land was inhabited and used by Aboriginal people.'

By 2004, a new plaque was installed, which reads: 'The City of Melbourne acknowledges that the historical events and perceptions referred to by this memorial are inaccurate. An apology is made to indigenous people and to the traditional owners of this land for the wrong beliefs of the past and the personal upset caused.'

Perceptions, of course, are changed and modified. But if Batman's name is to be erased forever from public spaces, no doubt it will be a difficult and lengthy process.

*

JOHN FAWKNER OPENED Melbourne's first hotel on the corner of William Street and Flinders Lane, and published the *Melbourne Advertiser* in 1838. While that paper was short-lived – it lacked a licence – he started up a new one, the *Port Phillip Patriot and Melbourne Advertiser,* in 1839. In 1851 Fawkner was elected to the first Victorian Legislative Council of the Port Phillip District, and in 1856 he was elected to the first parliament of the self-governing colony of Victoria.

Fawkner became involved in just about every issue that vexed the colony and was known for expressing his liberal views, albeit with a certain dogmatic and vitriolic style. He became heavily involved in the problems of the goldminers in the 1850s, and expressed alarm at the vast number of Chinese and American immigrants, seeing both groups as potential sources of disorder. He never saw any hypocrisy in his statement about the Americans and their colonising ways: he described them as 'wild Americans, who know no law but the Bowie Knife, the Rifle or lynch practice'.

Fawkner wanted to be known as the godfather of Melbourne. In the 1860s, shortly before his death, he wrote that in March 1835, 'I made up my mind to venture across the straits and commence the world again.' He was given to self-congratulation and heavily involved in his own self-glorification. Fawkner never accepted that the people who had lived in the region for many tens of thousands of years had any stake in the land itself. He died in September 1869, reviled by many while others saw him as a respected founding father. There were over 200 carriages present at his funeral, and 15,000 persons lined the streets to watch his cortege.

*

John Pascoe Fawkner in later life. (State Library of Victoria)

THE PRESENCE OF the Kulin nation rapidly disintegrated from the late 1830s onwards. There has been plenty of conjecture about the number of people killed by frontier violence in Victoria in the mid-nineteenth century; the latest scholarly research puts the number at about a thousand Indigenous people and eighty whites who died between 1835 and 1850. In the Western District, the number is around 430 Indigenous casualties.

The factor that had the most debilitating effect on the Kulin was the degree to which colonisation deprived them of food. By 1840, just five years after the Yarra was populated by Europeans, there were 700,000 sheep grazing in central and western Victoria. The tide of sheep didn't stop, and two years later had doubled to 1.4 million. William Thomas was told by one Indigenous person in 1844: 'The bush big one hungry, no bellyful like it Melbourne.' Livestock compacted the ground and verges of waterholes. They monopolised native grasses on which emus, kangaroos and bush turkeys thrived. Sheep dug up murnong with their noses as they grazed on the plains and open forests where the plant was rife. The Wadawurrung and other Kulin peoples complained bitterly about the near total destruction of murnong, which had occurred in just a few years. In 1840, James Munro, a squatter, told the Chief Protector of Aborigines George Augustus Robinson that the millions of murnong he had seen over the plain just eighteen months before, as well as abundant kangaroos and emus, were now nowhere to be seen – the sheep had driven them away.

There were squatters who were well aware of the Kulin people's need for their staple food. Some of these white people demanded sex with Indigenous women in exchange for giving their tribes unfettered access to murnong. Near Bacchus Marsh in central Victoria, Robinson saw 'many native huts about Cadden's station. These natives [Wadawurrung] are enticed about the huts by the men for the sake of the women. Said the natives were quiet enough, all they wanted was *noorong* [murnong]'.

In 1836, the explorer Major Thomas Mitchell travelled through the western fringes of Wadawurrung country. He described the western plains as a 'sea of gold', almost certainly referring to the flowering murnong. By 1846 it was practically extinct. 'No murnong, no yam at Port Phillip, too much by one white man bullock and sheep, all gone murnong,' lamented one Wadawurrung man. The Kulin people were starving under British rule in a way that wasn't dissimilar to what the Irish were experiencing around this time. In Ireland it was a dearth of potatoes, in Port Phillip, the people experienced a yam famine.

By the 1840s, as the graziers and their sheep pushed the Indigenous people off their land, hundreds converged on the only place where food could be found: Melbourne. Many lost their bush skills and became dependent on government handouts. Crowding also took its toll. In 1840, the town's population was around four thousand, and the medical officer Dr P. Cussens found Indigenous people who had sought refuge there suffering from dysentery, typhus fever and all manner of respiratory infections. Syphilis, too, was a major problem; the doctor noted that 'if unchecked, [the disease] would render them extinct in a very few years'.

The 'bad disorder', as venereal disease was then called, had been rife for years. Only seventeen months after Batman and Fawkner arrived, Robinson, on his first visit, recorded that: the Aborigines in Melbourne 'are dreadfully afflicted with venereal ... Some of the children are afflicted by it and the old persons can hardly walk'.

Men like Billibellary, the most senior Wurundjeri elder who had fervently strived to keep the tenets of Batman's treaty intact, suffered from a severe cough for nearly a year and was given European medicines, which he ultimately rejected. He and William Thomas, the senior protector of Indigenous people at this time, discussed the growing number of infanticides among the Kulin, and while he promised to try to reduce them, he claimed that his people didn't want children born into this new world. Billibellary told Thomas that of eight children born to Kulin women in 1839 only two had survived – the rest had either been strangled or smothered. Billibellary's explanation has since become famous: 'Blackfellows all about say that no good have them Pickaninneys now, no country for blackfellows like long time ago.'

Derrimut had said much the same thing: 'All along here Derrimut's once … you have all this place, no good have children, no good have lubra, me tumble down and die very soon now.' Derrimut, who was Fawkner's close friend, had become seriously displaced by the late 1830s and heavily embittered by what had happened to his people, the Boonwurrung. There was a story of him arriving in the Yarra camp in 1839 roaring drunk, yelling abuse at the whites and then threatening to spear his own mother. He became a strong advocate for Boonwurrung rights and when his request to continue living at Mordialloc was refused in 1863, his already poor health, exacerbated by alcohol, declined rapidly. He died at the Melbourne Benevolent Asylum a year later, believed to be around fifty-four years of age. His head stone at the Melbourne General Cemetery reads: 'This stone was erected by a few colonists to commemorate the noble act of the native Chief Derrimut who by timely information given October 1835 to the first colonists Messrs Fawkner, Lancey, Evans, Henry Batman and their dependants saved them from massacre, planned by some of the up-country tribes of Aborigines …'

Derrimut was not forgotten. There is a suburb and a mountain named after him as well as a state electoral district and there are Derrimut streets in Albion, West Footscray and Hoppers Crossing.

When Batman and Fawkner first staked their claims, there were said to be at least 6000 to 7500 Indigenous people in the Port Phillip area, although some scholars believe there may have been as many as ten thousand. By the early 1850s, this had been reduced by 80 per cent to under two thousand.

The Wadawurrung, who had so expertly tended to their beloved green fields for thousands of years, had been at the sharpest end of the graziers' expansion. Buckley's adopted people had been heavily culled. Those around Geelong numbered just 375 in 1837 then 118 in 1842, and by 1853 only nine women, seven men and one child remained. The population of those living in country had been almost entirely destroyed. William Thomas, who made extensive journals of the Woiwurrung and Boonwurrung people from 1839 to 1859, said he only witnessed twenty-eight births in the twenty-year period. Deaths outmatched births by a ratio of five to one.

One of the great tragedies of this history is that the people whom Buckley found as a flourishing community in 1804 – the proud people who perplexed Buckley but whom he ultimately loved – had been scattered and deracinated in the course of two generations.

*

THE 1850s WERE described as a period of almost complete government neglect of Indigenous peoples. In 1858, the Victorian Legislative Council set up a select committee to enquire into the state of the Indigenous population and in a report the following year recommended the establishment of government reserves. In 1860, the Central Board for the Protection of Aborigines was established, which ushered in a series of reserves onto which the Aboriginal people would be compelled to move. These reserves included Lake Tyers, Framlingham, Lake Condah, Ebenezer, Ramahyuck, Yelta and Coranderrk.

The most famous of these was Coranderrk, established in 1863. Elders Simon Wonga (the son of Billibellary) and William Barak (Wonga's cousin) led around forty Woiwurrung, Taungurong and Bunwurrung people to a traditional camping site on Badger Creek north-east of Melbourne and requested ownership of the site. They sought control of about 5000 acres of fertile mountain country in Victoria's Yarra Valley.

They were granted the land and thus began a period of self-government that would last twenty-five years. The station manager, Pastor John Green, wanted the residents to control decisions that affected their lives – they were given autonomy and self-determination. The station ran successfully for many years as an Aboriginal enterprise, selling agricultural produce and crafts, such as cloaks, baskets and boomerangs.

In its day, it became something of a tourist attraction on the upper Yarra. Photographers came to document the life there and anthropologists to examine the culture and the people, but it wouldn't last. Its rich grazing lands were coveted and there was a strong lobby to shut it down. William Barak stirred the first Coranderrk Rebellion, marching with residents into Melbourne to claim ownership of land he called 'my father's country'. It was one of the earliest attempts to regain land stolen from traditional owners.

The Kulin residents, self-reliant and proud, successfully protested official treatment during the 1870s and 1880s, and gained some support from politicians and the public. When the residents were threatened with removal to the Murray River region in the 1870s,

William Barak drawing a corroboree at Coranderk, c 1895. (La Trobe Picture Collection, State Library of Victoria)

Barak launched a campaign with the famous words: 'Me no leave it, Yarra, my country. There's no mountains for me on the Murray.' They delayed attempts to close the station until the late 1880s. Some refused to leave and simply stayed and died there. There were those who had been born there who stayed well into the next century. Only a half-acre cemetery was ever given back to the Kulin people.

Barak, the great artist and fighter for his people, was not forgotten. In December 2005, the William Barak Bridge, on the Yarra, was declared open, the bridge a metaphor for the man who always tried to ease the divide between himself and the newcomers.

There are stories of those, perhaps lesser known, who doggedly avoided Aboriginal reserves and remained in country. William Buckley and his adopted kin would have known the three spits or fingers at the end of Edwards Point on the shores of Swan Bay. One of those fingers is still commonly known as Black Billy Point. It was named after King Billy, the name Europeans gave to Willem Baa-Ni-ip. He was born near a lagoon in Geelong in 1836. That day, his father was said to have seen a bunyip while hunting at Waurn Ponds (the same area in which Buckley said he saw one), and his name means 'Home Bunyip'. Billy's family had some pedigree, and it was said that his grandfather Waa Waa was present when Matthew Flinders climbed the You Yangs in 1802, the very first contact between the Wadawurrung and Europeans.

King Billy is said to have made occasional visits to Portarlington where he begged for food, often swearing at Europeans who ignored his requests. He and his mate Dan Dan Nook were at times forced into virtual destitution, but they always resisted attempts by Europeans to remove them to one of the Aboriginal reserves at Duneed or Coranderrk. They were determined to stay in country.

When Dan Dan died in 1870, King Billy was alone. By the 1880s he was often seen camped on Edwards Point, where he was still living as well as possible off the land as his ancestors had done. He died in 1885 at the age of just forty-nine, and was buried with belated honours in the West Geelong Cemetery. A monument stands there to him and his people. While nobody can be totally sure, he was among the last of the Wadawurrung people of Geelong to have known the world of William Buckley.

Epilogue

Every now and then a sentence pushes through in the Morgan–Buckley account that brings Buckley's thinking to life. Among them is his quote about how he dealt with growing anger among Wadawurrung tribespeople when they felt that the men at Batman's camp at the place they knew as Nearnenenulloc (St Leonards) weren't sharing their goods. Buckley had to think quickly to prevent bloodshed. He wrote, 'The policy I adopted was to seem to fall in with the views of the savages.' Buckley told his kinsmen that killing the white intruders now would avail them nothing – it would jeopardise the much better booty that would come in greater amounts later. This stalling tactic worked, but it required Buckley to deceive his people. When the next ship came in, the locals were supposedly so mesmerised by the food, axes, blankets and clothing, they were in no mood to attack. In the back of his mind, Buckley must have known that with the arrival of each boat, the British foothold on Wadawurrung land grew slightly firmer.

The great writer Graham Greene once said that once you enter the territory of lies, there's no return passport. So much of this story is about lying or, perhaps more accurately, about being two-faced to keep the peace. John Batman's treaty was a similar stalling tactic. He and his Port Phillip Association members needed to *seem* to be generous and protective for long enough to see off possible acts of aggression and to assuage government scepticism. Their policy was to keep the locals hooked on European accoutrements while slowly growing in power and strength. When the colony reached the required critical mass, all pretence of magnanimity could be dropped. The coming spate of massacres, dislocation and environmental upheaval, named by some Aboriginal people as 'the killing time', was originally designed to look like Christmas.

Even John Fawkner came around to these ideas. At first he espoused fighting fire with fire. He was threatened twice in the first three months of his arrival but survived due to being forewarned. It's thought that Billibellary was behind the warnings issued through Derrimut, which shows tremendous forbearance on the elder's part. Lesser men might have had such a recalcitrant and clearly unapologetic invader as Fawkner killed. Why the Kulin desisted has always been unclear, but perhaps the elders were still hoping to form an alliance. It became clear even to Fawkner that to conquer this new world the best weapon was dissimulation – to pay tribute only for as long as that was useful. He and Batman didn't share very much, but they shared that view and worked to that end.

Therein, for me at least, lies the great tragedy of the Kulin's dispossession of Port Phillip. I am not naive enough to think there would ever have been an alliance of equals, but I find it shocking that one side gave so much and the other so little. I'm not talking here about the trinkets exchanged by Batman for land. We still talk about

European explorers 'discovering' and 'naming' places in the region, but it was always a Kulin person or Buckley who guided them. This was the same all over Australia: European exploration amounted to continental dispossession. Every single act of 'discovery' in the Port Phillip region, in every place that was 'named' and later colonised, was aided by Indigenous guides. It was their diplomacy, knowledge and bush skills that enabled white people to reach the parts that would have otherwise been closed. It was in this 'discovery' period that the deception had to hold. Buckley knew when he and Gellibrand went travelling to stake out 'Gellibrand's country' he was in a dilemma – the more he helped the colonists to discover, the quicker he ushered in the destruction of his adopted people.

Buckley's real job was to maintain the lies to maintain the peace. He may have believed that if he could solve all the minor flare-ups with bandages, he could somehow prevent a more calamitous interracial explosion somewhere down the line. But his efforts would never be enough against the squatters' unrelenting pressure to possess, control, consume and rewrite. They'd said Port Phillip would be different, and predictably it wasn't. But the tipping point wasn't when the British government repudiated Batman's cynical treaty – it was Franks's murder. War was declared when one of their own was killed. Franks was wealthy. He was one of them. His killing couldn't be excused because it represented a threat to themselves, the monied squattocracy. It was the signal to excuse the conquest.

There is a view I have heard that by leaving Melbourne for Hobart Town, Buckley sold out his adopted people. I don't agree. He had been selling them out much longer, for the right reasons.

But it was to no avail. Every time he issued a white man's order in the Wadawurrung language or guided a colonial party through country, he was compromised. He left because he couldn't continue being Judas. At the heart of it was a wretched self-awareness that his job was to deceive the people he loved.

There are other great stories of white men and women who lived for long periods with indigenous peoples, but none that place the central character so strategically at the heart of the racial divide and at such a critical colonial juncture as Buckley's story. Buckley was at the sharpest point of competing interests. He must have known that if he had stayed on, he wouldn't have survived either physically or morally.

Buckley's family had been driven out of rural Cheshire in a similar way to the ejection of the Wadawurrung from the Bellarine Peninsula. He'd been inducted into the army and then sent as a prisoner to a land that couldn't have been more alien to him – and yet he survived. He had also, arguably, been inducted into Kulin culture. And he hadn't asked for any of it. This man had been beholden to others and dragooned into roles for almost all his adult life. He understood dispossession and powerlessness.

It's why Buckley escaped at the age of twenty-three, and it's also why he 'escaped' Port Phillip thirty-five years later. Buckley's departure wasn't a weak capitulation or an act of treachery, it was his way of freeing himself from the egregious narratives of the rich, powerful and aggressive. He simply came to an existential question: was he willing to remain the instrument of forces he could not control? Buckley chose a quiet life with no money or prospects as the only means to be free.

What, then, of the expression 'Buckley's chance'? That chance didn't happen in 1803 or 1835, but it may have happened in 1837 when he left his past behind. What kind of 'chance' was ever handed to him? The expression feels ironic to me. Chance was not something William Buckley ever had much of.

Acknowledgements

T HE NAME 'BUCKLEY' has been on Australians' lips for decades. The expressions 'You've got Buckley's' and 'You've got Buckley's chance/hope' are firmly entrenched in Australian everyday vernacular. They, of course, mean: 'You've got about zero chance of achieving this or fat chance of getting that', but as in all things, context is king. The expression usually has a sharper meaning: 'Don't get above yourself' or even more precisely, 'Who do you think you are?'

I never bothered to ask why we used the expression until late 2018 when my oldest friend in the world, Sydney art aficionado Jonathon Lee (known in the business as Jono Lee 'The Hangman') called me excitedly. 'You've got to do the Buckley story, mate.' 'Who's that?' I asked.

Jono had been at a gallery showing of some local painters, some of whom had drawn their version of William Buckley, and had heard the story about his 32-year vigil with the Wadawurrung. Not only does Jono have an eye for good paintings, he knows a Courtenay story when he hears it.

A little bit of research later and the idea grew. Nobody at that point had written a full-length non-fiction and the more I read, the more I was convinced (as was my publisher) that William Buckley would succeed James Porter as my next convict anti-hero.

While I was touring *The Ship that Never Was* in Victoria, I asked an audience at Mornington Peninsular Library whether they thought the expression related to the now defunct but once famous Melbourne department store Buckley and Nunn or to William Buckley himself. The audience was split down the middle. Despite its uncertain origins, the expression has never lost its bite.

There are always special people who help an author make the big breakthroughs in a book. First and foremost is Dr Fred Cahir, Associate Professor in Aboriginal Studies at Federation University in Ballarat. Fred was not just lead researcher, continuity reader and spelling checker, he was mentor-in chief for a clueless Sydney boy looking into the life and ways of an astounding people who once graced the land from Geelong to Ballarat.

It just so happened that Fred had published a history of these very people, the Wadawurrung, at the same time I was writing this book. *'My Country all gone, the white men have stolen it'* gives far greater detail and context that I could ever promulgate about Buckley's adopted kin. Fred's input has been invaluable and this wouldn't be half the book it is without his guidance, knowledge and advice.

Clueless from the start, my very first port of call was to a hero of mine – Dr Mark McKenna, Professor of History at the University of Sydney, who wrote two books (among many others) that inspired me: *From the Edge* and *Looking for BlackFellas' Point*. William Buckley is pretty well known, he said, so you need to peruse the academic journals and seek out the more obscure references. He was right, of course. Therein lay the gold.

I then spoke to veteran ABC Radio National broadcaster Michael Cathcart who told me all Buckley roads should start with Des Cowley, the History of the Book manager at the State Library of Victoria.

Des is curator of all the rare printed material relating to early Victorian history and he showed me many original artefacts of the Buckley-Batman epoch, including notebooks, drawings and works or art. I soon realised Buckley and Batman not only inspired stories, they moved people to art. Here was Buckley depicted as Robinson Crusoe or John the Baptist; there was John Batman pictured as the prophet of civilisation. History is about impressions, and only art conveys these most succinctly. This book acknowledges the rampant iconography of its subjects.

I am also grateful for the help of Melinda Kennedy at the Wadawurrung Aboriginal Corporation, a traditional owner and expert in indigenous knowledge systems. Melinda put me straight on a number of matters relating to indigenous customs and beliefs while her colleague, Wadawurrung language officer Stephanie Skinner, generously explained (in layman's terms) how Buckley might have grappled with the language. My thanks also go to Bruce Pascoe, the prolific author and commentator on all manner of indigenous subjects, who lent his views on some of the vexing issues a book such as this is bound to throw up.

Big mentions also go to award-winning author and historian Peter Cochrane for letting me use an excerpt from his exceptional novel *The Making of Martin Sparrow* and to the great Kay Saunders, polymath and professor emerita of history at the University of Queensland, who kindly read the initial draft.

There are so many professionals who give time freely and generously. These include Lana Capon at the Geelong Heritage Centre, who offered some excellent tips on the Buckley background, and to the librarians at Geelong Library, who amassed everything they could muster on Buckley ahead of my visit there.

There were also my researchers who did some brilliant detection work on diverse parts of the book. Michelle Blake, who was so instrumental to the research of *The Ship that Never Was*, was given leave this time to verify anything and everything. Anna Kelly helped me resurrect facts on John Batman and the Tasmanian sides to this story. Helene Manger-Hofhuis looked into the experiences of other European men and women who had lived with various Aboriginal tribes.

Thanks also go to my wife Gina, continuity reader and soother-in chief of the male ego, who had to put up with a man who became progressively less helpful and gradually more irritable as the book evolved. Her sister Mary McManus has also been a godsend, helping me book library talks and signing me up for literary events.

Others just show enormous interest and that is all an author can ever ask for. These include Di Bracey, Marcus McRitchie, Irene Appollonov, Alexandra Cain, George Holman, Djo Hillaire, Nic Carroll, Ben Courtenay, Bill McManus, Andy Miles, Annie Herro, John Eastman, Matthew Sweeney, Rupert Jeffrey, Gayle Bryant, Father Pax Scarf, Beverly Chandler, Nada Herro, Michael Girdis, Rowan Bosworth-Davies, Irene Grootendorst, Andrew Travers, Michelle Brooks, Pete Heininger, Chris Thynne, Matthew Ellks, Jo Pybus, Andrew Penfold, Delysia Ashwood McNair, Merridy Eastman, Ingrid Villata, Amy Butler and Colleena Presnell.

A big note of gratitude to all those behind the scenes pulling the strings. Chief among these are James Kellow, Harper Collins CEO, who helped me with US connections and Harper's senior editor Lachlan McLaine, who literally puts the whole thing together. There's also the man who never fails to get the show on the road, campaign manager Matthew Howard.

Last but not least, a book must have backbone. This one would have ossified without the ever stalwart Jude McGee, my publisher at ABC Books. It could easily have withered and crumbled without Kate Goldsworthy, the best structural and copy editor on the planet. Both Jude and Kate can smell sloppiness, incoherence and conjecture (not to mention plain old boring writing) from a thousand paces. I may have been the writer, but the rhythm and vitality of the book is theirs.

Adam Courtenay, March 2020

Bibliography & Sources

Primary Sources

Batman J. *The Settlement of John Batman in Port Phillip* (Batman's journal), George Slater, 1856

Bride, FT (ed). *Letters from Victorian Pioneers*, Robert S Brain, 1898

Bonwick, J. *John Batman, The Founder of Victoria*. Samuel Mullen, 1867

Bonwick J. *The Wild White Man and the Blacks of Victoria*, Fergusson & Moore, 1863

Bonwick J. (Edited by Anderson H) *Discovery and settlement of Port Phillip: Being a history of the country now called Victoria* (1839) Red Rooster Press, 1999

Bunce, D. *Australasiatic Reminiscences of Twenty-Three years' Wanderings in Tasmania and the Australias*, JT Hendy, 1857

Cary, JJ. *Vocabularies of the Geelong and Colac tribes (collected in 1840)*, Australasian Association for the Advancement of Science, 1898.

Clarke A. *A Year's History of the Settlement of Port Phillip in 1836: Containing reminiscences of Batman, and correspondence of Mr. J.P. Fawkner during that period, compiled from authentic sources*, Henry Franks, Geelong, 1867

Clark, ID. (Ed) *The Port Phillip Journals of George Augustus Robinson: 8 March - 7 April 1842 and 18 March - 29 April 1843*, Melbourne, Monash University Press, 1988

Curr, EM. *The Australian Race (vol 1): It's languages, Customs, Place of Landing in Australia and the Routes by which it spread Itself over that Continent.* John Ferres, 1886

Dawson J. *Australian Aborigines – the languages and customs of several tribes of Aborigines in the Western District of Victoria*, George Robertson 1881 (Facsimile edition 1981)

Fawkner, JP (ed Billot, CP) *Melbourne's missing chronicle: being the Journal of Preparations for Departure to and Proceedings at Port Phillip.* Quartet Books, 1982

Gellibrand, JT. *Memorandum of a trip to Port Phillip*, State Library Victoria, Australia, 1836

Langhorne, G. *Reminiscences of James Buckley Who Lived for Thirty Two Years among the Wallawaroo or Watourong Tribes at Geelong Port Phillip, Communicated by Him to George Langhorne* (1837). First published in The Age, 29 July, 1911

Morgan, J. *The Life and Adventures of William Buckley, Thirty-Two Years a Wanderer amongst the Aborigines of the Then Unexplored Country around Port Phillip, Now the Province of Victoria.* (Archibald MacDougall, printer) 1852.

Morgan J. (ed Flannery, T) *The Life and Adventures of William Buckley* (with Langhorne, G 'Reminiscences'). Text Publishing, 2002

Pateshall, N. (Tipping M ed): *A short Account of a Voyage around the Globe in HMS Calcutta, 1803-1804.* Queensbury Hill Press, 1980

Pyke, WT. *Thirty Years Among the Blacks of Australia: The Life and Adventures of William Buckley the Runaway Convict,* EW Cole, 1889

Rusden, GW. *The History of Australia, Vol 1* (1883) Cambridge University Press, 2011

Shillingshaw, JJ. *Historical records of Port Phillip:The first annals of the Colony of Victoria,* Government Printer Melbourne, 1870

Smyth, RB. *The Aborigines of Victoria; with notes relating to the habits of the natives of other parts of Australia,* Melbourne, 1878

Todd, A. *The Todd Journal. Andrew alias William Todd, John Batman's Recorder and his Indented Head Journal 1835* (ed, Geelong Historical Society, 1989)

Thomas, W. (Edited by Stephens M). *The Journal of William Thomas: Assistant protector of the Aborigines of Port Phillip & Guardian of the Aborigines of Victoria 1839-1867. Vols I-IV,* Victorian Aboriginal Corporation for Languages, 2014.

Tuckey, JH. *An account of the Voyage to Establish a colony at Port Phillip, in Bass's Strait, on the South Coast of New South Wales in his Majesty's Ship Calcutta, in the years 1802-3-4.* Longman and Co, 1805

Wedge JH. *On the Country around Port Phillip,* (Communicated to the Colonial Office) London 1836.

Wedge, JH. *Map of Port Phillip From The Survey of Mr Wedge and Others,* National Library of Australia, nla.obj-416707851 (1856)

Wedge JK. *'Narrative of William Buckley'* in Labilliere, FP. *Early History of the Colony of Victoria.* Sampson Low, Marston, Searle, & Rivington, 1878.

West, J. *The History of Tasmania (vol 2),* Henry Dowling, Launceston, 1852

William Buckley papers 1835–1836, State Library Victoria

Secondary Sources

Alexander, A *Tasmania's colonial years,* Hodder & Stoughton, 1986

Annear, R. *Bearbrass: Imagining Early Melbourne,* Black Inc, 1995

Barrett, C. *Whiteblackfellows: The strange adventures of Europeans who lived among savages,* Hallcraft, 1948

Billot, C. P (Ed). *Melbourne's Missing Chronicle by John Pascoe Fawkner.* Quartet Books, 1982

Billot, CP. *John Batman: the story of John Batman and the founding of Melbourne,* Melbourne, 1979

Boyce, J. *1835: The founding of Melbourne & the conquest of Australia,* Black Inc, 2011

Braybrook J. *John Batman: An inside story of the birth of Melbourne,* Xlibris, 2012

Broome, R. *Aboriginal Victorians: A History since 1800.* Allen & Unwin, 2005

Butlin, NG. *Our Original Aggression*, Allen &Unwin, 1983

Cahir, F. *My Country All Gone The White Men Have Stolen It*, Australian History Matters, 2019

Cahir, F, Clark, ID & Clarke, PA. *Aboriginal biocultural knowledge in south-eastern Australia: perspectives of early colonists*, CSIRO Publishing, 2018.

Campbell, AH. *John Batman and the Aborigines*, Kibble Books, 1987

Christie, MF. *Aborigines in Victoria 1835-36*, Sydney University Press, 1979

Clark ID. *"That's my Country, belonging to me": Aboriginal Land Tenure and dispossession in nineteenth century Victoria*, Heritage Matter, Melbourne 1998

Clark ID. *Aboriginal Languages and Clans: An Historical Atlas of western and Central Victoria 1800-1900*, Monash Publications in Geography, no 37, Clayton, Vic.

Cochrane P. *The Making of Martin Sparrow*, Penguin Random House, 2018

Davison, G. *The companion to Tasmanian History*, Centre for Tasmanian Historical Studies, 2005.

Davison, G, Hirst, J & Macintyre, S. *The Oxford Companion to Australian History*, 2003.

Eidelson, M. *Melbourne Dreaming*, Aboriginal Studies Press, 1997

Fels, M-H. *'I succeeded once': The Aboriginal Protectorate on the Mornington Peninsula, 1839-1840*, Australian National University E Press, 2011

Flannery, T (Ed). *The Birth of Melbourne*, Text, 2002

Flood, J. *The Original Australians*, Allen & Unwin 2006

Hiatt, LR *Arguments about Aborigines, Australia and the evolution of social anthropology*, Cambridge University Press, 1996

Hughes, R. *The Fatal Shore: A History of the Transportation of Convicts to Australia 1787-1868*, Harper Collins, London, 1987

Linnell, G. *Buckley's Chance*, Penguin Random House, 2019

Manly, S. *Language, Custom and Nation in the 1790s: Locke, Tooke, Wordsworth, Edgeworth*, Ashgate 2007

Maynard, J & Haskins, V. *Living with the Locals: Early Europeans' Experience of Indigenous Life*, National Library of Australia, 2006.

McKenna, M. *From the Edge: Australia's Lost Histories*, Miegunyah Press, 2016

Munster PM: *Putting Batman and Buckley on the Map of St Leonards*, St Leonards, 2004

Pascoe, B. *Dark Emu*, Magabala Books, 2018

Pascoe, B. *Convincing Ground: Learning to Fall in Love with Your Country*, Aboriginal Studies Press, 2007

Pascoe, B. *Wathaurong – the People Who said No.* Wathaurong Aboriginal Co-operative, 2003

Pickering M. *Consuming Doubts: what some People Ate? Or What some people swallowed?* in Goldman, R. *The Anthropology of cannibalism*, Bergin & Garvy, 1999

Presland G. *Aboriginal Melbourne: The lost land of the Kulin people*, Penguin 1994

Reynolds, H. *The other side of the frontier: Aboriginal resistance to the European Invasion of Australia*, UNSW Press, 1982.

Reynolds, H. *Fate of a free people*, Penguin, 1995.

Robertson, C. Buckley's Hope, Scribe, 2002

Robson, LL. *A History of Tasmania Volume I. Van Diemen's Land From the Earliest Times to 1855*, Oxford University Press. (1983).

Rogers, TJ. *The Civilisation of Port Phillip, Settler ideology, violence, and rhetorical possession*, Melbourne University Press, 2018

Shaw AGL. *A History of the Port Phillip District: Victoria before Separation*, Melbourne University Press, 1996

Tipping, M. Convicts Unbound: The Story of the Calcutta Convicts and Their Settlement in Australia, Viking O'Neil, 1988

Wadawurrung Aboriginal Corporation. *Wadawurrung Country of the Victorian Volcanic Plains* (2019)

Journals and online sources

Boucher L. and Russell, L. *Colonial history, postcolonial theory and the 'Aboriginal problem' in Colonial Victoria cited in Settler Colonial Governance in 19th Century Victoria*, ANU Press, 1979

Boyce, J. *Return to Eden: Van Diemen's Land and the Early British Settlement of Australia*, Environment and History Vol 14, No 2, Australia Revisited, 2008

Brumm, A. *'The Falling Sky': Symbolic and Cosmological Associations of the Mt William Greenstone Axe Quarry, Central Victoria, Australia*, Cambridge Archaeological Journal 20:2, 2010

Cahir, F. *Murnong: Much more than a food*. The Journal of the Archaeological and Anthropological Society of Victoria, vol 35, 2012

Cahir, F. *The Wathawurrung People's Encounters with Outside Forces 1797-1849: A History of Conciliation and Conflict*, MA Thesis, University of Ballarat, 2001

Clark, ID. and Cahir, DA. *Understanding Ngamadjidj: Aboriginal Perceptions of Europeans in nineteenth century Western Victoria*, Journal of Australian Colonial History vol 13, 2011

Clark ID. *'You have all this place, no good have children' ...Derrimut: traitor, saviour, or a man of his people?* Journal of the Royal Australian Historical Society Volume 91 Issue 2, December 2005

Eldridge, R. *The Cultural Interactions of Aborigines with Whales, Whalers and Whaling in southwest Victoria*, Federation University, 2015

Everts, S. *Europe's Hypocritical History of Cannibalism*, Smithsonian Magazine, April, 2013

Frank, JAB. *Private Enterprise and the Peopling of Australasia, 1831-50*, The Economic History Review, vol 35, no 2 ,1982

Hill, B. *Buckley, Our Imagination, Hope* in *William Buckley Rediscovered*, Geelong Gallery, 2002

Huber, B. *A Curator's Perspective* in *William Buckley Rediscovered*, Geelong Gallery, 2002

Izett, EK. *Breaking New Ground: Early Australian Ethnography in Colonial Women's Writing*, University of Western Australia, 2014

Peacock, A. *Reflections and Shadows: Picturing William 'Murrangurk' Buckley*. Australian and New Zealand Journal of Art; Canberra vol 13, Issue 1, 2013

Stephens, M . *Infanticide at Port Phillip: Protector William Thomas and the witnessing of things unseen*, Aboriginal History, Vol 38, 2014

Stern, WM. *The Bread Crisis in Britain, 1795-96'*, Economica, vol 31, no 122, 1964

Xiao, B. *Morality in the Victorian Period,* Theory and Practice in Language Studies Vol. 5, No. 9, September 2015

Online Sources

Annear R. 'Still to rise above the quagmire, early Bearbrass was quite a different place' www.smh.com.au/entertainment/books/still-to-rise-abovethe-quagmire-early-bearbrass-was-quite-a-different-place-201201081pq5g.html

Clements N. 'The truth about John Batman: Melbourne's founder and "murderer of the blacks"' theconversation.com/the-truth-about-john-batmanmelbournes-founder-and-murderer-of-the-blacks-1025

Culture Victoria 'William Buckley, "The Wild White Man"' cv.vic.gov.au/stories/immigrants-and-emigrants/william-buckley/william-buckley-the-wild-white-man/

Edmonds P. 'Founding Myths' www.emelbourne.net.au/biogs/EM00603b.htm

Ganitis, G. 'The Stubborn myth of Batman's Treaty' overland.org.
    au/2019/04/the-stubborn-myth-of-batmans-treaty/

Sparrow J. 'Melbourne from the Falls' overland.org.au/2012/07/melbourne-
    from-the-falls/

Taylor, R. 'The Wedge Collection and the conundrum of Humane
    Colonisation' meanjin.com.au/essays/the-wedge-collection-and-
    theconundrum-of-humane-colonisation/

White, M. 'Popular politics in the 18th century' www.bl.uk/
    georgianbritain/articles/popular-politics-in-the-18th-century

Calcutta Convict Record. Libraries Tasmania stors.tas.gov.au/CON22-
    11$init=CON22-1-1_0656

Calcutta voyage to New South Wales [Port Phillip], Australia in 1803 with
    292 passengers. convictrecords.com.au/ships/calcutta/1803

Djillong Timeline ww w.djillong.net.au/images/Djillong_Timeline_
    Banner_-_update_FINAL _Aug18-compressed_2.pdf

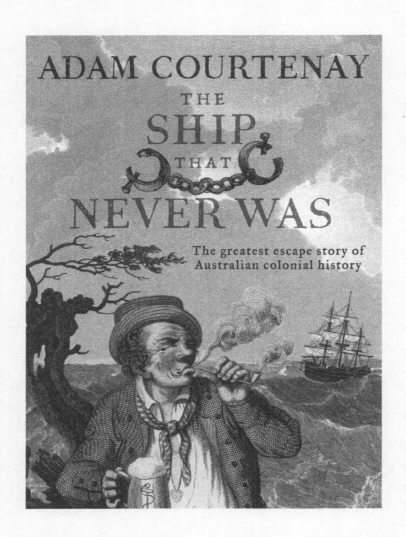

ADAM COURTENAY

THE
SHIP
THAT
NEVER WAS

The greatest escape story of
Australian colonial history

The greatest escape story
in Australian colonial history

In 1823, cockney sailor and chancer James Porter was convicted of stealing a stack of beaver furs and transported halfway around the world to Van Diemen's Land. After several escape attempts from the notorious penal colony, Porter, who told authorities he was a 'beer-machine maker', was sent to Macquarie Harbour, known in Van Diemen's Land as hell on earth.

Many had tried to escape Macquarie Harbour; few had succeeded. But when Governor George Arthur announced that the place would be closed and its prisoners moved to the new penal station of Port Arthur, Porter, along with a motley crew of other prisoners, pulled off an audacious escape. Wresting control of the ship they'd been building to transport them to their fresh hell, the escapees instead sailed all the way to Chile. What happened next is stranger than fiction, a fitting outcome for this true-life picaresque tale.

The Ship That Never Was is the entertaining and rollicking story of what is surely the greatest escape in Australian colonial history. James Porter, whose memoirs were the inspiration for Marcus Clarke's *For the Term of his Natural Life*, is an original Australian larrikin whose ingenuity, gift of the gab and refusal to buckle under authority make him an irresistible anti-hero who deserves a place in our history.

Available from all good book shops